DISPLACEMENT AND ERASURE IN PALESTINE

DISPLACEMENT AND ERASURE IN PALESTINE

The Politics of Hope

Noa Shaindlinger

EDINBURGH
University Press

Edinburgh University Press is one of the leading university presses in the UK. We publish academic books and journals in our selected subject areas across the humanities and social sciences, combining cutting-edge scholarship with high editorial and production values to produce academic works of lasting importance. For more information visit our website: edinburghuniversitypress.com

© Noa Shaindlinger, 2023, 2025

Edinburgh University Press Ltd
13 Infirmary Street
Edinburgh EH1 1LT

First published in hardback by Edinburgh University Press 2023

Typeset in 11/15 Adobe Garamond by
Cheshire Typesetting Ltd, Cuddington, Cheshire

A CIP record for this book is available from the British Library

ISBN 978 1 4744 8972 0 (hardback)
ISBN 978 1 4744 8973 7 (paperback)
ISBN 978 1 4744 8975 1 (webready PDF)
ISBN 978 1 4744 8974 4 (epub)

The right of Noa Shaindlinger to be identified as author of this work has been asserted in accordance with the Copyright, Designs and Patents Act 1988 and the Copyright and Related Rights Regulations 2003 (SI No. 2498).

CONTENTS

List of Figures	vi
Acknowledgements	viii
Introduction: Who's Afraid of the Right of Return?	1
1 Jaffa: From the Blushing 'Bride of Palestine' to the Shamed 'Mother of Strangers'	25
2 The 'New Normal'	47
3 Itineraries of Exile	70
4 Living in Memory: Exile and the Burden of the Future	97
5 Broken Tiles and Phantom Houses: Urban Intervention in Tel Aviv-Jaffa Now	118
6 Feeling Palestine in South Africa	151
7 The Palestine of Tomorrow	183
Conclusion: The Way Home	219
Bibliography	229
Index	252

FIGURES

1.1	Jaffa's pre-1948 neighbourhoods superimposed on a current map of the city	40
4.1	'Football with the martyrs': children playing football in the narrow alleys of Balata refugee camp	106
4.2	A mural inside the Yafa Cultural Centre, Balata refugee camp, depicting a baffled Israeli soldier	106
5.1	A screenshot from an Israeli manufacturer of 'Jaffa style' decorative tiles	120
5.2	*Derekh Hasafa*, a visual dictionary: Jaffa, Yefet street, December 2009	123
5.3	Jaffa 2030 'Map no. 1' showcasing Palestinian Jaffa	124
5.4	The Bibi family house on Gaza Street, Jaffa, April 2016	129
5.5	Bibi's house, 'My Jaffa' installation	134
5.6	'Pedagogic Acts': Miniature Arab architecture in Charles Clore Park, formerly Manshiyyeh	136
5.7	A student's design for Bibi's house after the return	138
5.8	'Arab Homes for Sale' at Platform art fair	141
5.9	Miniature Arab houses, glued to a piece of broken arabesque-style floor tile	142
5.10	'For Sand thou art, and unto Dust shalt thou Return': Fishermen village/Tel Aviv-Gaza, 1948–2014	149

6.1	District Six memory map covering the floor of the museum	171
6.2	The inscription '*a'idun*' on the ruins of District Six	175
6.3	Waving the Palestinian flag in District Six	175
7.1	Members of the Dajani family with an activist from Zochrot	185
7.2	The 'green house' at the heart of Ajami (built 1934), until recently used as a military court	200
7.3	'Beit Gidi' – the Etzel (Irgun) Museum in Irshid	202
8.1	'Umar introducing the history of demise of Manshiyyeh in front of Beit Gidi	221
8.2	The sign at the Israeli–Lebanese northwestern border in Ras al-Naqurah	221

ACKNOWLEDGEMENTS

This book is dedicated to the memory of Hamed al-Sa'id, a refugee from Jaffa, who died in exile, in Balata camp, to Salah Ajrama, a refugee from 'Ajur/Aida refugee camp, and to all the Palestinian refugees who have suffered the pangs of longing for the homeland.

This project would not have been completed without the immense help I have received from Palestinians in Jaffa and in Nablus, in particular all the refugees, young and old, that I met at the camps and who shared their personal histories with me. 'Tell them we are still here, in these overcrowded and crumbling camps. Don't let the world forget about us,' they pleaded with me time and again. This project was carried out, then, with an eye to echo the voices of the refugees, to demand the world does not abandon them to their fate and side with their oppressors. In Balata, I am particularly thankful to the al-Sa'id family, my generous hosts and most intimate interlocutors and companions; to Muhammad 'Ayash for spending so much of his precious time introducing me to countless people and sitting in on interviews; to the staff of the Yafa Cultural Centre and the young men who kept me company each morning, greeting me with coffee and cigarettes (which I have since quit) and offering stimulating conversations and riveting gossip.

This book (and the dissertation is it based on) would not have been written if it were not for the mentorship and guidance of Jens Hanssen, a diligent and caring supervisor, who, with lots of tough love helped me through writer's blocks and other hurdles, constantly challenging and demanding better from me. I hope some day I will do unto others what he has done for me. Amira Mittermaier introduced me to anthropological thinking and to rigorous ethnographic methodologies, and continued to challenge me, offering her critique of my chapters, forcing me to rethink that which I had taken for granted or at face value. Ato Quayson welcomed me to the Diaspora and Transnational Studies collaborative programme, introducing me to a whole body of scholarship I previously was not familiar with, and constantly asking me questions, challenging my analytical framework to make it more resilient. Alejandro Paz offered extensive review of my completed project, providing me with several excellent new trajectories for my book manuscript. Serving as an external reviewer, Julie Peteet has been supportive of my research from the first time I presented from it at the American Anthropological Association (AAA) through the defense process, pressing me on a few of my most fundamental questions.

In Palestine, I owe a debt of gratitude to many for their hospitality, companionship and assistance: Haim Schwarczenbrg, Chen Misgav, Lizi Sagie, Neria Biala, Tamar Freed, Ronnie Barkan, Yudit Ilani, Sami Abu Shehadeh, Iris and Yoav Bar, Shosh Kahn, Tali Shapira, Halleli Pinson, Moran Barir, Ami Asher, Ayat Abou Shmeiss and so many others. Daniel Monterescu who has been a friend and a scholarly collaborator while in the field, and my cheerleader during the long write-up period. Eitan Bronstein Aparicio and Eleonore Merza-Bronstein for the many hours of discussing the Nakba, the right of return, and the response of Israelis. The entire staff at Zochrot, especially 'Umar al-Ghubari and Liat Rosenberg, for bringing me into the fold and allowing me to participate and to ask so many questions. To my friends at Badil for their companionship and insight, as well as all the wonderful people we met in Cape Town, especially Heidi Grunebaum and Aslam Levy.

Back in Toronto, I must thank my friends for their continued support over the years: Susan Benson-Sokmen, Oscar Jarzmik, Mathew Gagne, Ian Costa and Usman Hamid. I would have never made it through those long years of writing if it weren't for your friendship. To the wonderful and dedicated administrative staff at NMC, especially Anna Sousa, who worked tirelessly behind the scenes making sure our graduate experience is a pleasant and productive one. This research was supported through generous funding from

SGS at the University of Toronto, OGS (Ontario Graduate Scholarship), SSHRC (the Social Sciences and Humanities Research Council) doctoral awards, Charles and Andrea Bronfman Award for Israeli Studies and Friends of Hebrew University Travel Grant. Indexing funding was provided by the Worcester State Foundation.

At the College of the Holy Cross, I owe a debt of gratitude to Ed O'Donnell and Sahar Bazzaz for their encouragement and friendship, and to the history faculty for embracing me since day one. Special thanks to my friend, colleague, co-conspirator and fellow traveller Liat Spiro for our brainstorming and tea sessions, and to Nico Sillitti and Flor Carril for their never-ending faith in me.

Finally, many heartfelt thanks to my family: my parents, Klara and Hillel, and my sister Liron for their continued support, material included, for repeatedly picking me up and dropping me off at the airport, and for hosting me for so long while doing fieldwork; to my feline companions Sookie, Shlomo and Jon Snow for the most welcome distractions and for keeping me sane.

INTRODUCTION: WHO'S AFRAID OF THE RIGHT OF RETURN?

We will return
that is not a threat
not a wish
a hope
or a dream
but a promise.

                    Remi Kanazi, 'Nakba'[1]

On 15 May 2011, hundreds of Palestinians gathered on the Syrian border with the Israeli-occupied Golan Heights to protest the sixty-third anniversary of the *Nakba* (Arabic, 'catastrophe'), the mass expulsion of Palestinian Arabs from those parts of mandatory Palestine that became Israel.[2] One man, whose parents were exiled from Jaffa back in 1948, managed to evade the Israeli

---

[1] Remi Kanazi, *Before the Next Bomb Drops: Rising up from Brooklyn to Palestine* (Chicago: Haymarket Books, 2015), p. 4.
[2] On the Nakba and its aftermath, see below in this introduction. That day, four demonstrators were killed when the Israeli army opened fire on the demonstrators. See Karma Nabulsi, 'Nakba Day: We Waited 63 Years for This', *The Guardian*, 19 May 2011, http://www.theguardian.com/commentisfree/2011/may/19/nakba-day-palestinian-summer (last accessed 26 May 2016); less than a month later, on 5 June 2011, another march, this time marking the Naksa, or the 1967 Arab defeat, ended in tragedy when the IDF shot and killed twenty-three demonstrators.

army and hitchhike his way to his ancestral city, where he attempted to locate his family's house and reconnect with his lost homeland. He then voluntarily surrendered himself to the police, not before being interviewed by Israeli journalists. Israeli news outlets considered the affair an embarrassment for the state, as a mixture of shock, fear and disgust echoed through social media online and in conversations on the streets and on buses.[3] Hijazi's daring return journey was widely and immediately dismissed as an attempt to 'infiltrate' the country by a Syrian, obscuring his Palestinianness and his profound affective connection to a homeland that he had only heard of from his exiled parents.

Denouncing Palestinian returnees as 'infiltrators' is not a new practice. In fact, Palestinians who attempted to return to their villages and towns after the formation of the Israeli state, even before the creation of the armistice lines in 1949, were called *mistanenim* (Hebrew, 'infiltrators'), denoting their illegal status as non-citizens and as a security threat that must be removed.[4] The fear of being engulfed by Palestinian returnees marching through Israel's borders is also not a novelty. In fact, in 1952, only four years after the Nakba, Israeli security apparatus was alarmed by reports of a potential 'march of the refugees', which was understood as an 'insidious plot' against the state of Israel by Arab governments. Internal correspondence stressed that

> We must reiterate that we view the march of the refugees as a political and security threat. Preventing the return of the refugees is a question of life and death to our state. Of particular danger are those refugees who wish to enter with the intention of being a fifth column ... our response to the 'march' will have to be attempting to stop it at any cost.[5]

---

[3] See Sal Emergui, 'Returning to Jaffa: the Triumphant Odyssey of Palestinian Refugee Hassan Hijazi', *MR Zine*, 17 May 2011, http://mrzine.monthlyreview.org/2011/emergui170511.html (last accessed 26 May 2016); for Israeli news coverage of the affair, see Reuters, '"It Was Always my Dream to Reach Jaffa," Syrian Infiltrator Says', *Haaretz*, 16 May 2011, http://www.haaretz.com/news/diplomacy-defense/it-was-always-my-dream-to-reach-jaffa-syrian-infiltrator-says-1.362166 and 'Syrian Infiltrator Recounts Journey to TA', *Ynet*, 16 May 2011, http://www.ynetnews.com/articles/0,7340,L-4069686,00.html (last accessed 26 May 2016).
[4] Palestinians attempted to enter Israel throughout the 1950s for various reasons, see Chapter 3 as well as Benny Morris, *Israel's Border Wars, 1949–1956: Arab Infiltration, Israeli Retaliation, and the Countdown to the Suez War* (New York: Oxford University Press, 1993).
[5] Israeli state archives (ISA), 'March of the Refugees', 20 November 1952, GL 17117/28.

The Palestinian right of return has remained a specter of Israeli political discourse; its presence lingers even several decades after the Nakba and the establishment of the state though it is rarely publicly discussed. However, occasionally it resurfaces to invoke fear and mobilise the Jewish masses against such possibility. Recently, in the context of the Syrian refugee crisis in Europe and calls to allow a limited number into the country, opposition MK member Yair Lapid explicitly claimed that admitting Syrian refugees would be 'opening a backdoor to the right of return for the Palestinian refugees', revealing once again the deeply ingrained fear of being engulfed and perhaps 'submerged' by returnees.[6]

Fast-forward to March 2018; Gaza-based youth grassroots organisers launched a new wave of popular protests adjacent to the demarcation line, commonly dubbed by the media as the 'border' between Israel and the Gaza Strip. In reality, though, it is an Israeli-constructed barrier aimed at maintaining the ongoing blockade of the Strip, controlling the movement of commodities and people, and imposing forms of collective punishment against a besieged civilian population of over 2 million, most of whom are refugees.[7] The organisers of the 'Great Return March', as it became known, wished to draw the world's attention to the plight of the besieged population but emphasised the root cause of their misery: their expulsion from their places of origin in 1948.[8] Indeed, the Great Return March is the most recent chapter in a

---

[6] Robert Tait, 'Israel Prime Minister Benjamin Netanyahu Rejects Calls to Admit Syrian Refugees', *The Daily Telegraph*, 6 September 2015, http://www.telegraph.co.uk/news/worldnews/middleeast/israel/11847304/Israel-prime-minister-Benjamin-Netanyahu-rejects-calls-to-admit-Syrian-refugees.html (last accessed 26 May 2016).

[7] Much has been written about the Gaza blockade since its imposition in 2007. Scholars have debated its legality, for instance Noura Erakat, 'It's not Wrong, it's Illegal: Situating the Gaza Blockade between International Law and the UN Response', *UCLA Journal of Islamic and Near Eastern Law*, vol. 11, no. 37 (2011–12), pp. 1–34; others have studied the adverse impact of the blockade on the quality of life of Gazans: David Mills *et al.*, 'Structural Violence in the Era of of a New Pandemic', *Lancet*, 26 March 2020, doi:10.1016 S0140-6736(20)30730-3; see also Alison Martin *et al.*, 'Israel Tightens the Blockade, Civilians Bear the Brunt', *Oxfam*, 27 July 2018, http://hdl.handle.net/10546/620527 (last accessed 3 August 2021); UNCTAD Report, 'The Economic Costs of the Israeli Occupation for the Palestinian People: The Gaza Strip under Closure and Restrictions', 13 August 2020, UN A/75/310 (Geneva: UNCTAD).

[8] Jehad Abusalim, 'The Great March of Return: An Organizer's Perspective', *Journal of Palestine Studies*, vol. 47, no. 4 (2018), pp. 90–100.

longer history of similar actions, as I mentioned above. The Israeli media dismissed the marches, describing them as 'violent riots' that endangered Israeli troops and undermined the security of Israeli settlements beyond the barrier.[9] A year and a half later, in the autumn of 2019, the marches ceased, but not before Israeli snipers killed 234, and injured over 36,100.[10]

'Too Much History'

In a recent case brought before the Israeli Supreme Court, Justice Daphne Erez-Barak accused the attorney of Palestinian families set to be evicted that his clients are 'loading too much history' onto the case.[11] The Justice's uneasiness about the deeper history of ethnic cleansing implicated in this case is emblematic of the state of mind of the Israeli public. After all, Palestinian refugees have been the ghosts of peace diplomacy haunting every configuration of negotiated solution to the lingering conflict in Israel/Palestine. While international law as well as United Nations General Assembly resolution 194 of November 1948 were squarely on the side of the displaced Palestinians,[12] the Israeli state

---

[9] For example, Yoav Zeitoun and Elior Levi, 'The IDF Killed Terrorists that Fired on Soldiers; 16 Killed Yesterday in Gaza', *Ynet*, 31 March 2018, https://www.ynet.co.il/articles/0,7340,L-5211505,00.html (last accessed 3 August 2021). In the Israeli media parlance, Palestinian protests are habitually coded as 'violent disturbances of the peace', and protesters described as 'rioters' or 'terrorists', especially if troops end up killing them.

[10] Orly Noy, 'Gaza's Great Return March: 234 Killed, 17 Investigations, One Indictment', *+972 Magazine*, 25 November 2020, https://www.972mag.com/gaza-return-march-idf/ (last accessed 3 August 2021); Office for the Coordination of Humanitarian Affairs (OCHA), 'Two Years on, People Injured and Traumatized During the "Great March of Return" are Still Struggling, *United Nations*, 6 April 2020, https://www.un.org/unispal/document/two-years-on-people-injured-and-traumatized-during-the-great-march-of-return-are-still-struggling/ (last accessed 3 August 2021).

[11] Haneen Majadala, 'Your Honour, This is a History Lesson', *Haaretz*, 4 August 2021, https://www.haaretz.co.il/opinions/.premium-1.10084247 (last accessed 5 August 2021). The case involved several Palestinian families, who, after being expelled from their homes in the Haifa area in 1948, settled in the East Jerusalem neighbourhood of Sheikh Jarrah. In the past decade, Israel has been aggressively removing these families from the neighbourhood at the behest of Jewish settlers who are claiming they are the rightful owners of these properties. See also 'Israel asks US to push Palestinians to accept Sheikh Jarrah "Compromise"', *The New Arab*, 5 August 2021, https://english.alaraby.co.uk/news/israel-asked-us-apply-pressure-sheikh-jarrah-case-0 (last accessed 5 August 2021).

[12] United Nations archives UN A/RES/194 (III) and UNCCP, 'Analysis of paragraph 11 of the General Assembly's Resolution of 11 December 1948', UN A/AC.25/W.45, 15 May 1950.

successfully managed to evade the issue of repatriation entirely[13] and relegate memory of violent uprooting to oblivion. Moreover, the Palestinian state-building project has grappled with the idea of repatriation as it evolved since the inception of the Palestine Liberation Organization (PLO) in 1964 as an Arab League-sponsored organisation. Since its takeover by Yasser Arafat's Fatah faction in 1969, the PLO has gradually shifted the Palestinian revolution from the struggle of return to state-building. Although the idea of return was, for a time, foregrounded in official rhetoric, no concrete plans have been drawn up by the PLO leadership to facilitate discussion about its practicability.[14]

In the foundational Palestinian National Charter of 1968, the state-building project was articulated as intimately linked to a particular and clearly defined ethno-national identity (Palestinians are 'Arab nationals who, until 1947, normally resided in Palestine'[15] and their descendants). It calls for the restoration of a status quo ante. Liberation, in this formulation, consisted of the 'elimination of Zionism' and 're-establish[ing] peace and security'.[16] The implication of the totality (but also vagueness) of Palestinian liberation meant a return, not just in the sense of physical repatriation of exiles, but also reversing the effects of settler colonialism. The Charter further distinguished between Jews who resided in Palestine before 'the beginning of the Zionist invasion'

On the applicability of international law norms, and especially humanitarian law, to the Palestinian case, see Victor Kattan, *From Coexistence to Conquest: International Law and the Origins of the Arab-Israeli Conflict, 1891–1949* (New York: Pluto Press, 2009), especially chapters 7 and 8; John Quigley, 'Displaced Palestinians and the Right of Return', *Harvard International Law Journal*, vol. 39, no. 1 (Winter 1998), pp. 171–229; Thomas Mallison and Sally V. Mallison, 'The Right of Return', *Journal of Palestine Studies*, vol. 9, no. 3 (Spring 1980), pp. 125–136, and Thomas Mallison and Sally V. Mallison, *An International Law Analysis of the Major United Nations Resolutions Concerning the Palestine Question*, UN ST/SG/SER.F/4 (New York: UN, 1979).

[13] Arik Ariel Leibovitz, *The Sanctity of the Status Quo: The Palestinian Refugee Issue in the Israel Foreign Policy, 1948–1967* [in Hebrew] (Tel Aviv: Resling, 2015).

[14] Menachem Klein, 'Between Right and Realization: The PLO Dialectics of "The Right of Return"', *Journal of Refugee Studies*, vol. 11, no. 1 (1998), pp. 1–19.

[15] 'Palestine National Council: The Palestinian National Charter (July 1968)', in Walter Laqueur and Barry Rubin (eds), *The Israel-Arab Reader: A Documentary History of the Middle East Conflict* (New York: Penguin, 2008), p. 117.

[16] Ibid., p. 118.

and were part of the envisaged Palestinian state, and those who settled as a consequence and were not and, presumably, would be forced to leave.[17]

Subsequent declarative resolutions were forced to recalibrate the PLO leadership's understanding of liberation; thus, for instance, the 1974 Palestinian National Council (PNC) resolution introduced the idea of a mini state 'in every part of the Palestine territory which will be liberated',[18] which ultimately became the first articulation of the idea widely known as the 'two states solution'. In his famed UN address of the same year, Yasser Arafat made explicit overtures to Israeli Jews, as equal citizens in the 'Palestine of tomorrow'. The Declaration of Independence (1988), a remarkable document of diasporic politics penned by two towering Palestinian exiles (Mahmoud Darwish and Edward Said, Arabic and English versions respectively), represented the acceptance of political realities which by the late 1980s seemed incontestable: that the state of Israel was there to stay for the foreseeable future.

The height of the popularity of the two-states solution vision was, no doubt, during the 1990s and the 'Oslo Process', that hailed the Palestinian Authority as a state-in-waiting witnessed the return of thousands of Palestinian political functionaries and neoliberal entrepreneurs into the West Bank and Gaza.[19] Under the Oslo Process, the question of the refugees was indefinitely deferred to 'final status' negotiations that never materialised. Unsurprisingly, the most vociferous opposition to Oslo came from the 1948 refugees, especially in Lebanon, who sensed that their right of return was traded for the PLO's building of a state in the West Bank and Gaza. After the demise of Oslo, the so-called 'two-states solution' continued to feature in formal diplomatic

---

[17] Ibid., p. 117. The cut-off date of this putative indigeneity after which the Jewish cannot be considered authentically Palestinian was left vague, perhaps on purpose, and has been interpreted as 1917 (before the Balfour Declaration), though it can definitely be read by some as prior to the first wave of Zionist migration, 1881–2. For more on the 'Jewish settlers' debate: Alain Gresh, *The PLO, the Struggle Within: Towards an Independent Palestinian* State (London: Zed Books, 1988), pp. 30–52; on the democratic state of Palestine, see David Hirst, *The Gun and the Olive Branch: The Roots of Violence in the Middle East* (London: Faber and Faber, 1984), pp. 289–94; Rashid Khalidi, *The Iron Cage: The Story of the Palestinian Struggle for Statehood* (Boston, MA: Beacon Press, 2006), pp. 190–3.

[18] 'Palestine National Council: Resolutions (June 1974)', in Laqueur and Rubin, *The Israeli-Arab Reader*, pp. 162–3.

[19] On these returnees and the tensions with the local population in Gaza, see, for instance, David Hirst, 'Shameless in Gaza', *The Guardian Weekly*, 21 April 1997.

platitudes, with American and European officials paying lip service to the idea that a viable solution was just around the corner if the peace process could be implemented. Unlike the hollow gesture of Western diplomacy toward the two-states solution, the Israeli liberal-Zionist left (sometimes self-identified as the 'peace camp') deployed the partition discourse out of fear that the Palestinian population would soon outnumber the Jews between the Jordan river and the Mediterranean.[20] This discourse of demographic panic was not coincidentally reminiscent of the age-old colonial fear of engulfment. My research project was conceived, researched and penned between 2008 and 2016, at the time when the PLO's state-building process ran its course, and new actors mobilised around the right of return and a single democratic state.

In the seven decades since the violent Palestinian exodus, the Israeli state has embarked on a massive project of erasures; while that project is multi-faceted, this book focuses on two of its manifestations: the spatial/physical and the symbolic. In the aftermath of the events of 1948, Israel systematically demolished depopulated villages and towns, a process that continued apace well after the 1967 war and the occupation of the West Bank and the Gaza Strip, where refugees were forced into decrepit United Nations Relief and Works Agency (UNRWA)-administered camps.[21] Existing archive-based scholarship has revealed these consistent demolitions were intended to render the repatriation of the refugees impossible. In the city of Jaffa, the focus of my research, demolitions were accompanied by spatial appropriations: the state and the municipality presided over decades-long processes of Judaicisation, shorthand for settling

---

[20] See Tikva Honig-Parnass, *False Prophets of Peace: Liberal Zionism and the Struggle for Palestine* (Chicago: Haymarket Books, 2011), pp. 35–52.

[21] A few examples of the vast scholarship on Israel's systemic destruction of Palestinian villages and towns in the aftermath of the Nakba: Meron Rapoport, 'History Erased: the IDF and the post-1948 Destruction of Palestinian Monuments', *Journal of Palestine Studies*, vol. 37, no. 2 (Winter 2008), 82–8; Susan Slyomovics, *The Object of Memory: Arab and Jew Narrate the Palestinian Village* (Philadelphia: University of Pennsylvania Press, 1998); Noga Kadman, *Erased from Space and Consciousness: Israel and the Depopulated Villages of 1948* (Bloomington: Indiana University Press, 2015); Ghazi Falah, 'The 1948 Israeli-Palestinian War and its Aftermath: The Transformation and De-Signification of Palestine's Cultural Landscape', *Annals of the Association of American Geographers*, vol. 86, no. 2 (June 1996), pp. 256–85; on the post-1948 demolitions in a broader context of systemic state-initiated destruction, see Penny Green and Amelia Smith, 'Evicting Palestine', *State Crime Journal*, vol. 5, no. 1: Palestine, Palestinians and Israel's State Criminality (Spring 2016), pp. 81–108.

Jewish migrants in properties owned by Palestinian refugees, thus radically altering the character of the city. In their later stages, these spatial appropriations resulted in the embeddedness of Jaffa in global tourism circuits through the marketability of its oriental antiquity; the concomitant overtaking of the city by the forces of the real estate market has accelerated the rate of further displacements and further shrunk the remaining Palestinian community.[22]

These physical erasures were accompanied by symbolic ones: the Israeli state archives (ISA) have kept the bulk of evidence documenting its violence of 1948 behind lock and key, in some cases reclassifying previously public-facing documents ostensibly for security reasons.[23] In this sense, the Israeli archives defy what Achile Mbembe claimed is the purpose of archives and instead seem to be hellbent on the destruction of the past rather than allow for its reassembly. In other words, these particular archives are designed for the permanent internment of history's debris, since it is the latter that poses 'constant threat to the state'.[24] Clearly, anxiety over a possible unearthing of evidence of the constitutive violence of the Nakba mobilises considerable state resources in efforts to conceal the 'story made possible'[25] by the documents in its vaults.

Salvaging Hope

In light of this, my book offers a departure from questions of state-building, and instead focuses on people's affective attachment to place and concomitant concrete ideas about remaking micro-realities and lived places, that put

---

[22] Yara Sa'di-Ibraheem, 'Settler-Colonial Temporalities, Ruinations and Neoliberal Urban Renewal: The Case of Suknet al-Huresh in Jaffa', *GeoJournal*, vol. 87 (2020), pp. 661–75, https://doi.org/10.1007/s10708-020-10279-0; Sharon Rotbard, *White City, Black City* [in Hebrew] (Tel Aviv: Bavel, 2005); Daniel Monterescu, *Jaffa, Shared and Shattered: Contrived Coexistence in Israel/Palestine* (Bloomington: Indiana University Press, 2015).

[23] Ilan Pappé, 'An Indicative Archive: Salvaging Nakba Documents', *Journal of Palestine Studies*, vol. 49, no. 3 (Spring 2020), pp. 22–40; Seth Anziska, 'The Erasure of the Nakba in Israel's Archives', *Journal of Palestine Studies*, vol. 49, no. 1 (Fall 2019), pp. 64–76; Adam Raz, 'History in Shreds', *Haaretz Weekend*, 25 June 2021, pp. 5, 11; see also reports on archive inaccessibility on the Akevot Institute website https://www.akevot.org.il/en/publications/.

[24] Achile Mbembe, 'The Power of the Archive and its Limit', in Carolyn Hamilton *et al.* (eds), *Refiguring the Archive* (Dordrecht: Springer, 2002), pp. 19–27.

[25] Ibid., p. 21. The traces of these silenced documents in the archives' catalogue have given us substantial clues as to what it is they hide. See Ofer Aderet, 'War Crimes and "Unpleasantness": Israel's Censorship List', *Haaretz*, 20 October 2021, p. 7.

negotiations and geopolitical concerns into perspective. Against the failures of their political leadership and Israel's efforts to elide them from the annals of history, Palestinians have forged alternative archives as a means to resist both physical and symbolic erasures. Inscribing their presence against the ongoing Israeli colonial project, Palestinians retell histories of rootedness and exile, staking their claim to place, and demand a role in shaping its futures. This project of imagining the return of the refugees that is at the heart of this monograph is fundamentally different from historical and ongoing debates about the nature of Palestine's political formation, also known as the one/two-states debate. With the majority of Palestinians displaced from their places of origin, the experience of prolonged exile has been identity-endowing and has provided the most concrete understandings of national liberation.

The book will further explore the intersection between displacement and the imagination as a politically mobilising force. My analysis reveals a constant tension between forms of activism that Palestinians forge and the temporalities they imply. The return has not happened yet, and Palestinians are still waiting for it to occur. This waiting, which by now has spanned at least three generations, has produced a temporal break between what is perceived as a 'golden past' in the homeland, cut abruptly by occupation and expulsion, and an undetermined point in the future that signals restoration of the homeland and a reversal of exile. These two temporal breaks are separated by an ever-expanding present marked by violence, struggle and shame. This book will therefore focus on displacement as historically and geographically specific, and how these differences reconfigure Palestinian understandings of temporality and forms of belonging. My analysis will therefore consider hope as the production of histories and temporalities that refuse elisions and appropriations. Informed by Ernst Bloch's lengthy ontological study of hope within the Western cultural and political canon, hope, in the context of this book, is recognising the liberatory potential in assembling archives that are outside the reach of the coloniser and therefore cannot be classified; hope is the performance of submerged memories, staking claim to expropriated urban spaces through artistic and literary interventions. Sustaining hope through the production of history is not just a response to violence and despair. Rather, it is a liberatory project that re-articulates multi-generational Palestinian belongings, and offers potential paths to return and reclamation.

Bloch was interested in hope as an affective state of mind that propels humans to 'venture beyond' the here and now and 'throw themselves actively into what is becoming, to which they themselves belong'.[26] My concern is with the ways in which Palestinians understand hope as a core political concept, re-fashion and imbue it with particular meaning, and deploy it for their own liberatory projects. In this way, I am trying to avoid preconceived notions of hope with their own Eurocentric and Christian genealogies, that Bloch traces, and instead am attempting to gage how hopefulness is contingently produced on the ground, through mundane social encounters, and people's responses to their positionality within settler colonial power structures. Approaching hope as a performative and productive of histories helped me to be attuned to the particular contexts in which Palestinians cope and venture beyond the here and now.

The contingency of hope eschews ideas about the difference between optimism, as an attitude towards the mundane and the immediate, and hope as relating to more ambitious visions for structural changes. In the particular context of the Palestinian lives I study, I noticed that my interlocutors refused a binary between the 'small' acts in the present and revolutionary 'grand gestures' that are designed to overhaul reality. Their social interactions are informed by what they view as viable possibilities for their future. The visibility of these possibilities is what imbues forms of sociability and courses of action with meaning.[27]

This approach has a clear temporal dimension: if hope is future-oriented, and actions are informed by ideas about what can be, then, as Bloch himself argued, everyone lives in the future. To tweak William Faulkner's oft-misquoted aphorism 'the past is not dead; it is not even past': the present is not even present. When Bloch claimed that we all live in the future, he meant that a broad array of human emotions that guide our choices, be it fear, hope

---

[26] Ernst Bloch, *The Principle of Hope*, trans. Neville Plaice, Stephen Plaice and Paul Knight (Cambridge, MA: MIT Press, 1986), p. 3.

[27] See Joel Pearl, *The Question of Time: Freud in the Light of Heidegger's Temporality* (Amsterdam: Rodopi, 2013), pp. 51–3; Claude Romano, *Event and World*, trans. Shane Mackinlay (New York: Fordham University Press, 2009); Bloch himself eschews the divide between a more distant future and the 'darkness so near it of the just lived moment' (*Hope*, p. 12), locating hopefulness in the immediate and the tangible.

or desire, are always oriented towards what might be. Thus, our actions only make sense when considered against what we see as viable possibilities for our future, both those we favour and the outcome we wish to avoid. In this sense, we are in constant process of becoming, or rather, trying to become.[28] This horizon is also not 'mysterious', distant or unknown,[29] but rooted in and emanating from the conditions of the present, the vantage point from which we cast our gaze.

For Palestinians, this vantage point is the realities of settler colonialism and dispossession, differentially experienced across class, gender and political divides. As subordinates in a colonial state, let alone as stateless refugees, Palestinians actively strive to carve out their horizon against the designs of the Israeli state, aimed to cement the status quo and foreclose potential subversive ideas and avenues for political engagement. Under these conditions, Palestinians (and their Israeli-Jewish allies I also discuss here), seek to invoke both that which is 'no longer conscious' and, more importantly, what Bloch calls the 'not yet conscious', the 'forward dawning' of Jaffa's (and Palestine's) future that unsettles the colonial order and its project of the new normal.

Bloch defined the no longer conscious as 'old content that has merely sunk below the threshold and may cross it again by a more or less straightforward process of being remembered'.[30] This 'old content', in the Palestinian context, is histories of violent displacement and spatial elisions, through which the state has attempted to de-Arabise Palestine in their stead. It is not just a question of remembering these histories, as both refugees and those Palestinians who remained in Jaffa have not simply 'forgotten' about the circumstances that created statelessness and second-class citizenship. For Palestinians, the act of remembrance is not confined to the private realm, nor does it entail merely internal processes of reminiscence of the past. Put differently, Palestinians take up the conscious act of recollection, which denotes 'a way of destroying

---

[28] Jonathan Lear explored the diminishing of the horizon of possibilities as a result of cultural extinction, or the catastrophic ending of a way of life that renders past traditions meaningless. See his *Radical Hope: Ethics in the Face of Cultural Devastation* (Cambridge, MA: Harvard University Press, 2006); Vincent Crapanzano, 'Reflections on Hope as a Category of Social and Psychological Analysis', *Cultural Anthropology*, vol. 18, no. 1 (2003), p. 15.
[29] See Crapanzano, 'Reflections on Hope', p. 10.
[30] Bloch, *Hope*, p. 115.

or eradicating'[31] what the Zionist state attempts hard to preserve, namely the normalisation of occupation and its own self-identification as a liberal, democratic nation state. Rather, the effect of the act of recollection undertaken by Palestinians elucidates the settler colonial nature of the state and falsifies its founding myths. In the context of settler colonialism and violent spatial expropriations, remembrance as recollection is politically charged active engagement in public, openly challenging Israeli narratives of national rights over place. Invoking the 'no longer conscious' in public spaces is therefore intended to elicit responses from Israeli Jews and solicit new and contingent forms of political engagement.

While Bloch's main concern was to interrogate the manifold ways through which humans engage with the future, Walter Benjamin's 'Theses on the Philosophy of History' pointed to the failure of the European left to stand up to fascism and find inspiration in revolutionary traditions. Benjamin's sense of urgency and obvious despondency are evident throughout the essay: the theses were written in early 1940, even before the fall of France and the Vichy regime, but after the disastrous Molotov-Ribbentrop pact of August 1939, which, for the time being, left the USSR outside of the war and moreover, abandoned European anti-fascists to their fate. Already in exile in France, Benjamin was sensing the storm heading his way, as vast sections of the continent fell into Nazi hands.[32] In his 'moment of danger', Benjamin voiced his scathing critique of his generation and its fascination with 'progress' as a teleological understanding of human history. According to that logic, fascism is a mere exception in what is otherwise a progress of humanity towards a glorious future. In fact, Benjamin warns, this outlook, which had plagued the Weimar Social Democrats, had pawned the well-being of the oppressed classes for the promise of future liberation, which had not come. Benjamin implied that the modernist obsession with the future was, in the final analysis, what gave rise to Nazism and its attendant horrors, because the German Social Democrats and their ilk neglected to tackle fascism head on and study its appeal to the masses.

---

[31] Frederic Jameson, *Marxism and Form: Twentieth-Century Dialectical Theories of Literature* (Princeton, NJ: Princeton University Press, 1971), pp. 62–3.

[32] See Michael Löwy, *Fire Alarm: Reading Walter Benjamin's 'On the Concept of History'*, trans. Chris Turner (London: Verso, 2005).

Fascism in its different variants, then, was not an exception to modernity but part and parcel of it.

Walter Benjamin, then, was much more interested in the dialectical relationship between the past and the present, than with the future. The key to undermining the destructive 'progress' narrative is through illuminating the dark corners of history that the victors willed into oblivion: failed uprisings as well as moments of unspeakable loss. The politics of 'remembrance as recollection' operates to, in the words of Walter Benjamin, 'fan the spark of hope in the past'[33]: Palestinians who consciously and publicly dredge up that which Israelis refuse to remember – histories of mass expulsion, the ugliness of occupation, with its attendant act of violence and looting – strive to reconcile the disappointments of the past. The failures of the past also inhabit the seed of future salvation, and it is to the past that the oppressed turn to find unfulfilled hope and 'seize hold of a memory as it flashes up in the moment of danger'.[34] That memory, of failed struggles and trauma, but also of tremendous resilience and creativity, is brought up to bear on the present and point the way towards a future that rectifies the 'maimed present'.[35] For Palestinians, that 'moment of danger' is the present, as it has been since the 1948 Nakba. Benjamin reminded us that for the oppressed, there is no 'state of emergency' that is somehow the exception to the rule, as the history of the victors' claims. The act of 'fanning the spark of hope', then, is designed to undermine that illusion of 'exception', and, like Angelus Novus facing the destructive form of progress, stand at the threshold of the future while at the same time paying homage to the past.[36] The appearance of the angel in Benjamin's text writes human agency back into history: the angel may be forced to leave the pile of ruins behind, since the storm is mightier than his wings, but critical historians and oppressed peoples themselves are able to make the past a transformative force in the present. As Benjamin warned us, the Israeli state threatens even the dead: on the one hand, since 1948, Israel has systematically destroyed the physical remains of Palestine, through massive demolitions of Palestinian villages and towns and

---

[33] Walter Benjamin, 'Theses on the Philosophy of History', in W. Benjamin, *Illuminations*, trans. Harry Zohn (New York: Schocken Books, 1968), p. 255.
[34] Ibid., p. 255.
[35] Jameson, *Marxism and Form*, p. 61.
[36] Ibid., p. 83; Benjamin's image of the angel of history appears in 'Theses', p. 258.

transforming them into Jewish settlements. On the other hand, Israeli historians have been producing hegemonic narratives that celebrate the state as a bastion of democracy and Zionism as a liberatory force for oppressed Jews. As I will demonstrate in this book, Palestinians and their Israeli Jewish allies have been fighting to wrest history away from the state by staging spatial interventions in expropriated urban spaces and through the recollection of Palestine's pre-1948 past and its traumatic loss.

These acts of remembrance are also not spontaneous, and are precipitated by the invocation of the yet to become:

> The Not-Yet-Conscious itself must become *conscious* in its act, *known* in its content, as the process of dawning on the one hand, as what is dawning on the other. And so the point is reached where hope itself, this authentic expectant emotion in the forward dream, no longer just appears as a merely self-based mental feeling ... but in a *conscious-known* way as *utopian function*.[37]

My research clearly demonstrates that the past and the future are not mutually exclusive in the context of the struggle for liberation as Benjamin might have argued. Indeed, already in 'The Theses', the futuristic dimension is invoked through Benjamin's engagement with the concept of redemption, as he implies at the end of his essay. The future is not predictable, especially if we eschew the modernist teleological approach to history. Yet our understanding of the past, and through it our potential for revolution and liberation, creates opportunities for a future redemption.[38] In the context of Palestine, the new horizon of possibilities that emerges despite the Israeli state's efforts at foreclosure also elicits memories of a forgotten and submerged past that reinforce and bring visions of a redeemed world into focus. What is perhaps new here is the fissures of linear temporality: it is not that past memories make the future knowable, nor is it a simple call for a return to a real or imagined 'golden age'; rather, the forward dawning, or the drive to create a better world is what unearths that which was suppressed or made forgotten, because it was inconvenient or too traumatic, and imbues these memories with new meaning and purpose: overcome forced removals and the denial of rights by the settler colonial state.

---

[37] Bloch, *Hope*, p. 144.
[38] Benjamin, 'Theses', p. 264.

Hope as a utopian function and as a politically mobilising force operates as a way to imagine a better world and provide Palestinians an avenue for concrete actions designed to 'overwhelm', remake reality and reclaim the homeland.

The horizon, argued Reinhart Koselleck, 'is that line behind which a new space of experience will open, but which cannot yet be seen'.[39] Koselleck's main concern here is the vexed relationship between the past and the future, memory and hope, and experience and expectation. Futurity is produced within the tension between these categories: the space of experience, the 'present past', is the totality of human action, 'within which many layers of earlier times are simultaneously present'.[40] The horizon of expectation, the 'future made present', is oriented towards the 'not-yet', but at the same time, has a dialectical relationship with experience: although one cannot predict one's future based on the past, still, the layers of human experience provide guidance or 'counsel' what we may expect to happen to us next. Nevertheless, Koselleck clearly leaves ample space for human agency and for the possibility that things may turn out completely different than what we expect, based on past experiences. This is what he means when he stresses that the future 'is scattered among an infinity of temporal extensions'.[41] The 'tradition of the oppressed', or the 'space of experience' (to return to Benjamin) for Palestinians provide the layered historical memory they need in order to generate new visions, raise new hopes or anxieties from which a new space or horizon will open up. As I will show in Chapter 6, the resources my interlocutors draw on extend beyond the history of the Palestinian liberation struggle, and include other experiences of collective struggle against forms of oppression that occurred elsewhere, but that nevertheless are familiar to Palestinians.

Finally, my choice to interrogate hope as liberatory is clearly a political one. Hope as a category of analysis and as an anthropological object has come under criticism. First, Bloch's ontology of hope is based exclusively on the archaeology of the Western cultural canon, which produces a highly Eurocentric

---

[39] Reinhart Kosellek, *Futures Past: On the Semantics of Historical Time*, trans. Keith Tribe (New York: Columbia University Press, 2004), pp. 260–1. Notably, Koselleck was on the opposite end of the political spectrum. A conservative, he was more interested in preserving the social and political status quo than in the potential for revolution.

[40] Ibid., p. 260.

[41] Ibid., p. 260.

understanding of hope which might not make sense from different 'loci of enunciation', to quote Mignolo,⁴² and their own histories of knowledge production and meaning-making practices. Second, in recent decades, hope seems to have been hijacked by neoliberal promise of happiness and prosperity. Consider, for instance, President Barack Obama's 'audacity to hope' in an age of deregulation, climate erosion, border policing and high-tech warfare. Obama's hopeful visions seem to address the American (mostly white) middle class who consider the election of an African American for the grandest position a sign of utopian social progress and overcoming race. Yet his hopefulness would be greeted with ample cynicism from outside its intended audience and from different corners of empire: consider, for instance, the African-American working class and the rise of the Black Lives Matter movement at the height of Obama's presidency. It is no coincidence so many black organisers and protesters sense they were left beyond the pale of the president's hopeful fantasies, abandoned to fend for themselves against police brutality and systemic violence in dystopic inner cities. Other useful examples to the utter sense of abandonment by Obama's hope would be the president's authorised drone attacks in Yemen, and his carte blanche for Israel, thus carrying on the policy of his predecessors. Indeed, the illusion of a post-racist America shattered in November 2016 when Donald Trump carried the presidential election with the votes of millions of former Obama supporters.⁴³ Just like Bradley Whitford's character Dean Armitage in the film *Get Out* (2017), these newly minted Trump supporters tried to convince black Americans they were not 'really' racist since they voted for Obama twice and would have voted for him again if they could.

Viewed from within a Eurocentric and Christian tradition, hope has been identified as the 'passive counterpart' of desire, a human affective disposition that espouses 'constraint and resignation' and therefore abdicates human

---

⁴² Walter Mignolo, *Local Histories/Global Designs: Coloniality, Subaltern Knowledges and Border Thinking* (Princeton, NJ: Princeton University Press, 2000).

⁴³ Studies suggest that a sizeable portion of the Obama–Trump switchers found the latter's racial grievances appealing. See, for instance, Zack Beauchamp, 'A New Study Reveals the Real Reason Obama Voters Switched to Trump', *Vox*, 16 October 2018, https://www.vox.com/policy-and-politics/2018/10/16/17980820/trump-obama-2016-race-racism-class-economy-2018-midterm (last accessed 29 December 2021).

agency in favour of an outside intervention, be it a deity or just fate.[44] If we follow the logic of this critique, hope can become a category devoid of politics, with a feeble articulation of a wish or vague optimism in its stead. Similarly, feminist critics remind us that hope is a fragile project, and that furthermore, patriarchy might couch sexist and oppressive projects in the language of hope and further undermine emancipatory visions for women.[45] As recent scholarship already demonstrated, the circulation of the neoliberal valences of hope from the US into the Arab world through massive PR campaigns was designed to depoliticise and divert the attention of their intended audiences from political economy to 'culture talk' as a strategy to maintain the status quo and avoid popular uprisings.[46] The Palestinian Authority (PA), especially under former Prime Minister Salam Fayyad, embraced its own local variant of crony capitalism that benefits a small group of Palestinian businessmen and their Israeli counterparts, and undermines effective resistance to military occupation. The PA markets its neoliberal regime to West Bank Palestinians as an 'economic miracle' of growth (despite staggering poverty rates, food insecurity and land loss) and as a phase of state-building that would lead to liberation. This neoliberal pipe dream of hope is pushed by the PA and capitalist elite as an active promotion of 'economic peace' with Israel (through, among other means, the non-governmental organisation – NGO – industry) that would eventually 'trickle down' and benefit broader sectors in Palestinian society, while in reality, this strategy only serves the political status quo.[47]

I chose to focus on the ways in which Palestinians salvage hope from neoliberalism and counterinsurgency and reproduce it in concrete and meaningful terms as part of future-oriented, liberatory vocabulary and practices. Hope in this context is not a 'pie in the sky', a faint gesture of optimism or resignation to fate, but a clear articulation of a goal – the end of exile and a return to the

---

[44] Crapanzano, 'Reflections on Hope', p. 6.
[45] Amy Billingsley, 'Hope in a Vice: Carole Pateman, Judith Butler, and Suspicious Hope', *Hypatia*, vol. 30, no. 3 (Summer 2015), p. 598.
[46] Mayssoun Sukarieh, 'The Hope Crusades: Culturalism and Reform in the Arab World', *PoLAR: Political and Legal Anthropology*, vol. 35, no. 1 (May 2012), pp. 115–34.
[47] See Raja Khalidi and Sobhi Samour, 'Neoliberalism as Liberation: The Statehood Program and the Remaking of the Palestinian National Movement', *Journal of Palestine Studies*, vol. 40, no. 2 (Winter 2011), pp. 6–25.

homeland – that produces a set of practices and strategies designed to achieve it. Under these circumstances, *sumud* (Arabic, 'steadfastness'), a term that has become synonymous with the moral fortitude that enables Palestinians to cope with the precarity of refugeehood, statelessness and continued marginality, is reconfigured to denote the sheer creativity and the ability to shift tactics with the changing circumstances.

Contingencies and unknowability that are wound up in hopeful practices have shifted hegemonic discourses among Palestinians back to international law. If, in the first few years after the Nakba, international pressure and diplomacy were resources of hopeful anticipation for repatriation, these soon dissipated with staunch Israeli intransigence, and were replaced with the resurgence of Palestinian nationalism, ready to confront the occupier through armed struggle. As my fourth chapter demonstrates, the era of a Palestinian 'global offensive' with the support of newly formed developing nations came to a close by the end of the 1970s, and the armed struggle option was rolled back in the wake of the Israeli offensive in Beirut and the ousting of the resistance. After the Madrid Summit in 1991, the spectacular failure of the Oslo Accords and the massive devastation of the Second Intifada, Palestinians resorted to international law to stake their claims to place against an increasingly repressive military occupation. Their success in obtaining an International Court of Justice ruling against the separation barrier in 2004[48] fuelled the Boycott, Divestment and Sanctions (BDS) movement, a rights-based global campaign couched in international law that stipulates three basic demands, one of which is respecting the right of return of Palestinian refugees. This ongoing campaign has been gaining ground in the past few years, as it has gradually earned global recognition and support.[49]

The Right to Belong

While Palestinian refugees have been largely marginalised in the political and diplomatic spheres, camp dwellers have long been the objects of scholarship. In the past two decades, the figure of the refugee has attracted anthropologists

---

[48] Full documentation of the court's deliberations can be viewed here: http://www.icj-cij.org/docket/index.php?pr=71&code=mwp&p1=3&p2=4&p3=6&case=131&k=5a.
[49] The Boycott National Committee (BNC) has documented the campaign's successes, as well as its appeals and other public notices: https://bdsmovement.net/.

who have increasingly been interested in disaggregating refugees, previously configured as enumerable subjects. The political cultures in which refugees have found themselves in are interrogated as 'complex' and 'fluid'. The ethnographic 'arrival'[50] of Palestinians reconfigured the refugee as a political agent, and focused on questions of memory, place-making and identity formation at multiple intersections, including gender, generation, class and specific historical contexts.[51] On the other hand, the emergence of anthropological scholarship that treats hope as an analytical category has been rather incremental: Vincent Crapanzano began to explore the viability of hope deployed ethnographically and its pitfalls, Ghassan Hage argued that a 'caring' society distributes hope more effectively than a paranoid and defensive one, and Hirokazu Miyazaki treated hope as a 'method' that ties together different practices over time.[52]

---

[50] Recently, Sa'ed Atshan reframed the scholarly engagement with Palestine as a 'rise' rather than merely 'arrival' which gestures at de-exceptionalising the Palestinian lived experience. See Sa'ed Atshan, 'The Anthropological Rise of Palestine', *Journal of Palestine Studies*, vol. 50, no. 4 (2021), pp. 3–31.

[51] Diana Allan, *Refugees of the Revolution: Experiences of Palestinian Exile* (Stanford: Stanford University Press, 2014); Nina Gren, *Occupied Lives: Maintaining Integrity in a Palestinian Refugee Camp in the West Bank* (Cairo: The American University in Cairo Press, 2015); Juliane Hammer, *Palestinians Born in Exile: Diaspora and the Search for a Homeland* (Austin: University of Texas Press, 2005); Julie Peteet, *Landscape of Hope and Despair: Palestinian Refugee Camps* (Philadelphia: University of Pennsylvania Press, 2005); Sophie Richter-Devroe, '"Like Something Sacred": Palestinian Refugees' Narratives on the Right of Return', *Refugee Survey Quarterly*, vol. 32, no. 2 (2013), pp. 92–115; Rosemary Sayigh, *The Palestinians: from Peasants to Revolutionaries* (London: Zed Books, 1979) and R. Sayigh, *Too Many Enemies* (London: Zed Books, 1994).

[52] Crapanzano, 'Reflections on Hope'; Ghassan Hage, *Against Paranoid Nationalism: Searching for Hope in a Shrinking Society* (Annandale: Pluto Press Australia, 2003); Hirokazu Miyazaki, *The Method of Hope: Anthropology, Philosophy and Fijian Knowledge* (Stanford: Stanford University Press, 2004). The deployment of hope as an analytical category in the anthropology of the Middle East is still a work in progress: Schielke traces iterations of hope in contemporary Egypt to the Islamic revival, juxtaposing hope with experience: see Samuli Schielke, *Egypt in the Future Tense: Hope, Frustration, and Ambivalence before and after 2011* (Bloomington: Indiana University Press, 2015). In November 2015, Daniel Monterescu and I organised three panels on the anthropology of hope across two conferences, the American Anthropological Association (AAA) and the Middle East Studies Association (MESA) annual meetings concurrently held in Denver. The papers presented in these panels demonstrate a growing interest in hope as a viable anthropological subject, and those works in progress will no doubt emerge in the coming years.

My work draws on these shifts but offers a public history intervention into existing scholarship on place-making, forms of belonging and futurity. In contrast to anthropologists, historians of Palestine and Palestinians have largely limited themselves to archival research. In the absence of a Palestinian state and national archives, the bulk of historical research hinges on access to Israeli archives, which, as I noted above, has been less than reliable or robust. My book therefore begins in the Israeli state archives while identifying the deliberate silences they produce.[53] Palestinians have long resisted this deliberate elision of their presence and voices by producing their own historical narratives and memorialising the places they have been expelled from.[54] More recently, the Palestinian Authority has been engaged in more organised attempts at heritage preservation as a form of anti-colonial resistance.[55] While this scholarship is concerned with the ways in which colonised people memorialise their history as a strategy to undermine the colonial present, my work expands the perimeters of the discussion to include futurity. I am interested in the ways in which Palestinians articulate their understanding of belonging to 'home' as a displaced place through their relation to temporality: how are return and place-(re)making imagined differentially under conditions of settler colonialism, military occupation and forced dispersion? While I concur with Diana Allan's argument that anthropologists (and, I should add, historians) have largely neglected refugees' everyday camp experiences and community-building, foregrounding the idea of Palestine in their stead, my notes and recordings illustrate refugees' attachment to the idea of return and the temporariness of camp life. I conclude that living so long under perennially temporary international aid regimes means that refugees constantly reconfigure their forms of belonging and understanding of temporality.

The shortcomings of traditional archival research and the silences built into the Israeli archives in particular necessitated methodological creativity: oscillating between two main sites of ethnographic and oral history research,

---

[53] Michel-Rolph Trouillot, *Silencing the Past: Power and the Production of History* (Boston, MA: Beacon Press, 1995).
[54] Rochelle A. Davis, *Palestinian Village Histories: Geographies of the Displaced* (Stanford: Stanford University Press, 2011).
[55] Chiara de Cesari, *Heritage and the Cultural Struggle for Palestine* (Stanford: Stanford University Press, 2019).

Jaffa and Nablus-area refugee camps, amplified the voices of displaced Palestinians, and made visible the significance of place and distance to/from it. This project, therefore, interrogates received wisdom about home as clearly bounded and identifiable, and 'mixed cities' as places where racialised subjects (uncritically referred to as 'minorities') are 'trapped'.[56] Broadening the scope of my discussion of the local facilitates an ethnographic and historical exploration into claims of belonging that challenge not only normative thinking about place, but about temporality as well. Furthermore, insisting that Palestinians in 'mixed cities' (itself a highly problematic concept) are a national and municipal minority works to re-enforce methodological nationalism and obfuscate the working of settler colonialism that produced these urban spaces to begin with. Indeed, Daniel Monterescu's recent ethnographic monograph on Jaffa as a mixed city develops a 'relational analysis' to reveal not only mutually constitutive urban identities that displace sectarianism and nationalism, but are also productive of vibrant binational spaces that defy state-imposed ethnocracy.[57] Stressing forms of binational sociality works to reify Palestinians and Jews as national subjects rather than undermine it, and moreover, reproduces the illusion, advocated by apologists of the Zionist state, that rather than settler colonialism, there is 'conflict' between two territorial national movements warring over land. Stressing binationalism and using the language of 'national minority', then, obfuscate histories of dispossession and articulations of belonging from Palestinians who were forced to remain in exile.

Considering hope as the production of history that is future- and place-making and is potentially liberatory, I ask: how do Palestinians defy the settler colonial order, wrest history away from the state, and deploy and maintain hope for their return, especially in the context of their ongoing displacement and marginalisation in Jaffa? How do Palestinian refugees from Jaffa articulate their sense of belonging to the city, even if they had never lived in it, in a

---

[56] Dan Rabinowitz and Daniel Monterescu, 'Introduction: The Transformation of Urban Mix in Palestine/Israel in the Modern Era', in Daniel Monterescu and Dan Rabinowitz (eds), *Mixed Towns, Trapped Communities: Historical Narratives, Spatial Dynamic, Gender Relations and Cultural Encounters in Palestinian-Israeli Towns* (Aldershot: Ashgate, 2007), p. 20; Haim Yacobi, *The Jewish-Arab City: Spatio-Politics in a Mixed Community* (London: Routledge, 2009).

[57] Monterescu, *Jaffa*.

meaningful way? My work aims to point to the ways in which the settler colonial state has displaced Palestinians from their places of belonging and from history, obfuscated and foreclosed on the hope of return. More importantly, this book explores the creative responses of Palestinians (and their Israeli Jewish allies) that challenge and unsettle the present and aim to undo both aspects of displacement. I argue that by strategically unearthing traces of the 'no longer conscious' past and memories of violent displacement in addition to crafting imaginaries for the 'not yet conscious' future, Palestinians critique and challenge the colonial experience of the here and now. Moreover, this hopeful engagement with the future contracts the confining present, broadens the horizons of possibilities and works to mobilise others to action for world remaking and – reordering.

Structure and Content

The structure of this monograph reflects the imperfect tense and the pluperfect in the Jaffa refugees' experience as well as current residents of the city, both Palestinians and Jewish. The overarching process this book elaborates on is the production of history that is both outside the control of the state and that seeks to undo the effects of displacement and spatial appropriation.

The start of the book unpacks the aftermath of the 1948 mass displacement of Palestinians (or the Nakba, as it is widely referred to among Palestinians and their allies) and is based on extensive research in the Israeli state archives and the Israeli Defense Forces (IDF) archives. The first chapter introduces the history of Jaffa in the modern era, focusing on the city's final years as an important regional economic, political and cultural centre. This chapter ends with the fall of the city in the spring of 1948 and its annexation to the Israeli state and to Tel Aviv.

Chapter 2 elucidates the limitations of archival research in the Israeli state archives. In the course of this chapter, I flesh out the ways in which the new Israeli state enabled processes of public forgetfulness. I analyse how state institutions conquered urban spaces and their ability to 'bury' histories of mass expulsion, organised violence and en-masse appropriation of material goods, houses and lands, on the other. One concern in this chapter is to explore how this violent transformation assumed the guise of sanitised, inexorable normality. The making of the 'new normal' in Jaffa, then, constitutes routinising occupation, in ways that convincingly submerged the 'newness' of a rapid and radical urban transformation. Another concern here is to showcase the deliberate production of silence in the Israeli archives, the concealment of state violence, and the sedimentation of Palestinian voices and experience. Chapter 3 addresses the silences of the archives by tracing the Jaffa refugees along the different routes they have taken since 1948. These refugees experienced multiple displacements: first, from their places of origin in Palestine, then in the course of the decades since – from temporary place of refuge due to hostility, conflict and economic necessity. Furthermore, Palestinians have also experienced a displacement from official documents and therefore from traditional history. This chapter focuses on a few notable refugees whose displacement led them to revolution and public visibility. Based on memoirs and literary texts, this chapter explores the transformation of the figure of the stateless refugee, doomed to historical oblivion, into political agents that narrate their own histories and demand to be recognised.

Despite the path carved out by the Jaffa refugees I discussed in Chapter 3, itineraries of exile are far from being predictable: most refugees found themselves de-nationalised and precarious, confined to decrepit camps, while fewer pursued opportunities for meaningful political engagement and armed struggle. This chapter focuses on the fate of the former and explores the ways in which those refugees who have 'run out of place' dwell in their memories of loss, mourning and abandonment by Arab elites and the international community. Based on a variety of textual sources and interviews with refugees in the Nablus area, as well as second-generation refugees in Toronto, this chapter demonstrates how nevertheless these refugees reconfigured belonging by narrating roots and multiple routes, remaking refugeehood into a marker Palestinian identity and their exilic existence meaningful.

Chapter 5 is based on rich ethnographic material and zooms in on the artwork of Israeli-Jewish artist Gil Mualem-Doron and his urban intervention in public spaces in Jaffa and Tel Aviv. My discussion of Mualem-Doron's artistic engagement with realities of the continued displacement of Jaffa's Palestinians highlights the ways in which he seeks to provoke Israeli Jews' wilful amnesia and undermine the state project of the 'new normal'. My discussion points to Mualem-Doron's creative deployment of 'haunting' as a strategy to invoke the uncanny, or the 'no longer conscious', sedimented histories of violence and trauma and force the memory of Palestinian displacement into the public sphere.

Chapter 6 is based on extensive engagement with a project launched by two NGOs, a Palestinian and an Israeli, the highlight of which was a study visit to South Africa that was meant to provide lessons relevant to the future of Palestine and chart a shared vision for reality after the return of the refugees. These lessons, and the visions they engender, I argue, are contingent, in flux, and the result of multiple encounters and itineraries and the affective processes they are steeped in. Participants in this project pointed to commensurability of the current settler colonial realities in Palestine and apartheid South Africa. These identifications are largely divorced from structural comparisons and instead rooted in the realm of the affective and experiencing the uncanny and the eerily familiar by Israeli and Palestinian participants. Moreover, they engender narratives of both trauma and hope that crisscross between different temporalities, histories and places.

The final chapter draws on Jacques Derrida's engagement with the idea of 'living together', and seeks to explore visions for the future of Jaffa and the tangible imaginaries they produce. This chapter offers in-depth analysis of three sets of articulations: the 'Cape Town documents' that resulted from the project I described in the previous chapter; literary explorations of future-tense Jaffa by a Palestinian and an Israeli; and a tension-fraught workshop I conducted in the Balata refugee camp with young Palestinians who stake their claim to Jaffa and Tel Aviv, articulate their understanding of belonging and imagine the realities of return while at the same time, casting doubt over the possibility of a postcolonial 'shared homeland'.

1

JAFFA: FROM THE BLUSHING 'BRIDE OF PALESTINE' TO THE SHAMED 'MOTHER OF STRANGERS'

You who remove me from my house
have also evicted my parents
and their parents from theirs.
How is the view from my window?
How does my salt taste?
Shall I condemn myself a little
for you to forgive yourself
in my body? Oh how you love my body,
my body, my house.

Fady Joudah, 'Remove'[1]

In the annals of history, Jaffa is often written as a coveted prize, a *terra irredenta*, an object of desire for warlords and invading armies.[2] The city has been claimed by almost every conqueror that set his eyes on Palestine as a loot of war. Its current status as a real estate boomtown for Israeli developers can be read as yet another chain in that long history.[3] Yet, reducing Jaffa's history

---

[1] https://lareviewofbooks.org/article/my-palestinian-poem-that-the-new-yorker-wouldnt-publish/.
[2] See the Preface of S. Tolkowsky, *The Gateway of Palestine: A History of Jaffa* (London: G. Routledge and Sons, 1924), n.p.
[3] On Jaffa's current attractiveness to real estate developers and investors, see, for instance, Lyle Plocher, 'Foreigner's Guide to Property Market: Living in Jaffa', *The Jerusalem Post*,

to a chain of military conquests, however formative those have been for the city, elides its people and their lived experiences, and obscures how humans have constantly redefined their relationship to its changing urban landscapes. Narrating the *longue dureé* history of Jaffa as a site of military victories and defeats ultimately serves the interests of the Israeli state and its claims to the city as wartime conquest, sidestepping the human catastrophe of mass displacement and the continued attachment of Jaffa's refugees to their lost homes.

Drawing mostly on secondary sources, this chapter traces the history of Jaffa in the modern age until its fall in the spring of 1948. Despite the perceived linearity of this chapter, its purpose is to provide a counter-narrative to Israeli ones that position the founding of the state and the Judaicising of the city as their telos. Instead, this chapter reminds us of that which is 'no longer conscious', the local history suppressed and silenced by the state, a story with Palestinians as its agents, highlighting their creativity and resourcefulness, as well as suffering and eventual expulsion.

Jaffa: A Hub of Modernity

The question of modernity in the global South and the Middle East in particular has long been a subject of historiographical debate. Orientalist as well as Zionist historians identified Europe as the 'true' locus of modernity and the sole historical agent undertaking the 'white man's burden' of modernising and civilising the rest of the world.[4] In this vein, colonial narratives dismiss

---

12 May 2011, http://www.jpost.com/Business/Real-Estate/Foreigners-guide-to-property-market-Living-in-Jaffa (last accessed 26 May 2016); Imogen Kimber, 'Gentrifying Jaffa', *Middle East Eye*, 17 September 2015, http://www.middleeasteye.net/in-depth/features/gentrifying-jaffa-1476207527 (last accessed 26 May 2016). See also Mark LeVine, *Overthrowing Geography: Jaffa, Tel Aviv and the Struggle for Palestine, 1880–1948* (Berkeley: University of California Press, 2005), especially chapter 8.

[4] Bernard Lewis, *The Middle East and the West* (New York: Harper & Row, 1964), *The Muslim Discovery of Europe* (New York: W.W. Norton, 1982) and 'The West and the Middle East', *Foreign Affairs* vol. 76, no. 1 (January–February 1997), pp. 114–31; more recently, Thomas Sparr's *German Jerusalem: The Remarkable Life of a German-Jewish Neighborhood in the Holy City* (trans. Stephen Brown (London: Haus Publishing, 2021)) credits the British and then the Ashkenazi-Jewish migrants to Palestine as agents of modernity. For a comprehensive historiographical discussion of the periodization of modernity, see Dror Ze'evi, 'Back to Napoleon? Thoughts on the Beginning of the Modern Era in the Middle East', *Mediterranean Historical Review*, vol. 19, no. 1 (2004), pp. 73–94. I cite a few prominent Zionist historians

non-European claims for modernity as mere mimicry, a result of Western 'tutelage', though it never measured up to the origin. When it comes to Palestine, these narratives often choose the Napoleonic conquest as its point of departure, describe the purported herculean efforts of American, German, and other 'pioneers' of modernisation, culminating in the British Mandate and its achievements integrating the country into global markets. Zionist historians (as well as operatives and politicians) have taken up these colonial pretenses, casting the Zionist project as the primary agent of modernity and economic development, successful despite the intransigence of Palestine's 'traditional' Arab population. Indeed, within this logic, all that is Ottoman and Arab is considered an impediment for modernity that Zionists, and later Israelis, had to overcome in order to reinvent themselves as the 'startup nation'. Since 1949, the purported immutable 'backwardness' of Palestine's Arabs was deployed by Israel's diplomatic corps to explains the state's rejection of any solution to the refugee problem that entails their repatriation.

The consensus today among most historians of the region (and of Palestine), is that certain economic shifts identified with modernity in fact occurred prior to the nineteenth century, and that what was previously (mis)identified as a radical break with a static past took place in a much more haphazard and decentralised manner. Not only was Napoleon not the engine of rapid economic and political transformations (in fact, his army left mostly destruction in its wake), but changes in the production, circulation and trade of commodities hinged on multiple factors, most of which were region-specific. This is also why Palestine emerged as a hub for the production and trade of, for instance, olive oil, soap and citrus, with Jaffa as its main import and export gateway.[5] What follows is therefore a short history of modern Jaffa as a product

---

(such as Kark and Tolkowski) in this chapter, though I evaluate their scholarly contribution within a broader, more critical, context.

[5] Beshara Doumani, *Rediscovering Palestine: Merchants and Peasants in Jabal Nablus, 1700–1900* (Berkeley: University of California Press, 1995); Alexander Scholch, *Palestine in Transformation, 1856–1882: Studies in Social, Economic, and Political Development*, trans. William C. Young and Michael C. Gerrity (Washington, DC: Institute for Palestine Studies, 1993); Sherene Seikaly analysed the socio-economic dynamics in Palestinian society during the Mandate era and demonstrated that the flourishing of exports and business ventures were in spite of the British colonial administration rather than its byproducts. See her *Men of Capital: Scarcity and Economy in Mandate Palestine* (Stanford: Stanford University Press, 2015).

of intersecting, often contradictory, forces while remaining grounded in the lived experiences of the *Yafawiin* themselves.

In the wake of the short-lived Napoleonic conquest and devastation (1799), and Ahmed al-Jazzar's ensuing revolt against the Ottoman government (1799–1800), Jaffa entered a new phase of reconstruction and rapid growth. Under the rule of Muhammad Abu Nabbut, governor of Gaza and Jaffa (1807–18), the city's walls were fortified, the Mahmoudiyah mosque renovated, and public fountains and new marketplaces were constructed.[6] Efforts at urban renewal continued and intensified during Egyptian rule (1831–40). The Tanzimat, or the period of state reforms in the Ottoman Empire, slowly began to impact the Syrian provinces, and with the consistent presence of garrisons along the coastline and on major roads, security of trade routes improved, which also intensified the commercial activity in the city. By the mid-nineteenth century, Jaffa's significance as Palestine's main port and a commercial hub accelerated the movement of people and commodities in and out of the city, as the country's agriculture became integrated into global markets.[7]

Jaffa's port, however, was not just a commercial gateway of an emerging economy. It was also the primary entryway into the booming city that attracted settlers, investors and European and American missionaries. If at the end of the Egyptian occupation and the dawn of the Tanzimat, Jaffa's population numbered around 10,000, at the close of the nineteenth century, its number had increased fourfold.[8] Immigrants were attracted to Jaffa as a city of opportunity: merchants from Lebanon identified the potential as a global trade centre; peasants from as far as Egypt and from the Palestinian interior opted to settle outside the city proper and cultivate the land; American missionaries, for instance, believed one of their objectives was to teach modern agricultural techniques to

---

[6] Ruba Kana'an, 'Two Ottoman Sabils in Jaffa (c.1810–1815): an Architectural and Epigraphic Analysis', *Levant*, vol. 33, no. 1 (January 2001), pp. 189–204; Tolkowsky, *The Gateway*, 154–5; Ruth Kark, *Jaffa: A City in Evolution, 1799–1917*, trans. Gila Brand (Jerusalem: Yad Izhak Ben Zvi, 1990), pp. 18–20.

[7] For a more comprehensive analysis of the economic development of Palestine in the late Ottoman empire, see Roger Owen, *The Middle East in the World Economy, 1800–1914* (London: Methuen, 1981), pp. 173–9; on the economic development of Jaffa in the late Ottoman era, see Johann Bussow, *Hamidian Palestine, Politics and Society in the District of Jerusalem, 1872–1908* (Leiden: Brill, 2011), especially chapter 4.

[8] Kark, *Jaffa*, pp. 146–52.

the Jews, so that the latter would inherit the earth and bring about the Second Coming.[9] The German Templars, who replaced the Americans in 1868 after the spectacular failure of their nascent colony and subsequent hurried departure, prospered as both farmers (in Sarona) and industrialists (Valhallah), using imported farming machinery operated by local labourers.

Jaffa's demographic boom brought about the city's rapid spatial expansion in all directions, but especially to the north (Irshid and Manshiyyeh) and the south ('Ajami and Jabbaliyeh) as the old city walls were demolished in 1888.[10] East of the old city, the modern quarter of Nuzha was developed, and later, a European boulevard planted as the urban was creeping into the hinterland. Nevertheless, as Mark LeVine correctly noted, while the old city can be perceived as Jaffa's urban core, the boundaries between town and country were much blurrier, as the two spheres, the urban and the rural, constantly cut across each other and formed a symbiotic co-dependency.[11] This porosity is also reflected in interviews I conducted with elderly refugees from the villages around Jaffa and who, to this day, proudly self-identify as *Yafawiin*.[12]

The late Ottoman era also signalled a slow transformation of Jaffa's urban social relations. With the swelling of the population and the inevitable expansion beyond the city's old walls, there was a concomitant process of sectarianisation of urban space. Thus, for instance, Christian Maronites constructed their own quarter, while the Sephardic and Maghrebi Jews ventured north and founded Neveh Tsedek (1887) and Neveh Shalom (1890).[13] Yet although it seems sectarian belonging was the organising principle of the new modern quarters, inhabitants of Jaffa espoused a sense of shared identity, Ottomanism, and local pride and they collaborated to address concerns about public good (for instance, a planned tramway that would pass through Jaffa's major neighbourhoods).[14] What is clear from the sources we have is that Jaffa's emerging inter-confessional middle class consisted of entrepreneurs,

---

[9] Ibid., p. 76.
[10] Ibid., pp. 100–1.
[11] LeVine, *Overthrowing Geography*, pp. 52–3.
[12] See Chapter 4.
[13] Kark, *Jaffa*, pp. 126–7.
[14] Michelle U. Campos, *Ottoman Brothers: Muslims, Christians, and Jews in Early Twentieth-Century Palestine* (Stanford: Stanford University Press, 2011), p. 182.

merchants and builders who seized the opportunity to purchase lands and develop new housing and business quarters.[15]

The local Jewish community was made up of Maghrebi migrants, such as the Chelouch and Moyal families, and old Sephardi families (Amzaleg) who left Jerusalem for Jaffa despite an age-old rabbinical ban. These families not only became community leaders, but also shared much in common with their class counterparts across confessional lines. This is evident, among other things, from the memoirs of Yosef Eliyahu Chelouch, who self-identifies as a 'son of this land', just like his Muslim and Christian counterparts, and, like his generation, was culturally integrated, spoke Arabic and worked, with other community members (such as renowned journalist Nissim Malul), to quell any sign of sectarian strife. The life histories of the Maghrebi Jewish community of Jaffa are filled with anecdotes that demonstrate forms of belonging to locality that is decidedly Arab and that later Zionist histories attempted to erase.[16] These Maghrebi and Sephardi Jews oscillated towards Zionism very gradually in light of the failed universalism of Ottomanist ideas, and even then, they remained on the peripheries of Zionist activity, partly because they were perceived as 'ideologically suspicious'.[17]

With the commencement of Zionist migration into the country, Jaffa became the movement's launching pad and base of operations. As young idealists disembarked in Jaffa and divided into groups of 'pioneers' before heading out to the new agricultural colonies (Petakh Tikva, Gedera, Rishon

---

[15] Kark, *Jaffa*, p. 125.
[16] See Yosef Eliyahu Chelouch, *The Story of my Life* [in Hebrew] (Tel Aviv: Bavel, 2005); Mordekhai Elkayam, for another instance, emphasised the affinity between the Maghrebi Jews of Jaffa and their Muslim neighbours, which was clearly demonstrated through everyday forms of sociability and reciprocity. See Mordekhai Elkayam, *Jaffa, Neve Tzedek: The Beginnings of Tel Aviv* [in Hebrew] (Tel Aviv: Ministry of Defense, 1990), pp. 121–2, 140–1.
[17] Campos, *Ottoman Brothers*, p. 198, as well as Michelle U. Campos, 'Between "Beloved Ottomania" and "The Land of Israel": The Struggle over Ottomanism and Zionism among Palestine's Sephardi Jews, 1908–1913', *International Journal of Middle East Studies*, vol. 37 (2005), pp. 461–83; for more on the cultural integration of Jaffa's Mizrahi Jews and their claims for Arabness, see Menachem Klein, 'Arab Jews: Neither Oxymoron nor Aspersion', *Lives in Common: Arabs and Jews in Jerusalem, Jaffa and Hebron*, trans. Haim Wartzman (London: C. Hurst & Co., 2014), Digital Edition; Louis Fishman, *Jews and Palestinians in the Late Ottoman Era, 1908-1914: Reclaiming the Homeland* (Edinburgh: Edinburgh University Press, 2020).

LeZion), Jaffa became the seat of Zionist institutions and local leadership and the centre of the movement's educational, economic and political activities, until later on these were relocated to Tel Aviv.[18] The ambitions of the newcomers did not go unnoticed by the Arabic-language media. Palestinian notables and other members of the political and cultural elite proceeded to petition the Sublime Porte, organise anti-Zionist societies and publish numerous op-eds about the potential menace of Zionist colonisation in Palestine. By the beginning of World War I, Palestinian Arabs, and urbanites in particular, were well informed about the aims of Zionism and, perhaps mirroring similar attitudes among Sephardi Jews, gravitated towards local patriotism and nascent forms of Arab nationalism. After the Young Turks Revolution (1908), and with the rise of suspicions that Zionism ultimately sought to establish a state in Palestine, Jewish migration to the country was restricted.[19]

The Zionist Colonial Logic of Separation

The threat that Zionism posed for indigenous Palestinians lay in its particular nature as an exclusivist settler colonial nationalist movement that, despite humble beginnings and relative weakness at the outset, capitalised on certain vulnerabilities of Palestinian Arab society. As sociologist Gershon Shafir argues, Zionists acted 'with the express purpose of allowing the formation of

[18] A prominent example was the 'Gate of Zion' hospital in Jaffa; see Shifra Shvarts, 'B'nai B'rith-Sha'ar Zion Hospital in Jaffa (1891–1921): The First Jewish Community Hospital in Palestine', *Judaism*, vol. 47, no. 3 (Summer 1998), pp. 358–70.
[19] Neville J. Mandel, *The Arabs and Zionism Before World War I* (Berkeley: University of California Press, 1976), pp. 32–57; Rashid Khalidi, *Palestinian Identity: The Construction of Modern National Consciousness* (New York: Columbia University Press, 2010), pp. 89–104; see also Abigail Jacobson, 'From Empire to Empire: Jerusalem in the Transition between Ottoman and British Rule, 1912–1920', PhD dissertation, University of Chicago, 2006, pp. 26–8; Gershon Shafir, *Land, Labor and the Origins of the Israeli-Palestinian Conflict, 1882–1914* (New York: Cambridge University Press, 1989), pp. 202–11; Emanuel Beska, 'Political Opposition to Zionism in Palestine and Greater Syria: 1910–1911 as a Turning Point', *Jerusalem Quarterly*, vol. 59, no. 55 (2014), pp. 54–67; Rachel Hart, 'Jaffa and Tel Aviv through the Double Prism of the Arab Press, 1881–1930' [in Hebrew], *Kesher*, no. 39 (2009), pp. 92–101; on the Jaffa-based journalist 'Isa al-'Isa, his scathing criticism of Zionism in the press and his complex relationship with the local Maghrebi Jewish community, see Salim Tamari, 'Issa al-Issa's Unorthodox Orthodoxy: Banned in Jerusalem, Permitted in Jaffa', *Jerusalem Quarterly*, vol. 59, no. 17 (2014), pp. 29–31.

a pure or national settlement society, aimed at the reshaping of the land and labor markets'.[20]

Even though the conditions in Palestine and the nature of the Zionist movement were not favourable for the creation of a pure plantation colony, Zionist politicians and leaders carved out a project that entailed the creation of an exclusive national society explicitly through the 'conquest of land'. The discourse of 'conquest of land' reveals that although the Zionist colonial project lacked a metropolitan state or an occupying army, its leadership understood the link between nation-building in Europe and acquiring colonial possessions. Zionist desire to liberate the Jews from subordination and discrimination necessitated, in this view, proof that they were, after all, just as European and white as other nations. Zionism then, was premised on turning the idea of an ancestral land into an extra-European settler colony. Similarly, the 'conquest of labour' was also a means to an end: ending the dependency of Jews and its concomitant culture of lobbying (Hebrew, *shtadlanut*) with foreign rulers or benefactors, which was deemed demeaning and unworthy of white Europeans. Coming to one's own as a nation meant, therefore, economic and political independence that could only be achieved through exclusivist Jewish takeover of all economic activity.

Stressing the two-pronged conquest of Palestine also reveals the intentions of Zionists to permanently settle the land with European Jews, as a means to be acknowledged as a civilised nation. The desired permanence of the Zionist project in Palestine meant that this particular formation of settler colonialism was forced to engage with the land's indigenous population from the outset. Although agricultural colonies in particular extensively employed Palestinian labourers, Zionist leadership promoted and attempted to enforce ideas of labour exclusivity. In other words, rather than subordinate the indigenous populations, the Zionist variant of settler colonialism aspired to eliminate and replace them.[21]

---

[20] Shafir, *Land, Labor and the Origins*, p. 19.
[21] For a discussion of Zionism as a form of settler colonialism, see David Lloyd, 'Settler Colonialism and the State of Exception: The Example of Palestine/Israel', *Settler Colonial Studies*, vol. 2, no. 1 (2012), pp. 59–80; Zachary Lockman, 'Land, Labour and the Logic of Zionism: A Critical Engagement with Gershon Shafir', *Settler Colonial Studies*, vol. 2, no. 1 (2012), pp. 9–38; a nuanced discussion of Zionism in comparison to British-occupied Rhodesia: Seth J. Frantzman, 'The Dark Narrative of Israel's Rhodesia Fantasy', *+972*

The White City and 'Mixing'

This segregationist inclination was demonstrated through the establishment and further expansion of Tel Aviv. Originally named Ahuzat Bayit, Tel Aviv had a humble beginning as an exclusively Jewish suburb of Jaffa, just north of the city, on plots of land purchased by middle-class Sephardi and Zionist activists. The impetus for Tel Aviv's establishment, however, was its founders' nationalist fervour, and what they considered as the need for Jews to be separated from the *goyim* (Hebrew, 'non-Jews') in order to fully develop nationalist consciousness and the spirit of the 'new Jew', divorced from his past in the diaspora as a weak and subordinated other. Only in an exclusively Jewish suburb would Jews be able to learn and speak Hebrew and acquire the kind of education needed for the development of the nation.[22]

Stories circulated about the emergence of the 'first Hebrew city' often neglect to mention that in the years prior to the establishment of Tel Aviv, several Jewish neighbourhoods sprung up in its immediate vicinity, like Yefeh Nof (1897), Mahaneh Yosef (1904), Kerem Hateymanim (1905) and Ohel Moshe (1906).[23] What set the new suburb apart was its designation as a modern quarter that was inherently different, indeed, the opposite, of its forerunners, that, after all, resembled the unplanned and 'unsanitary' 'oriental' city. Ahuzat Bayit, then, staked its claim to modernity and to becoming everything that

---

Magazine, 24 September 2015, http://972mag.com/the-dark-narrative-of-israels-rhodesia-fantasy/111926/ (last accessed 26 May 2016); for an opposing argument that defines Zionism as diaspora nationalism rather than a colonial formation, see Arnon Golan, 'European Imperialism and the Development of Modern Palestine: Was Zionism a Form of Colonialism?', *Space & Polity*, vol. 5, no. 2 (2001), pp. 127–43.

[22] See, for instance, Joachim Schlor, *Tel Aviv*, trans. Helen Atkins (London: Reaktion, 1999), pp. 47–8.

[23] This criticism was levelled round the centennial celebrations, mostly online, on website such as Tel Aviv 100, the Urban Encyclopedia [in Hebrew], written and edited by Dani Recht, https://sites.google.com/a/tlv100.net/tlv100/tlv100?authuser=0; descendants of the original sixty-six families of Tel Aviv's founders created a website, now defunct, that advocated for public commemoration, http://www.ahuzatbait.org.il/העמותה-2/ [in Hebrew]; for the history of pre-Ahuzat Bayit Jewish neighbourhoods, see Hanna Ram, *The Jewish Community in Jaffa from Sephardic Community to Zionist Center* [in Hebrew] (Jerusalem: Carmel, 1996).

Jaffa was not, in the eyes of its founders.[24] The discourse of cleanliness and the link between urban planning and health already circulated in Europe at the time, and Tel Aviv was originally intended to become a 'garden city', a concept developed by Ebenezer Howard. Howard's Garden Cities were small suburbs in the countryside, consisting of single-family houses surrounded by greenery and arranged along wide avenues. This rationally planned new city, which is the opposite of the overcrowded industrial metropolis, was to develop healthier bodies and more disciplined, productive and morally improved citizens and workers.[25] Around the same time, and even into the World War I, Jaffa also went into a phase of urban modernisation, led by the local Ottoman authorities (and in particular governor Hassan Bey) and middle-class Palestinian entrepreneurs. Jamal Pasha Boulevard (later renamed King George V Boulevard), lined with median trees, was a prominent result of that modernisation impetus.[26] On the eve of World War I, Jaffa was a modern cosmopolitan city of 40,000 where one could comfortably get around speaking a mixture of languages, from Arabic and Ottoman Turkish to Yiddish and French, and where religious holidays often transformed into opportunities for popular celebrations for all.[27]

Despite the depravation of World War I, and the fact that many residents of Jaffa were forcibly removed by Jamal Pasha,[28] the modernisation impetus only increased once the country was taken over by the British. Everyday

---

[24] See Sharon Rotbard, *White City, Black City* [in Hebrew] (Tel Aviv: Bavel, 2005), pp. 112, 126–7.

[25] Ebenezer Howard, *Garden Cities of To-Morrow* (London: Swan Sonnenschein, 1902); see also Paul Rabinow, *French Modern: Norms and Forms of the Social Environment* (Chicago: University of Chicago Press, 1989), pp. 257–60; on Tel Aviv as a 'garden city' with a Zionist twist, see LeVine, *Overthrowing Geography*, pp. 159–61.

[26] Mark LeVine, 'Nationalism, Religion and Urban Politics in Israel: Struggles over Modernity and Identity in "Global" Jaffa', in Daniel Monterescu and Dan Rabinowitz (eds), *Mixed Towns, Trapped Communities: Historical Narratives, Spatial Dynamics, Gender Relations and Cultural Encounters in Palestinian-Israeli Towns* (Aldershot: Ashgate, 2007), pp. 283–4; LeVine, *Overthrowing Geography*, p. 175.

[27] For a vivid description of urban cosmopolitanism in Jaffa in the early twentieth century, see Menachem Klein, *Lives in Common: Arabs and Jews in Jerusalem, Jaffa and Hebron*, trans. Haim Watzman (London: C. Hurst & Company, 2014), pp. 67–72.

[28] About this brief 'first exodus', see Yusuf Heikal and Imad el-Haj, 'Jaffa ... as it was', *Journal of Palestine Studies*, vol. 13, no. 4 (Summer 1984), pp. 3–21.

urban lifestyle and forms of sociability also transformed, partly as a result of the encounters between civilians and British military personnel: men spent increasingly more time with their peers in coffee shops rather than entertain in the privacy of their homes; nightclubs and bordellos sprung up, particularly around the port area and in the vicinity of military barracks and bases. No wonder contemporaries lamented the visible 'deterioration of morals' inside the bustling metropolis.[29]

Under the British Mandate, the Zionist colonial logic of separation operated on several levels: Zionist institutions, for instance, continued to mobilise against all forms of 'mixing': from sharing lived spaces to moral panic over inter-ethnic sexual relations. The Histadrut, the Zionist labour federation in Palestine, was at once committed to the 'conquest of labour', advocating preference of Jewish workers over their Palestinian counterparts, but also, at least in theory, class over nationalist or confessional solidarities. The solution the Histadrut leaders found was supposed to reflect this duality: the organisation prioritised its commitment to Zionism, which meant filling a major role not only in the so-called 'battle' to 'conquer labour' but in the greater struggle to create a modern Jewish nation in Palestine. To this end, the Histadrut established a Hebrew-language newspaper and publishing house (Davar), theatre (Ohel), a bank (Hapoalim) and a construction company that built housing projects for Jewish labourers (Solel Boneh).[30] On the other hand, the Histadrut made some efforts to appeal to Palestinian workers, stressing class solidarity against their exploitative employers and nationalist propaganda, which, ostensibly, aimed at distracting them from everyday survival struggles they shared with their Jewish comrades. But instead of incorporating Palestinian comrades into its structures, the Histadrut opted to establish separate agencies to serve them, like Arabic-language newspapers that pontificated the benefits of Zionism for Palestinian Arabs and the country's prosperity. In 1932, the Histadrut established the Palestine Labour League (PLL), its own Arab union which was highly active in organising Palestinians in Jaffa, especially around the port. The PLL was moderately successful in Jaffa, partly because the Histadrut

---

[29] See, for instance, Salim Tamari, *Year of the Locust: A Soldier's Diary and the Erasure of Palestine's Ottoman Past* (Berkeley: University of California Press, 2011), pp. 11–12; LeVine, *Overthrowing Geography*, pp. 118–19.

[30] Lev Grinberg, *The Histadrut Above All* [in Hebrew] (Jerusalem: Nevo, 1993).

identified a vacuum in labour organising in the city and managed to insinuate itself into local struggles, such as the municipal employees' strike in the early 1940s. PLL was finally forced out of Jaffa in mid-1944, and the following year a Palestinian labour conference was held in the city, that brought former PLL members back into the national fold.[31]

The British mandatory authorities themselves were keen on ethnic and confessional demarcations. In May 1921, the British High Commissioner transformed Tel Aviv into an autonomous township.[32] From that point on, the Tel Aviv local council and its mayor Meir Dizengoff, tirelessly lobbied the British to make Tel Aviv into an independent municipality and argued for the expansion of its official boundaries to include other Jewish and mixed neighbourhoods.[33]

These urban borderlands between Jaffa and Tel Aviv were also sites of violent flare-ups, especially in the intercommunal strife of 1921, 1929 and 1936.[34] At the same time, these contact zones were also sites of everyday encounters and cooperation that cut across confessional and ethnic lines, defied official practices of border-making and belied nationalist histories of hostility.[35] In many ways, the Mandate years should be perceived as the continuation of Jaffa's modernisation surge. Despite financial fluctuations, the municipality carried on projects of construction, widening streets to improve traffic access, garbage collection and disposal, and other urban infrastructure. The city's population continued to swell, mainly as a result of internal migration and

---

[31] LeVine, *Overthrowing Geography*, pp. 90–5.
[32] Although the majority of the Zionists agreed that municipal separation would benefit Tel Aviv and the Zionist project in Palestine, some had doubts about turning Tel Aviv into an autonomous township, since, despite its impressive growth, the town was still depending on Jaffa. See Hart, 'Double Prism', pp. 94–5.
[33] Ram, *Jewish Community*, pp. 339–41; on Tel Aviv-Jaffa borders and their colonial imaginaries, see also Tali Hatuka and Rachel Kallus, 'Loose Ends: The Role of Architecture in Constructing Urban Borders in Tel Aviv-Jaffa since the 1920s', *Planning Perspectives*, vol. 21 (January 2006), pp. 23–44.
[34] LeVine, *Overthrowing Geography*, pp. 109–16.
[35] Ibid., chapter 4; Rotbard, *White City*, pp. 161–2; both Palestinian Arab and the Hebrew-language Zionist newspapers reported that many residents of Jaffa were in attendance during Tel Aviv's famed Purim celebrations: see Hart, 'Double Prism', pp. 97–8; see also Abigail Jacobson and Moshe Naor, *Oriental Neighbors: Middle Eastern Jews and Arabs in Mandatory Palestine* (Waltham: Brandeis University Press, 2016).

rapid urbanisation, that led many to seek better opportunities in Jaffa, the bustling core of commercial activity in Palestine. In the last few years of the Mandate, plans for the construction of a new 'garden city' (on its southern frontiers, close to the Jewish settlement of Holon) were drawn up, as well as ideas for enlarging and improving the port.[36] The Jaffa port was considered the city's economic base and a national symbol of longevity and rootedness. It is no wonder, then, that much of the popular mobilisation in the late 1930s focused on the port: keeping it Arab (i.e. resisting Zionist attempts to integrate more Jewish workers) and rejecting Tel Aviv's demands to build its own port. The 1936 Palestinian uprising and the strike that shut down all commercial activity at the port resulted in the construction of a jetty and then a more permanent dock in northern Tel Aviv; soon after, commercial liners began unloading wares at the new port. Even after the reopening of the Jaffa port, imports and exports were falling, and attempts in subsequent years were unsuccessful in reviving port traffic to pre-1936 levels.[37]

In terms of Jaffa's social make-up, while it is true that the middle and upper classes (many of whom made their fortunes in the citrus business) dominated the city's political, economic and cultural life, endowing it with a cosmopolitan allure, this rapid urbanisation also carried the seeds of Jaffa's defeat in 1948. Recently, Israeli historian Itamar Radai concluded that the gaping disparity between the rich and influential *Yafawiin* and the poor and marginalised newcomers that settled at the city's margins resulted in a catastrophic absence of a broad social base of urban resilience in the face of the encroaching enemy. This, Radai argues, explains the difference between the utter collapse of Jaffa in 1948 and the partial resilience of Arab Jerusalem.[38]

In retrospect, then, the Mandate era was fortuitous for the exponential growth of Tel Aviv; by the mid-1940s, its population reached 166,000 (see below). At the same time, Jaffa's fortunes were on the decline; first, with

---

[36] For a discussion of architecture and planning in Jaffa, see LeVine, *Overthrowing Geography*, pp. 171–9.
[37] Tamir Goren, 'The Struggle to Save the National Symbol: Jaffa Port from the Arab Revolt until the Twilight of the British Mandate', *Middle East Studies*, vol. 51, no. 6 (November 2015), pp. 863–82.
[38] Itamar Radai, *Between Two Cities: Palestinian Arabs in Jerusalem and Jaffa* [in Hebrew] (Tel Aviv: Tel Aviv University Press, 2015).

the loss of territory to Tel Aviv, and gradually to other Jewish settlements that, by 1947, surrounded it on three sides; the 1936 revolt resulted in the prolonged closure of the port and the loss of business to Haifa and then to the newly established Tel Aviv port.[39] The British penalised Jaffa for its popular support of the revolt with aerial raids that demolished substantial sections of the old city. Still reeling from the violent reprisals of the great revolt and plagued by financial troubles and surrounded by Jewish settlements that stunted its growth, Jaffa's residents were forced to watch on as the UN voted to partition Palestine and make Jaffa an Arab enclave inside a Jewish state.

Disaster

The most widely circulated term to describe the catastrophic Arab defeat of 1948 and its concomitant mass expulsions of Palestinians is *al-Nakba* (Arabic, 'the disaster'). It was coined by Syrian intellectual Constantine Zureiq while hostilities were still ongoing, even before several localities were completely depopulated. In *The Meaning of Disaster*, Zureiq warned his readers to look inward and locate the blame for the loss of Palestine in the corruption and ignorance of the Arab nation, and its inability to mobilise the masses and convince them of the danger of Zionist colonisation. It is not just that the Jews held superior military power, he argued, but that they were able to wage total war that encompasses every sphere of human lives, while the Arabs espoused outdated approaches to war as battlefield action.[40]

---

[39] On the rise of the Haifa port, see Jacob Norris, *Land of Progress: Palestine in the Age of Colonial Development, 1905–1948* (Oxford: Oxford University Press, 2013), especially chapter 3.

[40] Constantine Zureiq, *The Meaning of Disaster*, trans. R. Bayly Winder (Beirut: Khayat's College Book Cooperative, 1956), p. 21. A year later, Musa al-Alami, son and grandson of former mayors of Jerusalem, published his own analysis of the causes for the disaster, indicating that the Zionist side was engaged in total war, which the Palestinians were not ready for: Musa Alami, 'The Lesson of Palestine', *Middle East Journal*, vol. 3, no. 4 (October 1949), pp. 373–405, Alami mentions total war on p. 374; see also Moshe Naor, 'Israel's 1948 War of Independence as a Total War', *Journal of Contemporary History*, vol. 43, no. 2 (2008), pp. 241–57; Adel Manaa, 'The Palestinian Nakba and its Continuous Repercussions', *Israel Studies*, vol. 18, no. 2 (Summer 2003), pp. 86–99; Anaheed al-Hardan, 'Al-Nakbah in Arab Thought: The Transformation of a Concept', *Comparative Studies of South Asia, Africa and the Middle East*, vol. 35, no. 3 (2015), pp. 622–38.

For the Palestinians, the Nakba means the systematic and brutal removal of hundreds of thousands of civilians and the destruction of villages, towns and urban areas and their local cultures by Zionist troops. This expulsion and deliberate depopulation of whole regions were executed before the invasion of the regular Arab armies; moreover, the ethnic cleansing of Palestine was not done haphazardly, but followed a military blueprint known as Plan Dalet, which in many ways capped the Zionist settler colonial ambition of previous decades.[41] In other words, the Zionist political and military leadership brought the process of 'conquest of the land' to its logical conclusion through the removal of the indigenous population (or as many of them as they possibly could), replacing it with Jewish settlers.

The dire outcomes of the Nakba are still experienced to this day: about half of the Palestinian Arab population of Mandatory Palestine and 85 per cent of the territory that came under Israeli control were displaced, ending up as refugees in neighbouring Arab countries, in the West Bank and the Gaza Strip, and globally. Hundreds of villages, in addition to towns and urban neighbourhoods were either demolished to make way for new Jewish-only settlements or were repopulated with (in most cases) Jewish newcomers.[42]

The Fall of Jaffa

UN Resolution 181 of 29 November 1947 set an expiry date for the British Mandate in Palestine of 15 May 1948.[43] The resolution also stipulated the partition of Palestine and consigned Jaffa, the bustling cultural and economic urban centre of the Palestinian coast, to complete encirclement by Jewish settlements. In fact, the UN resolution effectively cut the city off from its

---

[41] Walid Khalidi, 'Plan Dalet: The Zionist Master Plan for the Conquest of Palestine', *Middle East Forum*, vol. 37, no. 9 (1961), pp. 22–8, and 'Why did the Palestinians Leave? Revisited', *Journal of Palestine Studies*, vol. 34, no. 2 (Winter 2005), pp. 42–54.

[42] For more extensive histories of the Nakba, see Ilan Pappé, *The Ethnic Cleansing of Palestine* (London: One World Publications, 2006); Rosemary Sayigh, *The Palestinians from Peasants to Revolutionaries* (London: Zed Books, 2007); Benny Morris, *The Birth of the Palestinian Refugee Problem, 1947-1949* [in Hebrew] (Tel Aviv: Am Oved, 1991); for the Nakba in its context, see Sami Hadawi, *Bitter Harvest: A Modern History of Palestine* (New York: Olive Branch Press, 1991); Michael Palumbo, *The Palestinian Catastrophe: The 1948 Expulsion of a People from their Homeland* (London: Quartet Books, 1987).

[43] UN A/RES/181 (II).

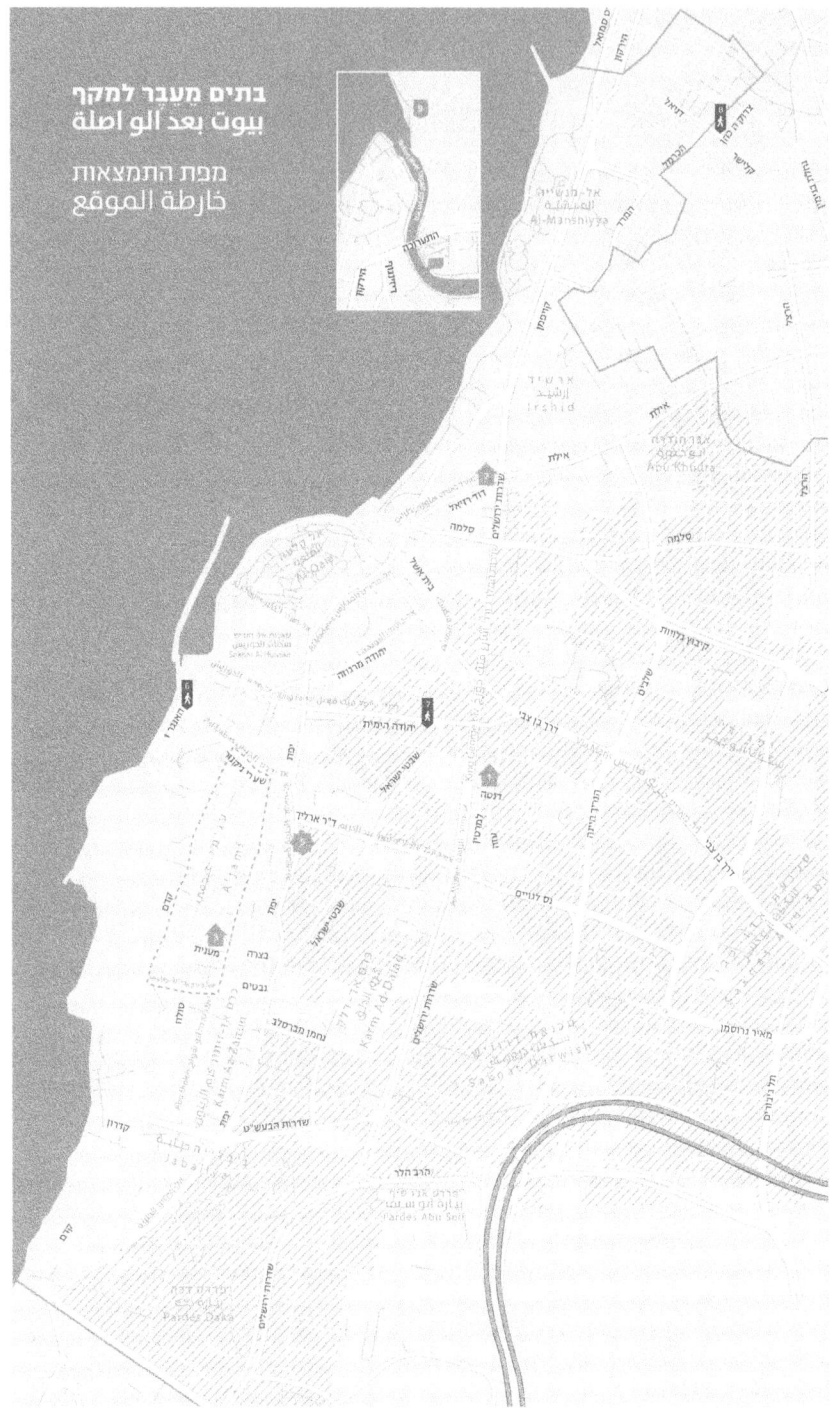

Figure 1.1 Jaffa's pre-1948 neighbourhoods superimposed on a current map of the city. (Photo courtesy of Zochrot.)

agricultural hinterland, as well as its satellite towns of Lydd and Ramla and the nearby religious site of Nabi Rubin. The immediate response of the Palestinians was to declare four days of general strike, as the Jewish Yishuv erupted in spontaneous celebrations. Soon, however, tensions exploded as the first in a series of hostilities broke out between Tel Aviv and Jaffa.

In the first few weeks following the UN resolution, violence mostly took the form of regular exchange of fire along the municipal boundaries of Jaffa, targeting some of the main traffic thoroughfares, in particular the road connecting Jaffa and Tel Aviv to Jerusalem, located between Arab Abu-Kabir and the end of Tel Aviv's Herzl Street. These long and winding boundary lines thus became the battlefronts in the weeks following the UN partition resolution.

From the west, the densely populated Arab-majority suburbs of Manshiyyeh and Irshid stood between the older, mainly Jewish quarters of just north of Jaffa, Neve Shalom, Neve Tsedek, and the Mediterranean coast. Bordering with the southern working-class neighbourhoods of Tel Aviv was Abu Kabir and its adjoining orange groves. The southeastern neighbourhoods of Tel Aviv (e.g. Hatikva and Yad Eliyahu) overlooked Salameh, the largest Palestinian village of the Jaffa region. The northern suburbs of Tel Aviv bordered with the villages of Sumayl, al-Shaykh Muwanis Jerisha and al-Jalil, the latter three along the 'Awja river; and from the south, Jabbaliyeh, which flourished along al-Hilweh road and was a natural continuation of Ajami, a mixed suburb of Jaffa built in the late nineteenth century which came to border with the Jewish municipality of Bat Yam during the Mandate period. Finally, Tel al-Rish, which consisted mostly of small agricultural landholdings, overlooked the Jewish township of Holon. Over the course of British rule, Jaffa became an Arab enclave besieged by Jewish settlements. Most importantly, Tel Aviv was a centre of significant military power in the form of the Hagana (est. 1920, the mainstream Zionist paramilitary organisation during the British Mandate), the Irgun (est. 1931, a breakaway guerilla group based on Jabotinsky's revisionist Zionism) and the Stern Gang (est. 1940, following a split from the Irgun).

The fighting along the Jaffa–Tel Aviv borderlands targeted vehicles travelling on these roads, and both sides made conscious attempts to bring traffic to a halt. Armed Palestinian militiamen based in Jaffa took positions in the tallest buildings along the municipal borders in order to fire onto adjoining Jewish neighbourhoods and beyond, and to cause panic among the civilian population that was fleeing the conflict zones.[44] The memory of Palestinian snipers gunning down pedestrians in Hakarmel Market from the Hasan Bek minaret is periodically invoked during times of increased tensions between Jews and Palestinians in the city.[45] Jewish militants, particularly the Irgun and the Stern Gang, captured strategic sites along main routes in order to target vehicle and pedestrian traffic and wreak havoc among the Palestinian civilian population. One strategically positioned Jewish sniper even managed to hit the white jeep owned by Hasan Salameh, the commander of the Arab militias in the Jaffa area.[46] In addition, Jewish militants also made extensive use of explosives along the border areas, particularly in the Manshiyyeh-Neve Shalom frontier, in order to remove buildings that obstructed their view or were deemed valuable for the Palestinian militias. Considering the superior firepower of the Jewish militias and the internal fissures among the local Palestinian leadership, and despite the claims of Zionist historians and politicians, as well as memoirs by veteran militants, Jaffa did not pose a real existential threat to Tel Aviv.[47]

The Hagana avoided a direct assault on the city of Jaffa, opting instead to secure their control over its suburbs and hinterland, imposing a tight siege on the Palestinian enclave. Their working assumption was that under such conditions, Jaffa would eventually fall once the British Mandate expired.[48] The Hagana's Kiryati brigade, which was in charge of the central region and based in Tel Aviv, focused instead on repelling attacks on Jewish settlements and neighbourhoods in the outskirts of Tel Aviv. One such battle over Hatikva,

---

[44] See Itamar Radai, 'Jaffa, 1948: The Fall of a City', *The Journal of Israeli History*, vol. 3, no. 1 (March 2011), pp. 27–8.

[45] In June 2001, following a suicide bombing in a night club across the street, a large Jewish mob surrounded the mosque, invoking its history of 'murder' and attempted to set it on fire. See Ali Waked and Yuval Peys, 'Severe Rampage around the Hasan Bek Mosque and 'Abulafiya' [in Hebrew], *Ynet*, 3 June 2001, http://www.ynet.co.il/articles/0,7340,L-783369,00.html (last accessed 26 May 2016).

[46] Yaacov Ben Gal, 'Defense and Offense', in Yosef Arikha (ed.), *Jaffa: A Historical-Literary Reader* [in Hebrew] (Tel Aviv: Tel Aviv Municipality, 1957), pp. 239–40.

[47] For a discussion of the disputes between Salameh and Yousef Haykal, the last mayor of Jaffa, regarding the course of action vis-à-vis Tel Aviv, see Palumbo, *Palestinian Catastrophe*, p. 84. For an assessment of the threat Jaffa posed for Tel Aviv, see Morris, *Palestinian Refugees*, p. 135, and Rotbard, *White City*, p. 174.

[48] Morris, *Palestinian Refugees*, p. 135; Haim Lazar, *The Occupation of Jaffa* [in Hebrew] (Tel Aviv: Misrad Habitahon, 1951), pp. 115–117.

a working-class Mizrahi suburb, took place on 8 December 1947 and ended when the Palestinian militiamen retreated back into nearby Salameh, aided by British forces who provided them cover while the Palestinian attackers evacuated their casualties.[49]

The Irgun and the Stern Gang pursued a different course of action than the official Hagana.[50] The first major attack at the heart of Jaffa was perpetrated by the Stern Gang. On 4 January 1948, two militants disguised as Arabs parked a truck full of explosives hidden under a pile of oranges next to the new Seray, which housed the municipal offices as well as meetings of the local Arab committee. The dignitaries were not in the building when the truck exploded. Instead, scores of children who were being fed on the premises were killed in the blast.[51] Isma'il Abu Shehadeh, who was working nearby, shared his memory:

> The place was destroyed on Sunday at nine a.m. in the morning, during breakfast. Not all of them died, some were injured ... it was raining. A vehicle came and parked by the Seray and detonated ... when the building collapsed we heard the people scream; I saw boys and girls with broken legs and exposed bones. When I saw them I fainted.[52]

---

[49] Ben-Zion Nachmias, *Tel Aviv as a Frontier and its Commander Michael Ben-Gal* [in Hebrew] (Tel Aviv: Irgun Havrey Hahagana, 1998), pp. 46–7.

[50] For a more comprehensive discussion of the Irgun's military assault on Jaffa, see Arnon Golan, 'The Battle for Jaffa, 1948', *Middle Eastern Studies*, vol. 48, no. 6 (November 2012), pp. 997–1101.

[51] See Palumbo, *Palestinian Catastrophe*, pp. 83–4; Radai argues no children were in the building at the time since the blast occurred on a Sunday, when the welfare kitchen did not operate: see Radai, 'Jaffa, 1948', p. 28. Palestinian historian al-Dabbagh does not mention any children welfare recipients, but argued that at least thirty people perished in the blast, among them 'quite a few of Jaffa's educated youth': see Mustafa Murad al-Dabbagh, *Our Country Palestine, Volume 4, Part 2: The Jaffa Area* [in Arabic] (Beirut: Dar al-Tali'ah, 1972), p. 278. Ibrahim Abu Lughod was nearby when the bomb detonated. He remembered the exact number of casualties: sixty-nine, nine adults and the rest were 'juvenile delinquents' cared for by the Social Affairs Department, which was located in the Seray. See Hisham Ahmed-Farajeh, *Ibrahim Abu Lughod: Resistance, Exile and Return* (Birzeit: Ibrahim Abu Lughod Institute of International Studies, 2003), p. 46.

[52] Haim Hazan and Daniel Monterescu, *A Town at Sundown: Aging Nationalism in Jaffa* [in Hebrew, my translation] (Jerusalem: Van Leer Institute and Hakibutz Hameukhad, 2011), p. 90. Another version of his testimony appears in Adam LeBor, *City of Oranges: Arabs and Jews in Jaffa* (London: Bloomsbury, 2006), p. 108.

Meanwhile, the Irgun began planning for a takeover of Jaffa in January 1948.[53] Unlike the Hagana, the Irgun's leadership, which included future prime minister Menachem Begin, considered Jaffa a strategic threat and therefore prioritised the military occupation of the city. The Irgun launched its assault on Jaffa from the north, targeting Manshiyyeh, on 24 April 1948. After three days of nonstop shelling of Jaffa, the Jewish militants invaded the city and pushed their way to the sea. The horrors of Manshiyyeh's destruction and the violence experienced by civilians reverberate in the memories of survivors. Iftikhar Turk recalled later how, when the last few families were advised to leave for fear of atrocities,

> [a]n elderly woman by the name of Sa'dyah Shakir and her daughter drove with us in the car from Manshiyyeh. The daughter and I were in the same class at school. We began driving towards Jaffa, when Sa'dyah said she left her money at her house and she must return there. The women in the car told her that if she does, the Jews would kill her, and she replied 'they won't touch me. I am elderly.' Sa'dyah left and the Jews shot and killed her. Her body remained in the house three days and could not be retrieved. Later, a few people from Jaffa drove there, tied the body with rope and dragged her all the way to Jaffa because they could not reach there [to Manshiyyeh] by car.[54]

After months of siege and growing anxiety about the future of the city, the Irgun's shelling was probably the most significant factor that led to the collapse of the Palestinian defence of Jaffa. In previous months, many of the city's notables, the well-off and much of the bourgeoisie trickled out of the city, mostly to Lebanon. Now, with horrors of the Irgun's shelling and the alarming number of civilian casualties, the terrified population was by and large trying to find ways out of the city in search of safety. Prisoners captured by the Irgun testified that as shells exploded all over the city, hotels became makeshift hospitals, and in their panic, many civilians attempted to board boats at the port.[55] Young Salah Khalaf, who was not yet fifteen at the time, witnessed a

---

[53] Lazar, *The Occupation of Jaffa*, p. 114. The Irgun also devised plans to conquer Jerusalem, Lydd and Ramla and the Tulkarm-Nablus-Jenin 'triangle'.
[54] Eyewitness testimony by Iftikhar Turk (Zochrot), *Remembering al-Manshiyyeh (Jaffa)* [in Hebrew and Arabic] (Tel Aviv: Zochrot, 2010).
[55] Morris, *Palestinian Refugees*, p. 137.

huge mass of men, women, old people and children, struggling under the weight of suitcases or bundles, making their way painfully down to the wharfs of Jaffa in a sinister tumult. Cries mingled with moaning and sobs, all punctuated by deafening explosions.[56]

The horror of this mass flight is reflected in Khalaf's memory of the 'piercing cries' of a woman who lost one of her children in the commotion and subsequently jumped into the sea and drowned, her husband following suit. Salah Khalaf grew up to become one of the most prominent leaders of the Palestinian resistance movement. I will return to his story in Chapter 4.

Even the British-initiated agreement forcing the Irgun to retreat from Manshiyyeh and allow the Hagana to take over its positions there did not persuade the Palestinians to stay, as they knew what was apparent to the Hagana all along: that the city would fall to Jewish hands as soon as the Mandate ended. The panicked exodus of civilians continued through early May.[57] Even Jaffa's mayor, Yousef Haykal, departed 'without bidding goodbye', complained one British official.[58]

A couple of aspects of the battle for Jaffa are important for understanding the mechanisms through which the Israeli state absorbed Jaffa into Tel Aviv's orbit in the first two years after the conquest, the subject of my next chapter. First, Jewish militants established facts on the ground that contravened UN Resolution 181 and induced the panicked flight of the Palestinian population of Jaffa. Second, the city's precarious position to begin with and the fact that it was surrounded by Jewish settlements provided the Zionist leadership ample time to plan for the days after Jaffa's immanent fall.

Conclusion

The modern history of Jaffa and the *Yafawiin* that I charted in broad strokes in this chapter flies in the face of received wisdom about 'the oriental city' ostensibly on an impending collision course with the vibrant and modern

---

[56] Abu Iyad with Eric Roulaeu, *My Home, My Land: A Narrative of the Palestinian Struggle*, trans. Linda Butler Koseoglu (New York: Times Books, 1978), p. 3.
[57] Basil 'Anab testified that the price of renting a vehicle to flee the city rose from 10 to 100 dinar. His testimony appears in (Zochrot) *Remembering Jaffa's al-Ajami Neighbourhood* (Tel Aviv: Zochrot, 2007), p. 45.
[58] Ibid., p. 142.

'white city' next door. These histories of inevitable nationalist contestation are too often uncritically reproduced and disseminated, cementing processes of elision and silence imposed by the settler colonial state apparatus.

If anything, attentiveness to the lived experiences of people who resided in Jaffa, Palestinians, Jews and otherwise, complicate these narratives of conflict and demonstrate that Tel Aviv, touted as a multicultural prosperous haven, benefitted from the wreckage of Jaffa and the catastrophe that befell its people. Displacing Zionist narratives of progress on the one hand, and of conflict on the other, reveals multi-directional and complex histories of urban identities and attachments made and unmade, and their intricate relationship to spatial practices, political economy and the contingencies of social dynamics. In the following chapters, I will zoom into the life histories of *Yafawiin* and their post-Nakba careers, as well as the experiences of the small Palestinian community that remained in the city and endured military rule, further displacement and political and economic marginalisation.

Finally, studying pre- and post-Nakba Palestinian demographics is crucial for any political project that is committed to the right of return. No Zionist reader can deny that Palestinians were not only present but formed the majority in both the urban and rural sectors of the country, and that their removal was a direct result of military action by Zionist militias and the IDF. Furthermore, the data clearly demonstrates that despite the hegemonic Zionist discourse and logic of separation, Jews and Palestinians shared lived spaces, and that experiences of 'living together' were diverse and reflected multiple and contingent social dynamics rather than just straight-up intercommunal conflict. But perhaps most importantly, both historical and current data are vital for the politics of hope that this book hinges on: it provides concreteness and even a sense of materiality to imaginaries about future forms of 'living together' that are the radical others of the present. Maps, census data and images are traditionally the registers of governmentality and the toolkit of the state; undermining the settler colonial state's project of the 'new normal', which I discuss in the next chapter, necessitates reclaiming and repurposing these forms of knowledge.

2

THE 'NEW NORMAL'

It is advisable to include the smallest possible number of Arab residents and the biggest possible number of Jewish residents in the Jewish state.[1]

The transformation of Jaffa was rapid and revolutionary. A new Hebrew seal has been impressed over the old Arab landscape. It seems that a giant hand was rocking the city, awakening it into new life ... in the streets the west has come to rule; it is lively, tumultuous and full of movement. The shops' windows and commercial ads make it [the street] look completely European. Yet cast your eyes upward to the buildings' upper stories and see the markers of an oriental city: shaded balconies, barred windows, and here and there old Arabic inscriptions, half faded, but their impression still remains.[2]

History has not known a case more just and more obvious than this: A country is snatched from its people to be made into a national home for remnants of mankind who settle on it from the various regions of the world and who erected a state in it despite its inhabitants and the millions of their brethren in the neighboring regions. Despite the pure right of the Arab's case, the

---

[1] ISA, 23.8.1948 G 5670/32.
[2] Haim Lazar, *The Occupation of Jaffa* [in Hebrew] (Tel Aviv: Misrad Habitahon, 1951), p. 250.

potentialities of their land, and the interests of other nations have in it ... the Arabs stand alone in the international arena.³

In May of 2013, while I was conducting fieldwork in Jaffa, hundreds of human remains were discovered in a mass grave at the local Muslim cemetery. As the news of the grim discovery circulated in the city, many residents turned to their elders for answers to the question on everyone's mind: who are those buried in these nameless tombs and how did they get there? The consensus reached by Palestinian historians, dignitaries and Islamic movement officials is that the remains should be traced back to 1948, to the period just before and following the fall of the city to Zionist forces and the mass exodus of its residents. While some of those bodies would have been of combatants, volunteers from as far as Bosnia and Iraq, the bulk of the dead would have been civilians, either buried alive under the ruins of their homes during the massive shelling or massacred by Zionist forces in the chaos that followed the occupation of the city.⁴

The outpouring of emotions percolating around Ajami, Jaffa's Arab-majority quarter, indicated many were shocked by the news. A press conference at the local office of the Tajamu' party was well attended, as people flocked to hear more about the mass graves, many learning about the fate of the city for the first time. While some Israelis also expressed their dismay and accepted the need to reassess nationalist histories of victory and urban 'reunification', others opted to profess doubt, denial and refusal to engage with the discovery, its meaning and possible political implications. Doubters claimed that it was impossible that a local story of massacre had remained hidden and unknown for so long in this age of 'free flowing information' and the opening

---

³ Constantine Zureiq, *The Meaning of Disaster*, trans. R. Bayly Winder (Beirut: Khayat's College Book Cooperative, 1956), pp. 2–3.
⁴ See AFP, 'Dozens of Bodies Found at Mass Grave in Jaffa', *The Jerusalem Post*, 1 June 2013, http://www.jpost.com/National-News/Dozens-of-bodies-found-at-mass-grave-in-Jaffa-315073 (last accessed 26 May 2016) as well as 'Up to Six Mass Graves Discovered in Jaffa, with Hundreds of Victims from 1948', *The Real News Network*, 11 June 2013, http://therealnews.com/t2/index.php?option=com_content&task=view&id=31&Itemid=74&jumival=10298 (last accessed 26 May 2016). Some historians concluded that the remains are of World War I Egyptian soldiers: Nir Hasson, 'Experts Battle over whether Jaffa's Mass Graves Stem from World War I or 1948', *Haaretz*, 10 June 2013, http://www.haaretz.com/news/national/.premium-1.528786 (last accessed 26 May 2016).

up of public access to knowledge about the past. Indeed, just like the skeletons, this buried material and mental history of catastrophe and trauma had to be excavated and revealed in order to become the subject of public review.

The mere act of excavation forces witnesses to face that which is 'no longer conscious', to deal with a sedimented history that challenges the pacified past and the reproductive normativity of the present.[5] In this context of survival under a colonial regime as second class citizens,[6] material evidence as well as archival sources work to reveal the 'unthinkable' history buried and silenced by various sites of historical reproduction: school textbooks and ceremonies, state-sanctioned commemorative rituals, monuments in public spaces and popular and semi-scholarly historical monographs.[7] In this chapter, the discovery of the skeletons and the array of emotions they elicited serve to index the potential for shifting political grounds, and for undermining the historical processes that sustained the 'new normal' in the aftermath of the Zionist conquest of Jaffa.

This chapter is about the ways in which, in the immediate aftermath of the Nakba (1948–9), the Israeli state enabled these processes of public forgetfulness that produced, on the one hand, a tangible reality of occupied urban spaces, and the ability to 'bury' (or silence, as Trouillot would phrase it) histories of mass expulsion, organised violence and en masse appropriation of

---

[5] Ernst Bloch, *The Principle of Hope*, trans. Neville Plaice, Stephen Plaice and Paul Knight (MIT Press, 1995).

[6] On the formation of Palestinian citizens of Israel as the state's internal 'others', see Shira Robinson, *Citizen Strangers: Palestinians and the Birth of Israel's Liberal Settler State* (Stanford: Stanford University Press, 2013). Salient examples of the prolific scholarship on the subaltern status of Israel's Palestinian citizens: Ismael Abu Saad, 'Separate and Unequal: The Role of the State Educational System in Maintaining the Subordination of Israel's Palestinian Arab Citizens', *Social Identities: Journal for the Study of Race, Nation and Culture*, vol. 10, no. 1 (2004), pp. 101–27; Sami Smooha, 'Minority Status in an Ethnic Democracy: The Status of the Arab Minority in Israel', *Ethnic and Racial Studies*, vol. 13, no. 3 (July 1990), pp. 389–413. In addition, NGOs such as Human Rights Watch and Adalah have documented the legal and formal discrimination of the Palestinians within Israel: Zama Coursen-Neff, *Second Class: Discrimination against Palestinian Arab Children in Israel's School* (New York: Human Rights Watch, 2001). Adala's ample documentation is available on their website http://www.adalah.org/en (last accessed 21 June 2016).

[7] Michel-Rolph Trouillot, *Silencing the Past: Power and the Production of History* (Boston, MA: Beacon Press, 1995).

material goods, houses and lands, on the other.[8] That these processes reconstituted Jaffa as a decrepit, Jewish-majority suburb of Tel Aviv is relatively well known in critical scholarship.[9] My concern in this chapter is to explore how this violent transformation assumed the guise of sanitised, inexorable normality. The making of the 'new normal' in Jaffa, then, constitutes normalising occupation in ways that convincingly submerged the 'newness' of a rapid and radical urban transformation. Recently, scholars have begun to study the normalisation of Israel post-1967 as the unfolding of a process that is not produced by a single agent in one fell swoop, but rather as multiple and partially intersecting processes that originated from multiple forces within Israeli society. Moreover, these scholars interrogated both the genesis and the consequences and lived reality it produced.[10] While these scholars have limited their inquiry to the post-1967 occupied territories, I propose broadening this framework to the colonisation of 1948. More specifically, this chapter aims to locate the genesis of the making of the 'new normal', or how Jaffa was remade as a Jewish-majority underdeveloped suburb of Tel Aviv. One way to begin thinking about the effects of creating this new normal as a success (from the point of view of the state), is the fact that even when I asked Palestinian residents in Jaffa about the prospects of the return of the city's refugees, my interlocutors expressed their doubts, or even outright rejection of the idea, citing the current urban reality of over-crowdedness, acute housing shortages and creeping gentrification. In other words, the work that the 'new normal'

---

[8] The systemic looting and expropriations in Jaffa were replicated in all territories occupied by Israel. See Adam Raz, *Looting of Arab Property during Israel's War of Independence* (Jerusalem: Carmel, 2020).

[9] See Sharon Rotbard, *White City, Black City* [in Hebrew] (Tel Aviv: Bavel, 2005); Daniel Monterescu, *Jaffa, Shared and Shattered: Contrived Coexistence in Israel/Palestine* (Bloomington: Indiana University Press, 2015); Dan Rabinowitz and Daniel Monterescu, 'Reconfiguring the "Mixed Town": Urban Transformations of Ethno-National Relations in Palestine/Israel', *International Journal of Middle East Studies*, vol. 40, no. 2 (2008), pp. 195–226; André Mazawi and Makram Khouri-Makhoul, 'Spatial Policy in Jaffa: 1948–1990', in Haim Lusky (ed.), *City and Utopia* [in Hebrew] (Tel Aviv: Israel Publishing Company, 1991), pp. 62–74; Kamal Al-Ja'fari, Hadas Lahav and Asaf Adiv, *Jaffa Facing the New Judaization Plan* [in Arabic] (Jerusalem: Dar al-Sharara, 1992).

[10] Marco Allegra et al., 'Introduction: The Politics of Everyday Life in the West Bank Settlements', in M. Allegra et al. (eds), *Normalizing Occupation: The Politics of Everyday Life in the West Bank Settlements* (Bloomington: Indiana University Press, 2017), p. 4.

does is turning urban residents into active agents in maintaining the status quo on behalf of the state; at the same time, this project also aims to foreclose alternative visions for the city and its people.

In what follows, I chart out the ways in which the state, following the conquest of Jaffa, managed to produce this 'new normal', through the appropriation and then redistribution of urban landscapes, goods, and of people themselves. In order to recreate Jaffa in its image and remake it into a Jewish city, the state of Israel used its military and legal apparatuses to facilitate a rapid takeover of everything and everyone that was previously under the jurisdiction of the Jaffa municipality. At the same time, Israel also had to manage the remaining Palestinian-Arab population by cordoning them off into what became the 'Arab quarter' of Ajami and create a physical separation between Arabs and the influx of incoming Jews.

State-sanctioned Looting

On 13 May 1948, following months of continuous shelling of the besieged city of Jaffa and the desperate flight of most of its population, four of the remaining local dignitaries were self-appointed as an ad-hoc 'emergency committee' acting as the legitimate representatives of the Arab population. These men, Ahmad Abu Laban, Salah al-Nazir, Amin Andraus and Ahmad Abd al-Rahim, were forced to drive to the centre of Tel Aviv to the Hagana headquarters and publicly sign a humiliating agreement, which constituted them as the only Palestinian authority respected by the remaining Arab population. On the one hand, as such, they were responsible to 'preserve and maintain the peace and welfare of the Arabs' in Jaffa. Whereas this part of the committee's authority remains vague, the next section of the agreement is quite clear: they were entrusted with the task to 'carry out all instructions given to be given by the Commander of the Hagana Tel Aviv, District, and/or by any officer designated and/or authorized by him, today [or] at any further date'.[11] It is this latter stipulation that clarified the first: the intention of Jaffa's new occupiers was to constitute the committee as its rubber stamp, lending a veneer of respectability and even consent to the military's new arrangements in the city.

---

[11] Israeli Defense Forces archives (IDFA) Agreement between the Commander of the Hagana and the Emergency Committee of Jaffa, 13.5.1948 321/1948-97.

By signing this 'agreement' which was effectively a decree of capitulation, the reluctant committee members handed over to what the very next day became the Israeli state complete control over the fate of what used to be one of the most vibrant cities in the Eastern Mediterranean and the lives of its remaining inhabitants.

The 13 May agreement has left traces, indeed – verbatim reproductions – among countless archival files. Both sides – the Israeli military apparatus and the Palestinians of Jaffa – keep conjuring the document but offering contrasting readings of it. Military officials, for their part, stressed the section specifying the purpose of the document is to 'preserve and maintain the peace and welfare of the Arabs'. Thus, in a letter dated 26 August 1948, the military governor rebuked the committee for addressing the international community and for relaying their plight and their sense of the realities on the ground because the communication had contravened the 13 May agreement as well as international law. Moreover, argued the second governor of Jaffa Meir Laniado, by turning to the outside world, it seemed the committee was doing its best to undermine his efforts at restoring 'normal life' in Jaffa.[12]

Laniado's consistent appeal to 'normal life' in official correspondence draws our attention to tangible realities in the city at the time. Although his authority was not uncontested, either by the Tel Aviv municipal bureaucracy or various governmental agencies, it was the military governor who was the ultimate policymaker in Jaffa. The policies contained in the 'agreement' quickly altered the city's physical and human geographies as well as its daily rhythms, and they reflected the governor's interpretation of the more abstract principles of rule guiding the newly installed Israeli provisional government.

As soon as the newly formed IDF (Israeli Defense Forces) took over from the Hagana and installed Itzhak Chizik as Jaffa's first military governor, the army deployed heavily guarded checkpoints along the boundaries with neighbouring Jewish municipalities (Tel Aviv and Bat Yam), scrutinising anyone wishing to enter the city, which was allowed only upon obtaining a special permit. Policing the city's boundaries and access to it was intended, among other things, to keep the small Palestinian population still trapped inside Jaffa from exiting the city, and those who had fled or remained in other towns and

[12] IDFA 292/1954-1737.

villages in the area and had maintained commercial, cultural and familial ties to the city from entering.

Cordoning off the city and turning it into a closed military zone provided the IDF with the means and opportunity to suspend not only every aspect of civilian life but also what is considered in liberal democracies the very basic tenets of individual liberties, all under the guise of 'security'. In the meantime, Jaffa became the site of a mass expropriation operation sanctioned by the military governor and the Ministry of Minority Affairs. Special storage facilities were set up in order to house the immense amounts of commodities, machinery and raw materials earmarked for confiscation by the governor's appointed inspectors. These facilities were then used to supply numerous government agencies, police stations and military bases and offices. The archives are replete with instances of such requisites; for instance, on July 11 1948, the department of Arab properties at the Ministry of Minority Affairs requested the military storage facilities 'confiscate from Jaffa ... a clock, a radio set, telephone switchboard, four fans and an electric refrigerator'.[13] In another instance, Gad Makhnes, general director of the Ministry of Minority Affairs specified that his office needed 'two good-quality German-manufactured English-language typewriters and two Arabic-language ones'. In another instance, Makhnes stressed that the 'borrowing-confiscation [of a paper cutting machine from a local print shop] should be executed in the friendliest possible manner'. The ambiguity of his wording perhaps reflects a moment of moral hesitation; he is aware that the requested machine is the private property of another, but at the same time, he feels compelled to prioritise what he deemed as the interest of the nation over respect for private property or basic human decency.

Governor Chizik himself made a distinction between the confiscation of equipment needed for the war effort and simple looting, and repeatedly complained that 'unauthorized personnel' were removing furniture from private dwellings.[14] The latter, he claimed, would pose challenges if Palestinians who 'fled' Jaffa were allowed to return, since 'it is necessary that returnees find

---

[13] ISA, Letter from Gad Makhnes, Ministry of Minority to the Jaffa Office, 11.7.1948 G 306/76.
[14] A report by the Emergency Committee provides greater detail about the extent of the looting which was perpetrated by military personnel as well as Jewish civilians. Looters are described as breaking into public offices and businesses (stressing the destruction of the local orange industry in the process), in addition to private residences, grabbing anything that could be

their apartments more or less in an acceptable condition, or else – the government will be forced to compensate them'. His concern for the image of Israel in the eyes of the international community echoes through correspondence as he ordered the confiscation of furniture to cease while the Red Cross and UN delegations were visiting the city during the first ceasefire (11 June–9 July 1948). Chizik could not prevent the looting of Palestinian property and the general chaos in the city and resigned shortly thereafter. Under the command of the next military governor, Laniado, the project of mass expropriations continued.

Both the random ('unauthorised') and systematic, state-sanctioned looting should be understood as part and parcel of the 'new normal'. The theft of movable property from homes, businesses, public offices and storage facilities reflected a more generalised attitude among Israel's leadership. Although officially Ben Gurion and his administration were committed to international mediation which left the question of the return of the refugees open for discussions, recently declassified correspondence reveals that posturing notwithstanding, the Israelis had no intention of letting the Palestinians return to the cities, villages and properties they left behind. As early as 26 June, the emergency committee provided a list of Jaffa residents who, at the time, were outside of the city, whether in areas under Israeli control (Lydd, Ramla), elsewhere in historic Palestine (Gaza, Ramallah) or across the border (Beirut, Saida), wishing to return to the city to the office of Bechor Chetrit, minister of Minority Affairs. Chetrit forwarded the request to Prime Minister Ben Gurion, who annotated the document himself:

> As long as the war is not over, and it isn't, and the enemy is at the gates of Tel Aviv, Jerusalem and Haifa, we cannot allow the return of Arabs to Jaffa, Haifa or anywhere else, unless there is an explicit decision by the whole government (to which I shall vehemently object).[15]

---

carried away into a truck in broad daylight. Whatever they could not carry, such as heavy furniture, they smashed and damaged (IDFA 71-1860-1950).

[15] ISA, Letter from Bekhor Chetrit to PM and FM, 30.6.1948 17103/35. Interestingly, the official response (of 5 July), signed by the government's secretary S. Kedar, omitted Ben Gurion's personal objection to the return of the Palestinians, and just stated that no return would be possible as long as war was still raging.

Moreover, ongoing discussions about the possibility of return reveal that Ben Gurion was not alone in his utter rejection of the idea of repatriation. In a letter addressed to Foreign Minister Moshe Shertok, Yaacov Shimoni from the Middle East Department in the Foreign Ministry candidly opined that while the government can openly object to the return of conscription-age males without repercussions in the international arena, 'our natural inclination' is to make the return of Arab refugees as difficult as possible. He went on to explain that the refugee problem would become a significant issue in future peace talks and suggested that Israel should not tip its hand and allow expatriation. Furthermore, he added, returnees would most probably refuse to sign an oath of allegiance to the Jewish state, and therefore, if allowed back in, could become a fifth column.[16] Internal discussions about the possibility of repatriation to Jaffa ended when in early October, the city's military governor decided that 'for the time being, for security reasons', all attempts to repatriate former Jaffa residents should cease immediately 'and would be resumed when the situation improves'. With the exception of very few individuals allowed back over the course of the following year,[17] the vast majority of *Yafawiin* remain in exile to this very day.

In light of this principled rejection of the possibility of return we should read and understand the particular course of action undertaken by the state of Israel in Jaffa, which ultimately produced the 'new normal'. The removal of moveable property and enclosing the city with checkpoints allowed the military governor to refashion the urban landscape and de-Arabise 'the Mother of the Stranger' (Arabic, *umm al-gharib*, a popular reference to Jaffa) through the redistribution of people throughout the city and by creating clearly

---

[16] ISA, Letter to Moshe Shertok from Yaacov Shimoni, 7.7.1948 G 307/51. Shimoni's rejection of the possibility of a mass repatriation to Jaffa also hinged on an abortive plan to remove around 6500 Palestinians from Acre and about 150 of the residents of Abu Ghosh (a village near Jerusalem whose inhabitants refused to cooperate with the resistance and therefore were allowed to remain) to Jaffa. The plan was abandoned since the city was already earmarked for the resettlement of Jews, as I will discuss below. Bechor Chetrit also added that displacing a whole city (in the case of Acre) would only cause unneeded hardship and suffering to its civilian population and therefore should be avoided.

[17] See, for instance, Haim Hazan and Daniel Monterescu, *A Town at Sundown: Aging Nationalism in Jaffa* [in Hebrew, my translation] (Jerusalem: Van Leer Institute and Hakibutz Hameukhad, 2011), p. 52.

demarcated ethnic (and physical) boundaries before allowing civilian life to resume. This process took place through two mutually constitutive elements: ghettoisation of the Palestinian population and Judaicising the rest of the city.

Beyond the Barbed Wires of Ajami

On Saturday morning in present-day Jaffa, one would try in vain to find an empty parking spot. Israelis from Tel Aviv, Bat Yam, Holon and other satellite cities crowd Jaffa's narrow streets enjoying a sunny weekend before heading back to the busy everyday routines. Groups of tourists in wide-brim hats, cameras at hand, are led by guides through the alleyways, listening to stories of the city's distant past told in every language under the sun. Others visit the countless tiny art galleries that offer Judaica artifacts as well as paintings of romantic orientalised landscapes. The old flea market is teeming with Israeli Jews, strolling about after a satisfying meal in a trendy bistro. Traffic along Yefet Street (formerly al-Hilweh) comes to a halt as incoming Jews and tourists stop to stock up on pita with za'tar in the tremendously popular bakery owned by the Abulafia family near clock tower square or drive up towards Ajami for hummus and falafel in one of the many 'authentic' Arab restaurants along the thoroughfare.

For the contemporary visitor, Jaffa has 'always' served as a playground of sorts for Israeli Jews, a destination for those seeking a taste of an authentic Middle Eastern flavour close to home. As far as Israeli Jews are concerned, local histories of military occupation and mass displacement have been relegated to the depth of collective amnesia as newer urban identities, including those of the hummus-serving Arabs and 'contrived coexistence' have flourished in their stead.[18] The remainder of this chapter seeks to highlight the processes by which, during military rule (1948–9), these profound transformations produced Jaffa as a weekend getaway tourist site for Israeli Jews.

Military governor Laniado's 'Operation Nine' ordered the removal and forced transfer of the Palestinian population into an enclosed 'security zone' in mid-August 1948.[19] This was a military operation, devised by Ben Gurion

---

[18] Monterescu, *Jaffa*.
[19] Governor Laniado exempted eleven notable Palestinian families who were allowed to remain in their homes and were provided with special permits (ISA, Letter to Ministers of Defense, Interior, Police, and Minority Affairs, 16.8.1948 G 96/306).

himself,[20] and conducted by supervisors appointed by the governor and IDF soldiers who were ordered to raid and search private residences – both those vacated and repopulated within 'the ghetto'. The new exclusively 'Arab' area, clearly referred to as the 'ghetto', earmarked for this operation was the neighbourhood of Ajami, which was established in the late nineteenth century as an extramural residential area by well-to-do Maronite artisans from Beirut.[21] By 1948, Ajami had expanded along al-Hilweh street to its east, becoming a lively heterogeneous commercial and residential centre, home to both Christians and Muslims. After the terrified flight of most Palestinians from Jaffa, Ajami was considered a prime location for such a 'ghetto' since most of its houses were uninhabited and because its western boundary was the Mediterranean. Moreover, Jabbaliyeh, the neighbourhood just to its south, bordered on the Jewish municipality of Bat Yam, and was therefore considered a potential 'security risk' by the Israeli military and political leadership.

Operation Nine created a new reality for the divided city: Ajami, surrounded by barbed wire and armed guards, became 'Arab Jaffa' whereas the rest of the city was rapidly transformed into 'Jewish Jaffa'.[22] This new division also produced new ethnicity-based modes of governance, which will be discussed below. The decision to concentrate the Palestinian population in an enclosed area did not pass without resistance. The Emergency Committee appealed to Chetrit, Minister of Minority Affairs, about the forced uprooting of civilians from their homes. But there were also minority voices within the Zionist political establishment that articulated unease at the creation of the Ajami ghetto. Moshe Erem (née Kazanovzky), a member of the Israeli Kenesset from the socialist MAPAM party, warned that the barbed wires around Ajami 'would make it look like a closed and sealed ghetto. It is difficult to accept that, since the idea is associated with enough atrocities.'[23] Erem referenced the Holocaust, which ended merely three years prior, as well as the British internment camps for Jewish refugees in Cyprus. A counter example is Haifa, where the remaining Palestinian population was indeed concentrated in Wadi Nisnas

---

[20] See Akiva Persitz's testimony, IDFA 5-1860-1950.
[21] See Chapter 1.
[22] For a recent discussion of the Ajami ghetto and its archival traces, see Adam Raz, 'Arab Citizens behind Barbed Wire', *Haaretz Weekend*, 28 May 2020, p. 11.
[23] IDFA, Letter to the Minister of Minority Affairs, 11.8.1948 1-1860-1950.

yet there was no need for barbed wire, walls or fences.[24] If we go ahead with this plan, claimed Erem, there will be far-reaching consequences in terms of intercommunal relations: 'Why is it necessary to pile on obstacles which will root bitterness, resentment and eternal hatred in the hearts of the Arabs?' And as for the Jews, barbed wires would serve as tangible markers of occupation and would amplify a sense of ethnic superiority, which may have 'undesirable' consequences.[25] Erem may have remained cryptic on this point, but in the very next paragraph he mentioned the 'official' pretext for the governor's policy of segregation – an appeal to the safety and security, not of the Jewish newcomers or even the state, but of the Palestinian residents themselves.

Erem was in complete denial of the mere possibility that Jews were capable of committing violent acts towards a minority population under occupation. However, there are multiple archival traces that confirm official concerns about the safety of Jaffa's Palestinians and shed some light over the vulnerability and precarity of Palestinians lives under Israeli occupation. These traces of everyday acts of unprovoked state violence indicate that Palestinians experienced a constant sense of vulnerability both before and after they were forced behind barbed wires in Ajami.

A formal complaint filed by the Emergency Committee mentions numerous cases of random assaults on Palestinians in the city's streets, as Israeli soldiers hurled insults at them and robbed them of their belongings. The same report details an arrest of a Palestinian man immediately after going through 'serious surgery' while others were shot and killed while in Israeli custody even though they posed no security threat.[26] The reported discovery of several dead bodies led medical examiners to the conclusion they were executed by Jewish forces after the formal capitulation and were left to rot without proper burial. The committee also complained about their exclusion from hearings for suspects arrested

---

[24] Ilan Pappé, *The Ethnic Cleansing of Palestine* (Oxford: Oneworld, 2006), pp. 207–8.

[25] The logic of this argument became popularised by liberal Zionists in the aftermath of the 1967 occupation of the West Bank and the Gaza Strip, repeatedly claiming that 'occupation corrupts' (Hebrew, *Hakibush Mashhit*). More on the ghetto as a spatial formation in Israel's 'mixed towns', see Daniel Monterescu, 'The Ghettoization of Israel's "Mixed Cities"', *+972 Magazine*, 5 December 2015, http://972mag.com/the-ghettoization-of-israels-mixed-cities/114536/ (last accessed 10 December 2015).

[26] IDFA, 71-1860-1950.

by 'various Jewish units' and about unnecessary searches and raids in private homes, without accountability. These raids occasionally resulted in sexual assault of women and girls in the presence of male family members, and the deliberate disgracing of unmarried girls ('virgins'), particularly targeting those from 'reputable families', by ordering them to accompany soldiers at night.[27]

Violence became a fact of life for the Palestinians who remained in Jaffa. Workers were afraid to leave their homes lest occasional Jewish invaders rob them of their meager possessions.[28] Local Palestinian leaders reported countless incidents of violence perpetrated by Jewish immigrants, often Mizrahim from Iraq and North Africa who were being settled on the urban frontiers until well after military rule in the city ended. Between June 1951 and January 1952 tensions rose between Palestinians and Jewish Iraqis recently resettled in Jaffa. Following the 1951 Baghdad riots, Palestinians had 'good reason to fear attacks from Mizrahi Jews, and that these well-founded concerns have led them to avoid leaving their homes alone after dark'.[29] It is not inconceivable that the scope of the violence was much greater than its archival traces, first and foremost, because these are state archives, in charge of the narrativisation of history and therefore producing its built-in silences.[30] The plight of the Palestinians in Jaffa was acknowledged just enough in the archives to reify the 'new normal': as chaotic as it was in the 'early days', the restrained security apparatus of Israel made the city safe and livable for everyone.

It is also highly likely that many Palestinians refrained from filing formal complaints, especially against members of the armed and police forces, fearing reprisals and sensing that Jews, and especially state agents, enjoyed impunity that rendered complaints futile.[31] Women in particular are vulnerable to

[27] Ibid.
[28] See IDFA, Letter from M. Shneorson, 24.2.1949, 2-1860-1950. The problem obviously persisted, since in a letter dated 23.6.1949, the Emergency Committee is complaining that both Jewish soldiers and civilians entertain the idea that Arabs and their properties 'have no right to be in Israel' (IDFA, 3-1860-1950).
[29] ISA, GL Report of the Regional Officer, June 1951 17115/23. For earlier incidents, see for instance a letter sent by religious leaders to the military governor, citing violence by Jewish newcomers (IDFA, 9.6.1949, 3-1860-1950).
[30] See Trouillot, *Silencing the Past*, pp. 48–9.
[31] Indeed, the Emergency Committee's reports specifically mentions that perpetrators of violence towards Palestinians have gone unpunished.

public disclosure of sexual violence perpetrated against them, as they had to face stigma, shame, and potential forms of community ostracism or risk their and their family's 'good name' and marriage prospects.

In this context of elisions and silences in the archives, a handwritten document from late May 1948, a fortnight after the fall of Jaffa, is indicative of the level of 'acceptable' violence and impunity. The document mentions a testimony by an Israeli policeman, who reported to his superior about a Palestinian man who had called him for help as he was being robbed by Israelis.[32] According to the policeman, his superior's response was to tell him he 'should have shot that Arab', presumably to silence a potential witness and save the state an embarrassment.[33] It attests to the level of impunity provided to perpetrators as well as to the extent of precarity experienced by Palestinians.

By October 1948, Laniado was reporting a sense of 'restrained discipline' (Hebrew, *mishma'at 'atzura*) among the ghettoised Palestinians in Jaffa.[34] His choice of words seems a little strange, even redundant. But by flagging his methods as 'restrained' Laniado implied to his superiors as much as to historians that he could have been much harsher with the occupied population had he wished. Lurking underneath this official's magnanimity and (temporary) successful pacification remained undercurrents of self-doubt and insurgency that could erupt at any time.

While 'Arab Jaffa' was being forged behind barbed wires in Ajami, the rest of the city was rapidly transforming: on the one hand, state-sanctioned processes of repurposing of private and public buildings as military bases and residences for 'authorised personnel'; simultaneously, many Jewish newcomers began to invade vacant apartments. The fictionalised memoir *The Bulgarians of Jaffa*[35] is suggestive of the real experiences of Bulgarian Jews upon their arrival in Israel, and the mass appropriation of Palestinian properties in the newly Jewish parts of Jaffa. The protagonist's cousin explains the new realities on the ground:

---

[32] Judging by the context, detailing looting by Israeli police and military personnel, we can assume the robbers were members of the armed forces.

[33] ISA, G Handwritten letter to the Minister of Police and Arab Affairs from Y. Geffen, 25.5.1948 77/306.

[34] See the military governor's weekly report from 13.10.1948, ISA, G 77/306.

[35] Rozalyah Pasi, *The Bulgarians of Jaffa* [in Hebrew] (Tel Aviv: Misrad Habitahon, 1993).

Jaffa is located near Tel Aviv ... the two cities share a border and a few streets. Thousands of Arabs escaped from it after its liberation, and almost all the houses are empty. Come, we occupied a two-bedroom apartment and locked the door, one room for you and the other for us.[36]

In the Hebrew source, 'occupied' (*tafasnu*, literally 'we caught') is instructive, since it suggests more than just settling an empty apartment, but squatting, invading the space of others without the owner's permission. Like a civilian occupation army, the Bulgarian immigrants stormed Jaffa: 'Hurry! People are wandering around, and when they see an empty apartment, they break the lock and occupy it. Then try to argue with them. Hurry, don't delay.'[37]

The military governor and his staff treated those 'unauthorised' Jewish newcomers who captured apartments on their own initiative as squatters that should be evicted. The military governor, as well as Defense Ministry officials and Akiva Persitz, who facilitated the resettlement of soldiers in 'abandoned' Palestinian houses,[38] were incensed upon the revelation that migrants squatted in a group of buildings in Nuzha earmarked for repopulation by families of military personnel. The governor even actively sought to redeploy forces to both reinforce the checkpoints to stop further incursions as well as evict as many of these unauthorised squatters. In a related instance, when a group of soldiers violently evicted Jewish women from houses in Jabbaliyeh, the governor sent soldiers under his command to remove the invaders.[39] These squabbles over living quarters in Jaffa were repeated again and again throughout the first year of occupation. The archives are replete with reports of battalions taking over buildings from other units, often moving in with their families. One such incident occurred in September 1948, when six military vehicles driven by men from the Kiryati brigade forced their way into buildings occupied by the air force, 'shoved the guards, hurling slurs such as "draft-dodgers

---

[36] Ibid., p. 14.
[37] Ibid., p. 17.
[38] Persitz is identified in these documents as the newly appointed chairman of the National Expropriation Committee. He demanded the Jaffa office of the Custodian of Abandoned Properties that vacant apartments be allocated to soldiers and their families rather than occupied by Jewish migrants. The ensuing furious inter-ministry dispute over those buildings left a long trail of documents in the IDF archives.
[39] IDFA, 5-1860-1950.

and parasites" and brought women, children and their belongings with them into the houses'.[40] Apparently, the Kiryati squatters felt their war efforts gave them greater entitlement to the loot than the air force, which had made less sacrifices in 1948.

The army seems to have won the day. For decades following these disputes, Jaffa was dotted with military bases, from Galey Tzahal, the IDF's radio mouthpiece, the military museum next to the Ottoman railway station in Manshiyyeh, to 8200 elite intelligence unit. Later on, the military court sequestered the home of Shaykh Ali in the heart of Ajami. On the one hand, the priority given to IDF units and individual soldiers in the process of dividing up the spoils of occupation reflects the military's sway over political life in Israel, as well as the blurring of the lines between military and civilian occupation. On the other hand, the archival documents that detail the disputes over the allocation of buildings in 'Jewish Jaffa' also reveal an emerging anxiety about the potential of rank-and-file IDF soldiers to mutiny and even to perpetrate violence against superior officers or high-ranking state agents. Indeed, the leadership of the fledgling Israeli state was well aware of the possibility of armed resistance by military factions, including former militants from the Irgun and the Stern Gang.[41]

As we have seen at the beginning of this chapter, the UN partition plan originally allocated Jaffa to the Arab state.[42] The new reality of occupation necessitated legislative and bureaucratic 'adjustments' that furnished the annexation of Jaffa with the veneer of legality. First, the pre-1948 Jewish neighbourhoods were to form their own local municipality and would receive essential services from Tel Aviv, while the rest of the city came under a committee appointed by the Minister of Interior Affairs.[43] In practice, though, the city's affairs were directed by the office of the military governor until that

---

[40] IDFA, 10.9.1948, 5-1860-1950.
[41] The fear of an armed mutiny against the state had some basis in reality. Just five weeks after the creation of Israel, the Altalena, a ship carrying arms for the Irgun, arrived near the coast of Tel Aviv. The refusal of the Irgun to surrender the massive amounts of arms on board to the IDF resulted in a battle with scores of casualties and the destruction of the ship. See Shlomo Nakdimon, *Altalena* [in Hebrew] (Tel Aviv: Idanim, 1978); Menachem Begin, *The Revolt* [in Hebrew] (Jerusalem: Achiasaf, 1950).
[42] UN, A/RES/181 (III).
[43] ISA, 7.9.1948, G 5670/32.

position was dissolved in 1949 and Jaffa officially and legally was annexed to Tel Aviv a year later.[44] The security apparatus, as well as civilian authorities, were adamant that the 'situation of Arabs is different than that of the Jews' and therefore it was 'impossible' to reconstitute the Jaffa municipality as it existed before the occupation. However, the real motivation behind this refusal was a vehement objection by Major General Elimelekh Avner, the Commander of Military Rule nationwide and Laniado, the local military governor, to include Palestinians in decision-making processes in the city, which would loosen their ability to control and surveil the Arab population. The consensus among the security establishment was that even if a local committee of municipal affairs was to be formed for 'Arab Jaffa' it would have to be headed by a Jewish military officer.[45] The 'new normal' for Arab Jaffa was therefore based on their ambiguous presence: they eventually were to become Israeli citizens, yet marked as an occupied population in constant need of military and police surveillance.

The logic of separation between Jewish and Arab Jaffa was inscribed onto each aspect of everyday life. Avner declared that the impending demilitarisation of Jaffa would take different forms for the Jews and Arabs in the city.[46] Normalcy in Jewish Jaffa meant receiving certain municipal services, such as electricity, water and sewage, from Tel Aviv as the city's affairs were to be overseen by the committee, while a civilian police force was to replace the military as the arbiter of public order. The military governor and his superiors were adamant that Jewish Jaffa would be rapidly normalised and facilitated the establishment of mundane services that served as the markers of normalcy: postal and bus services that linked the city beyond the barbed wires to nearby (Jewish) municipalities.

---

[44] In October 1949, the Israeli government decided on the annexation of Jaffa to Tel Aviv. This decision created controversy, as it stipulated the new municipality would be renamed 'Jaffa-Tel Aviv'. Israel Rokah, then Tel Aviv mayor, resented the decision to add Jaffa before Tel Aviv, not only because this decision was made without consulting him, but also because he felt it sidelines what he considered a symbol of the Zionist project. Eventually, though, a compromise was reached, and on June 1950 the municipality officially announced the annexation as well as its new name 'Tel Aviv-Jaffa' (see Tel Aviv Municipality Archives (TAMA) Yediot Iryat Tel Aviv, 5–6 (1949), p. 74).

[45] IDFA, 20.9.1948, 1-1860-1950.

[46] IDFA, 20.9.1948, 1-1860-1950.

In the meantime, the Palestinians in Arab Jaffa were confined to the ghetto, and their ability to communicate with the outside restricted: telephone services were unavailable; letters, collected and distributed only through the Red Cross and the office of the military governor, were heavily censored; the permits system, which required each Palestinian leaving the enclosure for any purpose to be scrutinised by the Israeli security apparatus in order to determine the level of threat they posed to the state further restricted mobility.[47]

The Israeli security apparatus envisioned a different form of 'normalcy' for Arab Jaffa. In October 1948, the military governor announced that owners of residential or business 'real estate properties within the Jaffa city limits' were to provide proof of their ownership to a committee in charge of registering such properties, ostensibly for the purpose of taxation. The registry prepared by the office of the military governor was, indeed, used to impose new taxes on the Palestinian population and thus fund its own operations. But this extensive registration project also served another purpose: keeping an inventory of valuables owned by Palestinians. For this purpose, Laniado also requested that the ownership of each radio set, automobile 'and other commodities' by Palestinians would require a special licence, which, as he admitted in his weekly report, would provide him with the most accurate information about the contents of each household, and allow him to assert control over the ways Palestinians spend their leisure time.[48] Around the same time, Laniado also ordered the closure of several Palestinian-owned coffee shops 'for obvious reasons'. If we consider the already severe restrictions on movement including that of the leadership, whom Laniado constantly suspected of 'meddling in politics', from the closure of coffee shops, registration of radio sets and the censorship over mail and publications it is clear that the Israeli security services intended to curtail any attempt at civil society formation – as much as political mobilisation.

Stranded in the city without an effective leadership and locked up under Israeli occupation, Palestinians were painfully aware of their precarious

---

[47] The military governor proposed a centrally located mail box for all incoming and outgoing letters that would be collected by the postal service and transferred to the office of the military governor for inspection and censorship before shipping (ISA, Letter to the Minister of Minority Affairs from Dr. Moshe Ophir, 11.10.1948 G 306/97).

[48] ISA, Weekly Report no. 7, 20.9.1948, G 306/77.

position. The Emergency Committee was, for the most part, powerless in the face of the state's security establishment, and its members were periodically subjected to detention and house arrest. Nevertheless, they continued to voice their opposition to the harsh measures of suppression imposed on them by the military governor: forced evictions and ghettoisation, expropriation of properties, and severe restrictions on their movement. They invoked the colonial past and present when they protested: '[You] should not treat us as if we were negroes in Africa. The Jewish people have suffered enough persecution, it cannot become the oppressor.'[49] This polyvalent statement should be read first within the immediate historical context of decolonisation: the UN recognised Israel only a few months prior to this letter of protest; the Indian subcontinent was partitioned into the independent states of India and Pakistan the year before, while the end of the French mandate in Syria and Lebanon just a few years prior (1946 and 1943 respectively) heralded the age of formal independence in the region. Not only were the old colonial powers perceived to be on the decline, but the ideologies that had conferred legitimacy over European rule in Africa and Asia were rapidly losing respect and appeal. By invoking colonial rule in Africa, the Palestinian leadership in Jaffa attempted to shame their Israeli readers for their tolerance of racism.

Yet this statement is curious when one reads it against the intellectual climate of the period. By the close of the age of what Albert Hourani glossed as the liberal age, unself-reflexive ideas of race and civilisation were popular among Arab intellectuals. Many of them turned the American and European missionaries' racial hierarchy in the 'family of mankind' into a developmentalist understanding of Arabness and Arab culture as halfway between white Europeans and black Africans and brown Asians. The Mandate System in the Levant, reflected this ideological geo-cultural one-upmanship: whereas British and French colonial rule in Africa and south and east Asia effectively continued, the former Arab provinces of the Ottoman Empire were 'subject to the rendering of administrative advice and assistance by a Mandatory until such time as they are able to stand alone'.[50] Read in that context, the invocation of colonial rule over Africans, then, was meant to do more than just shaming the Israelis.

[49] ISA, Weekly Report no. 22, 4.1.1949, G 306/77.
[50] Covenant of the League of Nations, Article 22.

It was a reminder that the authors of the letter, who are Arabs, should not be treated like colonised black subjects because they had, after all, already proved the required level of civilisation. For all intents and purposes, the Palestinian leadership reminded the European Jew, Laniado, that they should be treated as equals. After all, until recently European Jews were considered racially suspect, and as a result, persecuted, too.

The Emergency Committee also voiced its protest over the mass expropriation of houses in the city. In a letter dated 21 February 1949, the committee argued that since Jaffa was not allocated to the Jewish state to begin with, the seizure of properties was illegal, given the 'state ... claims to be ... democratic'. Moreover, the Custodian of Absentee Properties could not, neither morally nor legally, take possession of properties of Palestinians who were absent. This right should be reserved either to the relatives of absentees or to the committee itself. Furthermore, they charged the state with deliberate discrimination against the occupied Arab population by granting impunity to looters, whether they happened to be government agents or civilians.[51]

In addition to formal protest, Palestinians also devised other, less direct ways, to challenge Israel's attempts at appropriations and pacification through feet dragging, undermining procedures or finding alternative spaces for political engagement. For instance, when the military governor ordered the Arab population to submit documentation attesting ownership of properties, many refused to comply or to leave their documents at the Jaffa offices, fearing the occupying authorities would expropriate them and then deny their ownership rights. When the military governor realised this, he ordered his subordinates to prepare copies of these documents and return the original to their owners in order to allay such fears.[52] In another instance, Nicola Saba a member of the Emergency Committee, used his limited authority to register Palestinians as Israeli citizens in order to also register 'infiltrators', or Palestinians returning without obtaining the permission of the Israeli security apparatus. When his actions were revealed by an informant, an investigation launched into the affair discovered he may have registered several 'infiltrators'. Saba was

---

[51] ISA, G 5670/32.
[52] ISA, 8.11.48, G 77/306.

promptly replaced by a Jewish clerk.⁵³ Finally, the popularity of the communist weekly newspaper *al-Ittihad* was understood by the security authorities as a Palestinian response to their subordinate position, since it launched 'unrestrained attacks against the government. The Arab citizen derives pleasure from these attacks, as he blames the Israeli government for his bad situation, whether such blame is justified or not.' Palestinians found venues to articulate their opposition to the state and register their frustration at their subordinate position, whether through the publication and reading of such newspapers, or, as the same report noted anxiously, by meeting in local coffee shops engaging in political work with acquaintances and neighbours.⁵⁴

In July 1949, military rule was abolished in major coastal cities. In its stead, the department of Arab Affairs at the Ministry of Internal Affairs appointed Aharon Chelouche as the regional officer for the Palestinians of Jaffa, Ramla and Lydd.⁵⁵ Chelouche (1921–2004) was the grandson of Yosef Eliyahu Chelouche and the great-grandson of his namesake, Aharon Chelouche, who immigrated from Oran in French-occupied Algeria to become one of the leaders of the pre-Zionist Jewish-Maghrebi community in Jaffa and, with his son, founding father of Tel Aviv.⁵⁶ Yosef Eliyahu Chelouche (1870–1934) considered himself Arab and Jewish, both a native of the country (like the Palestinians) and a Zionist, but also chided the Zionist leadership for mistreating the Palestinians and slighting the Sephardic and Mizrahi Jews.⁵⁷ His grandson Aharon, however, managed to integrate into the state's security apparatus when he was appointed the regional officer, and served in this and other roles related to minority affairs within the Israeli police until his retirement in 1973.

The end of military rule in Jaffa entailed the removal of the barbed wire fences around Ajami. One Israeli newspaper's report that the 'Arabs are generally glad' as 'many have not left the area during the era of military rule' omitted

---

⁵³ ISA, GL 171103/44.
⁵⁴ ISA, n.d. GL 17111/29.
⁵⁵ IDFA, 29.6.1949, 104-1255-1953.
⁵⁶ Mordekhai Elkayam, *Jaffa, Neve Tsedek: The Beginnings of Tel Aviv* [in Hebrew] (Tel Aviv: Misrad Habitahon, 1990); Aharon Chelouch, *From Jalabia to Kova Tembel* [in Hebrew] (Tel Aviv: 1991).
⁵⁷ Yosef Eliyahu Chelouche, *The Story of my Life* [in Hebrew] (Tel Aviv: Bavel, 2005).

to mention the strict permit regime and the heavily armed guards along the fences. The reporter also claimed that since 'we are all Israeli now, there is no [legal] distinction between citizens'.[58] The removal of physical barriers and relaxing restrictions on movements were tangible signs of returning to civilian life and the reunification of the 'two Jaffas', the Arab and Jewish ones. Palestinians were now able to seek employment, shop and partake in the everyday cultures of leisure that developed in Tel Aviv. Yet, the 'new normal' of the Palestinians in Jaffa also entailed being closely surveilled by the regional officer, who produced detailed monthly reports about every aspect of everyday life in Jaffa, Ramla and Lydd. These reports reflect the interest of the Israeli security apparatus not only in economic, political or cultural activities of Palestinians, but also mundane social interactions, like idle conversations at local coffee shops.

In spite of the liberalisation of the state and the formal abolition of military rule in 1966, the close surveillance of Palestinians in Jaffa (and elsewhere) has only become more technologically and logistically sophisticated over the years and continues to this day. The notorious SHABAK (Hebrew acronym of the General Security Services or GSS) routinely detains and interrogates local activists who organise and participate in protests against state actions. This was the case during the Israeli assault in Lebanon in the summer of 2006, operations Cast Lead in the Gaza Strip (2008–9) and Protective Edge (2014). No wonder, then, that an elderly Palestinian interlocutor refused to provide direct answers to my questions about his experiences in 1948, because, as he apologetically explained to me, anyone can be a state agent and if he dares utter any criticism, he might lose his pension and benefits.

Conclusion

Despite its relative brevity, the era of post-occupation military rule was a formative one in the lives of Palestinians in Jaffa. The period 1948–9 marks a watershed not only in terms of their minoritisation and the precarity of an expendable colonised population under the direct rule of the military; the making of the 'new normal' meant a rapid transformation of familiar urban landscapes into unfamiliar and even hostile ones. And finally, these processes

[58] IDFA, n.d. 55-1255-1953.

were also designed to sediment the 'no-longer-conscious', and accelerate collective forgetfulness of the past, not only of pre-1948, but also that of loss, trauma and mass expulsion. These elisions that worked to normalise and reproduce the realities of occupation and subordination also foreclosed the potential to overcome the new normal and open up avenues for utopian imaginary and desire.

3

ITINERARIES OF EXILE

I'm looking for the true Palestine, the Palestine that's more than memories, more than peacock feathers, more than a son, more than scars written by bullets on the stairs ... for him, Palestine is something worthy of a man bearing arms for, dying for. For us ... it's only a search for something buried beneath the dust of memories.[1]

For me, a return home is not merely the redemption of my family's history and our pain, nor merely the absolute requirement of acknowledgement and apology, but a radicalisation of thought that endeavours to always speak truth to power.[2]

In a 1970 interview with Australian journalist Richard Carleton, prominent Palestinian intellectual and the editor of *al-Hadaf* Ghassan Kanafani pointedly responds to questions about 'peace talks' with the Israelis as an alternative to armed struggle. The tone-deaf questions and succinct, poignant responses seem almost hilarious in exchanges such as this:

---

[1] Ghassan Kanafani, 'Returning to Haifa', in G. Kanafani, *Palestine's Children: Returning to Haifa and Other Stories*, trans. Barbara Harlow and Karen E. Riley (Boulder: Lynne Rienner Publishers, 2000), pp. 186–7.

[2] Susan Abulhawa, 'Because We are not Children of a Lesser God', *Aljazeera*, 20 June 2015, http://www.aljazeera.com/indepth/features/2015/06/magazine-children-lesser-god-palestinian-refugees-150615110526283.html (last accessed 26 May 2016).

Carleton: Why don't your organization engage in peace talks with the Israelis?

Kanafani: You don't mean exactly peace talks. You mean capitulation. Surrendering.

Carleton: Why don't you just talk?

Kanafani: Talk to whom?

Carleton: Talk to the Israeli leaders.

Kanafani: That is the kind of conversation between the sword and the neck, you mean.

Carleton: There are no swords or guns in the room. You could still talk.

Kanafani: No. I've never never seen talk between a colonialist case and a nation liberation movement.

Carleton: But despite this, why not just talk?

Kanafani: Talk about what?

Carleton: Talk about the possibility of not fighting.

Kanafani: Not fighting for what?

Carleton: Not fighting at all, no matter what for.

Kanafani: People usually fight for something, and they stop fighting for something. So you can't even tell me what should we speak about what.

...

Carleton: Talk to stop fighting, to stop the death, the misery, the destruction, the pain ... of Palestinians, of Israelis, of Arabs.

Kanafani: Of the Palestinian people who are uprooted, thrown in the camps, living in starvation, killed for 20 years, and forbidden even to use the name Palestinians?

Carleton: It's better than death.

Kanafani: Maybe to you. Not to us. To us, to liberate our country, to have dignity, to have respect, to have our human rights is something as essential as life itself.[3]

Visibly irritated by the exchange, Kanafani masterfully demonstrates that making the Palestinian case for global audiences faces two interconnected

---

[3] The full interview can be watched here: https://youtu.be/3h_drCmG2iM (last accessed 15 June 2021).

major hurdles: framing and, to borrow from Edward Said, 'permission to narrate'.[4]

In terms of framing, it is clear that the interviewer's cookie-cutter formulae are utterly rejected by Kanafani. Thus, for instance, 'civil war', 'conflict' (in the Jordanian conflict) or 'peace talks' (with the Israeli colonisers) are insufficient as explanatory models, since Kanafani and the Palestinian guerillas identify as a liberation movement engaged in fighting both their colonisers and 'fascist' regional regimes that enable them. It is also painfully clear that Kanafani's alternate explanatory models were falling on deaf ears. But then again, one might assume Kanafani could have foreseen that. He might have agreed to the interview not in order to convince an intransigent journalist but to seize the opportunity to break through the hegemonic framework and achieve the fleeting 'recognition' Walter Benjamin was talking about.[5] In other words, Kanafani's goal here was to 'sneak' the Palestinian voice through the cracks and into the hearts and minds of global audiences that might acknowledge it. Primary among these global audiences are others in the global south locked in their own liberation struggles against Western colonialism and local (but often Western-supported) authoritarianism.

Kanafani, therefore, is speaking over the heads of Western media outlets, settler colonial regimes and their constituencies and international governing organisations to global audiences who might offer their support for the Palestinian liberation movement. Furthermore, Kanafani's goal here is not just undermining hegemonic colonial explanatory frameworks, but to provide an alternate, sedimented narrative that runs counter to what consumers of news media are accustomed to. When asked about what the armed confrontation with King Hussein's military achieved, Kanafani is explicit: 'we achieved teaching every single person in this world that we are a small brave nation who are going to fight to the last drop of blood, to put justice for ourselves after the world failed in giving it to us'. Here, Kanafani is referring to narration as an act of teaching the world the Palestinian perspective that has been silenced. His choice of the verb 'teaching' is not coincidental: Palestinians are

[4] Edward Said, 'Permission to Narrate', *Journal of Palestine Studies*, vol. 13, no. 3 (Spring 1984), pp. 27–48.
[5] Water Benjamin, 'Theses on the Philosophy of History', in W. Benjamin, *Illuminations*, trans. Harry Zohn (New York: Schocken Books, 1968), p. 255.

not merely fighting for their survival and liberation; their actions and words are public-facing, fostering critique of settler colonialism and inspiring others to resist oppression.

This chapter also treats narration as a transformative act: when Kanafani, Abu Iyad and Hisham Sharabi, the three *Yafawiin* I introduce here, narrate personal stories of exile, they intend not just to redeem history from the impersonal and the alienating and stir emotion in their readers; rather, these narratives are themselves a call to action – for Palestinians to resist their colonisers and reclaim the homeland, and for global audiences to oppose the violence of official histories and erasures and stand in solidarity with the oppressed.

The texts I chose demonstrate the gradual transformations in the ways these men understood their experience of exile and fashioned the means to overcome them. From the early clandestine infiltrations and isolated acts of revenge against Israeli soldiers and settlers, to organised military resistance against complicit Arab regimes and the production of revolutionary consciousness, the Palestinian authors on view in this chapter participated in one form or another in what Walter Benjamin called 'the tradition of the oppressed'. The textual interlocutors – including Ghassan Kanafani's fictional protagonists – will help me chart the contingent links between their itineraries of exile and forms of self-(re)constitution as political agents.

Making Refugees into Revolutionaries

For Palestinians driven out of their homeland, refugeehood meant finding themselves suddenly cut off from their sources of livelihood and from each other. Over a short period of time, Palestinians turned from a large majority into smaller and vulnerable minority groups dispersed in Arab states bordering with Palestine. Moreover, as most refugees used to be peasants who lived off the land, this sudden transformation into refugees also meant a shift from being producers into international charity recipients, residing in hastily erected tent camps, where Palestinians relied on rations based on calculated 'caloric intake', and subjected to 'techniques of discipline and control' such as enumeration and classification as refugees.[6] Palestinian refugees were then

---

[6] See Julie Peteet, *Landscape of Hope and Despair: Palestinian Refugee Camps* (Philadelphia: University of Pennsylvania Press, 2005), especially chapter two.

forced to endure the trauma of expulsion, the separation from extended family members, friends and neighbours, and the humiliation of their new refugee status, in addition to the harsh conditions of camp life.[7] These camps became 'spaces of bereavement', sites of creative coping with their new situation and places that enacted new collective identities through spatial memorialisation of the lost homeland.[8]

Even before the end of hostilities in the autumn of 1948, and throughout the 1950s, Israeli authorities repeatedly complained about the problem of 'infiltrators', individual Palestinians who transgressed the 1949 armistice lines into Israel for various reasons: refugees who wished to harvest their crops and reclaim possessions, visit relatives who remained 'inside' and return to their village irrespective of the diplomatic stalemate. Several of these cases also involved *fedayeen*, individual or small groups of fighters aiming to exact revenge, sabotage Israeli military installations or newly created border settlements, often on the lands of depopulated villages.[9]

The 1950s saw the rebirth of resistance first in the creation of the Arab Nationalist Movement (ANM), where George Habash (later Popular Front for the Liberation of Palestine –PFLP – leader) and Nayef Hawatma (later Democratic Front for the Liberation of Palestine leader) were prominent members. The ANM focused its activities on liberating the corrupt Arab regimes although they emphasised commitment to the liberation of Palestine. Mobilised by their motto 'unity, liberation and vengeance', the movement's Nasserist commitment dictated its pan-Arabist politics and deferral of armed struggle against the Israelis, with a few minor exceptions of support for guerilla raids along the Jordanian and Egyptian borders in the late 1950s. The birth of the ANM's 'Palestinian branch' that was highly critical of the movement's decentring of Palestine and pushed for more towards direct confrontation with the Israelis did not result in a shift towards armed struggle, and eventually

---

[7] Rosemary Sayigh, *The Palestinians: From Peasants to Revolutionaries* (London and New York: Zed Books, 1979), pp. 105–110.
[8] Peteet, *Landscape*, p. 95.
[9] See Benny Morris, *Israel's Border Wars, 1949–1956: Arab Infiltration, Israeli Retaliation, and the Countdown to the Suez War* (Oxford: Clarendon Press, 1993), pp. 28–68. Occasional archival documents mention 'Arab infiltrators' in Jaffa and the official policy of deportation, except for unique cases where they were allowed to stay and obtained citizenship.

brought about the demise of the ANM and the rise of Fatah after 1967, which I will discuss below.[10]

Literature of Resistance

The spectacular Arab defeat in the June 1967 war is known as *al-Naksa*, 'the setback' in Arabic. After the conquest of East Jerusalem, the West Bank and the Gaza Strip, the Israeli government decided to encourage Israeli tourism in the Occupied Territories.[11] For many Palestinian refugees and internally displaced persons, this too was a moment of 'opening up': historical Palestine became one again, even if under colonial rule, and the 1949 armistice lines were briefly dissolved, offering the promise of spatial expansion. While, for Israelis, the 1967 occupation meant physical and territorial expansion, which soon after morphed into the settlements projects, for Palestinians, and for those inside Israel, 1967 represented brief spatial release from the confines of the state and reconnecting with the Arab world. Thus, families were reunited, friendships rekindled, and many Palestinian refugees in the West Bank and Gaza seized the opportunity to cross back into the territories they were forced to leave nineteen years earlier and visit their lost homes.

Many Palestinian refugees exiled to the West Bank were eager to head into their places of origin, often retracing the same routes they travelled during the expulsion, except this time, in reverse. These visits, however, were rarely joyous occasions; rather they were fraught with tensions, between refugees and other Palestinians who remained, and between exiles to those inhabiting their homes. Two such bittersweet encounters are at the core of Ghassan Kanafani's short story *Returning to Haifa* (originally published 1969). Born in Acre and raised in Jaffa, Kanafani (1936–72) was forced into exile with his family,

---

[10] On the ANM and its internal struggles, see As'ad AbuKhalil, 'George Habash and the Movement of Arab Nationalists: Neither Unity not Liberation', *Journal of Palestine Studies*, vol. 28, no. 4 (Summer 1999), pp. 91–103; Walid W. Kazziha, *Revolutionary Transformation in the Arab World: Habash and his Comrades from Nationalism to Marxism* (London: C. Knight, 1975); Yezid Sayigh, 'Reconstructing the Paradox: The Arab Nationalist Movement, Armed Struggle, and Palestine, 1951–1966', *Middle East Journal*, vol. 45, no. 4 (Autumn 1991), pp. 608–29; Yezid Sayigh, *Armed Struggle and the Search for a State: The Palestinian National Movement, 1949–1993* (Oxford: Clarendon Press, 1997), pp. 71–80.

[11] Rebecca L. Stein, 'Souvenirs of Conquest: Israeli Occupations as Tourist Events', *International Journal of Middle East Studies*, vol. 40, no. 4 (2008), pp. 647–69.

initially relocating to Damascus, where he was certified as a teacher. His political commitment to ANM and personal affinity with George Habash forced him to abandon Syria for the Gulf, and finally for Beirut in Lebanon, where he devoted his time to editing and writing in pan-Arabist and leftist newspapers. From 1969 until his assassination, Kanafani edited PFLP's weekly magazine *al-Hadaf* (Arabic, 'the target') in addition to publishing his works of fiction.

Returning to Haifa is made up of two separate but interconnected subplots. The long one occurs in post-1967 Haifa: Said and Safiyya, a Palestinian couple who exiled from Haifa to a refugee camp near Ramallah, set out in search of their Halisa home and long-lost infant son, Khaldun. In contrast to the day they left Haifa, where they were literally swept up in the crowd, 'propelled toward the port',[12] ostensibly devoid of agency, this time, Said and Safiyya made the decision to make the trip. Moreover, while nineteen years earlier they seemed to have no choice but to follow the masses into exile, the couple made the return trip by car; the steering wheel in Said's hands symbolises agency and mastery over his itinerary, and as I demonstrate below – his fate.

Said and Safiyya's fictional 'return' to Haifa forces them to confront the demons of their past, in particular, abandoning their infant son Khaldun, their home and city. The pangs of guilt they both feel run throughout the story. Said finally articulated his guilt over the abandonment in the narrative lead-up to a peripatetic moment of meeting Dov/Khaldun, who returned home wearing his IDF fatigues:

> We shouldn't have left anything. Not Khaldun, not the house, not Haifa! ... I felt as though I knew Haifa, yet the city refused to acknowledge me. I had the same feeling in this house, here, in our house. Can you imagine that? That our house would refuse to acknowledge us? Don't you feel it? I believe the same thing will happen with Khaldun. You'll see![13]

The commensurability of son, house and city that Said imagined, led him to predict that just as his house and Haifa 'disowned' him, so would his flesh and blood, as indeed happened next. Yet only after Khaldun/Dov rejected his birth

---

[12] Kanafani, 'Returning to Haifa', p. 154.
[13] Ibid., p. 173.

parents and scoffed at what he perceived as the weakness that had precipitated their abandonment, it dawned on Said that homeland does not equal son, house and city. These, for Palestinians who lived through the Nakba, are the things of the past.

Khaldun's disavowal of his parents and of Palestinianness stands in stark contrast to their other son Khalid whom Said had forbidden to join the resistance for fear of losing him, too; Khalid's sense of belonging was less locked up in the past than that of his parents. For two decades the painful memories of happy days before the Nakba had impeded political action and produced only despair, mainly because they created a sense of pastness – that which has gone by, lost and irreversible. Moreover, what remained of it disavows the refugee couple, claiming they no longer belong in it. This is where the homeland-as-past had failed refugees, and in fact, reproduced them as stateless anomalies. Since refugees do not fit into existing spatial arrangement of the world as neatly bounded nation states, they are also outside of the present. With both past and present denied to them, the only salvation lies in the future. Khalid, the son who had never experienced life in Haifa before expulsion and had never met his older brother, and therefore free from the burden of nostalgia, was the first one to understand the role of past as a mobilising force: Palestinians should emancipate themselves from the stranglehold of nostalgic longings, which only keep them stuck in the past. Instead, memory of injustice should inform their struggle and propel them towards action. Longing for the status quo ante, which will never be restored, and wallowing in self-pity ought to be replaced with new identities that are rooted in the future, in the process of becoming. Kanafani's Khalid therefore represents the post-Nakba generation of Palestinians who realise that the actual return could only occur after Palestinians take up arms, collectively fight for their homeland, and thereby take ownership of the past in order to remake their futures.

But there is another layer to this realisation. Even Khaldun/Dov, who is entirely lost to his parents, intuitively understands this: 'man is a cause'.[14] Kanafani puts these words into the mouth of someone who is Palestinian by

---

[14] Ibid., p. 181. Arabic: *al-insan qadiyya*. *Insan* normally means human rather than the gendered 'man'; *qadiyya* can also be translated as 'matter' or 'issue' which further clarify the meaning of this statement.

birth but Jewish Israeli by choice. In other words, one's identity is not determined by birth, but by one's upbringing and more importantly – his (or her) actions. Khaldun makes a conscious decision not to return to a past he had never known and that his birth parents were holding onto; he becomes Dov, because he was brought up as an Israeli, by Israeli parents, in Haifa, a city that was mostly de-Arabised and remade an Israeli space.

The protagonist of the secondary plotline in *Returning to Haifa* is also from *jil Filastin*, the generation that experienced the expulsion. Faris al-Lubda, the couple's neighbour in Ramallah, Said informed his wife, had visited his old house in Jaffa just a week prior. Just like them, Faris arrived to his city of youth in a rental car, almost twenty years after he was forced out by sea. Kanafani knows this area from his own childhood and provides a detailed description of the whereabouts of the house in Ajami, the very quarter that had become the 'Arab ghetto' after the Nakba, as we have seen in Chapter 2, and the site we will return to in Chapter 7. Though born in Acre ('Akka) Kanafani was raised and educated in the modern Jabbaliyeh quarter in Jaffa and attended the Frères missionary school he mentions in the story, located just across from the former French hospital and the old city.[15]

The encounter at the core of Faris' story is between the exiled owner of the house, and another Palestinian from Jaffa who is internally displaced. Unlike Faris, this man is originally from Manshiyyeh, the northern Jaffa neighbourhood which, as we have seen in Chapter 1, was shelled by the Irgun in the spring of 1948 in the opening salvo of the Zionist conquest of Jaffa. This Palestinian, who is never named, had not left the city. He remained and bore the brunt of the Israeli occupation: made homeless after the destruction of Manshiyyeh, he fled, only to be incarcerated in Israel's prison camps and return, upon his release, to Jaffa, leasing an absentee's property from the state.[16] When the door

---

[15] Kanafani mentions his departure from Jaffa in passing in Ghassan Kanafani, 'The Land of Sad Oranges', in G. Kanafani, *Men in the Sun and other Palestinian Stories*, trans. Hilary Kilpatrick (Boulder: Lynne Rienner Publishers, 1999), p. 75. Rema Hamami's aunt remembered Kanafani as her childhood playmate, see Salim Tamari and Rema Hamami, 'Virtual Returns to Jaffa', *Journal of Palestine Studies*, vol. 27, no. 4 (Summer 1998), p. 70.

[16] On Israel's prison camps for Palestinian PoWs after the Nakba, see Salman Abu Sitta and Terry Rempel, 'The ICRC and the Detention of Palestinian Civilians in Israel's 1948 POW/Labor Camps', *Journal of Palestine Studies*, vol. XLIII, no. 4 (Summer 2014), pp. 11–38.

opens and Faris expects to see an Israeli, he goes off in a pre-rehearsed tangent, staking his claim to the house and stating he would return to repossess it 'by the power of the sword'.[17] But as it turns out, the man who opened the door was a Palestinian. The current occupants and the house seem to maintain a symbiotic relationship: it is unclear whether the family has taken over the place and made itself at home, or if it is the house that possesses the family. Kanafani makes this suggestion in several ways: for instance, the man had left the house virtually untouched for nineteen years since its original owners fled the city; the framed photo of Badr, Faris' martyred brother, remained hanging in the living room; and finally, the occupant's son was named after Badr, a practice that is usually reserved to family members of the deceased, especially if the circumstances of his death are considered honorable ones.

In fact, Badr al-Lubda had become part of the occupant's family, and when Faris removes the photograph, it immediately leaves a 'pale, meaningless rectangle, a disturbing void' not just on the wall, but in the lives of the family who embraced it as their own, as the occupant himself admitted.[18] The ghost of Badr may have possessed his former family home, but its absence, after Faris removes the photo, only produces anguish and anxiety rather than relief, as expected from exorcism, when one rids oneself of ghostly possession. In this case, Badr has not only become an integral part of the family, the house and Jaffa, but the memory of his martyrdom serves as a source of honour and pride for Palestinians, a symbol and marker of the way to liberation and return. This is, perhaps, what the occupant meant when he identified the photograph as a 'bridge' between the refugees and 'us', those who remained in place. Faris realised that collective armed struggle and the will to self-sacrifice are necessary to deliver Palestinian refugees from the humiliation of exile, return to the homeland and earn the right to reclaim past possessions like the photo of his martyred brother.

Returning to Haifa has often been read as a literary piece seeking to gauge the transformative role of the 1967 June war on Palestinian political consciousness and as a didactic piece, seeking to educate the readers and encourage

---

[17] Kanafani, 'Returning to Haifa', p. 174.
[18] Kanafani, 'Returning to Haifa', p. 177.

them to take up arms.[19] But in addition, the fraught encounters between the Palestinian returnees and the occupants of their former homes, whether Israeli or Palestinians, highlight potential problems pertinent to the implementation of the right of return. I will return to the very question of the 'second occupant' in Chapter 7.

While Kanafani's text may imply that the Palestinian revolutionary turn was abrupt, an unexpected result of the 1967 war, scholars have demonstrated that the transformation of political consciousness and action was in fact much more gradual, as Palestinians gravitated towards forming their own resistance movement in the second half of the 1960s long before the Naksa. The 'setback' of June 1967 certainly demonstrated to Palestinians that the Arab regimes were not their best bet if they wish to return to Palestine and end Israeli colonial rule. The revolutionary discourse of Nasser and the Ba'thists in Iraq and Syria amounted to an astounding defeat and a retreat from the promise of Arab socialism and national liberation. Moreover, politically, the 1967 Arab defeat meant that these regimes could no longer restrain the Palestinians.[20]

A key event in the transformation of Palestinian political consciousness was the battle of Karameh on 21 March 1968, which began as an Israeli cross-border reprisal for continuous PLO operations launched from Jordanian territory. On a tactical level, Israel indeed achieved its goal: the destruction of the Karameh PLO guerilla training camp. But politically, the battle boosted the aura of the PLO and its ability to do what the regular Arab armies failed to achieve less than a year prior: hold its own against the IDF.[21] The battle also signalled a diplomatic

---

[19] Muhammad Siddiq, *Man is a Cause: Political Consciousness and the Fiction of Ghassan Kanafani* (Seattle: University of Washington, 1984), p. 49.

[20] See Jamal R. Nassar, 'The Culture of Resistance: The 1967 War in the Context of the Palestinian Struggle', *Arab Studies Quarterly*, vol. 19, no. 3 (Summer 1997), pp. 77–98; Ibrahim Abu Lughod, 'Altered Realities: The Palestinians since 1967', *International Journal*, vol. 28, no. 4 (Autumn 1973), pp. 648–69.

[21] On the battle of Karameh and its legacy, see Sayigh, *Armed Struggle*, pp. 174–9; David Hirst, *The Gun and the Olive Branch: The Roots of Violence in the Middle East* (New York: Harcourt Brace Janovich, 1977), pp. 411–14; Paul Thomas Chamberlin, *The Global Offensive: The United States, the Palestine Liberation Organization, and the Making of the Post-Cold War Order* (Oxford: Oxford University Press, 2012), pp. 44–9; W. Andrew Terril, 'The Political Mythology of the Battle of Karameh', *Middle East Journal*, vol. 55, no. 1 (Winter 2001), pp. 91–111; Fuad Jabbar, 'The Arab Regimes and the Palestinian Revolution', *Journal of Palestine Studies*, vol. 2, no. 2 (Winter 1973), pp. 79–101.

defeat for Israel in the international arena, so much so that the American ambassador was quoted as saying that in historical perspective, twenty years down the line, the battle of Karameh will be remembered as the beginning of the end for Israel.[22] Yasser Arafat, the leader of Fateh, concluded:

> What we have done is to make the world ... realize that the Palestinian is no longer refugee number so and so, but the member of a people who hold the reins of their own destiny and are in a position to determine their own future.[23]

Palestinian revolutionary consciousness that emerged at Karameh began to shift to Lebanon where students, trade unions and leftist parties put pressure on the government to facilitate armed struggle from Lebanese soil. The state's security apparatus had clamped down on political mobilisation in the preceding years. A popular protest march on 23 April 1969 was an expression of the profound alienation of Palestinians. Triggered by a series of military assaults by the Lebanese army against the Palestinian guerilla fighters in southern Lebanon it ended the Lebanese military 'reign of terror' and brought about self-administration in all the Palestinian refugees camps in Lebanon.[24] In subsequent years, the Lebanese camps became sites where, in Arafat's dictum, Palestinian refugees aspired to 'hold the reins of their own destiny'. As Julie Peteet has argued, these camps transformed from places that secured bare life into landscapes of hope.[25] This shift from below came to be enshrined in the Cairo Accord of November 1969 in which the Lebanese government bowed to Egyptian government pressure to allow southern Lebanon to become a launching pad for Palestinian armed struggle against Israel.[26]

---

[22] Abba Eban quoted the US ambassador, Walworth Barbour, during a meeting of the Israeli government to the chagrin of Menahem Begin. See Tom Segev, 'It started in Karameh' [in Hebrew], *Haaretz*, 23 January 2008, http://www.haaretz.co.il/misc/1.1558623 (last accessed 26 May 2016).
[23] Quoted in Hirst, *The Gun and the Olive Branch*, p. 299.
[24] The march of 23 April 1969 was a response of camp Palestinians to the escalation of tensions between the Palestinian guerrillas and the Lebanese security forces, tensions that erupted with the Bint Jbeil siege earlier in the month. See Rosemary Sayigh, *The Palestinians: From Peasants to Revolutionaries* (London: Zed Books, 1979), pp. 164–73.
[25] Peteet, *Landscape*.
[26] Farid el-Khazen, *The Breakdown of the State of Lebanon, 1967–1976* (London: I. B. Tauris and the Centre for Lebanese Studies, 2000).

This combination of the liberation of the camps and Nasser's diplomatic pressure encouraged Palestinians and the wider Arab left to imagine their revolution as a project of world-making, refashioning selves from refugees to fighters, and in the process, recreating the image of the homeland as a horizon of liberatory possibilities, for the collective as well as the individual. In this context, Kanafani's 'man is the cause' is more than just didactic aphorism – it invokes the Palestinian revolutionary project as an empowering alternative to decades of dependency on international aid to Israel's delegitimisation of the refugees' right of return and the denial of Palestinian national identity. Eventually, Israel came to acknowledge the existence of a Palestinian people, albeit as a 'problem'. The right of return, however, remains a taboo in Israeli public discourse. This book aspires to open up the possibility to imagine Palestinian return as a practice.

The remainder of this chapter will follow the ways Palestinians from Jaffa grappled with exile on a spectrum between refugeehood and nostalgia for the past and a future-oriented self-fashioning project. Starting from a shared point of departure, the Nakba, the two autobiographies I selected are by a resistance leader and a public intellectual. They illuminate the range of responses to the expulsion among *jil Filastin*, first-generation refugees who experienced the Nakba. The next chapter will present the life histories of second-generation refugees while Chapter 7 will introduce third-generation perspectives on the practicability of the return of Palestinians.

From a Revolutionary to a Diplomat

When the French journalist Eric Rouleau recorded the autobiography of Abu Iyad (*nom de guerre* of Salah Khalaf, 1933–91) in 1978, Arafat's PLO was engaged in a public diplomacy offensive and assumed a role in international politics amidst the intense fighting during the Lebanese Civil War.[27]

---

[27] In fact, by 1978, the PLO was already embroiled in both internal and external crises, with dissenting factions (especially the 'rejection front') challenging the Fatah's leadership as a result of its shift to diplomacy and political compromise, while Egypt was in the midst of seeking a separate peace agreement with Israel, freezing out the Palestinians. For a comprehensive analysis of Abu Iyad's autobiography, see Elizabeth F. Thompson, *Justice Interrupted: The Struggle for Constitutional Government in the Middle East* (Cambridge, MA: Harvard University Press, 2013), pp. 239–74.

Abu Iyad's account of himself charts the transformation from a refugee, to revolutionary and – finally – a reluctant politician, as the initial romanticism of revolution faded for what he, in hindsight, considered as certain necessities of reality. This is also a story of fading hope: in 1958 Khalaf and his comrades (including Yasser Arafat and Khalil al-Wazir, known as Abu Jihad) founded Fatah as a clandestine liberation avant-guard. By the time of the book's original publication, Fatah had become the dominant group in the PLO that morphed into a heavily bureaucratised organisation with a global diplomatic presence.[28] In this process, the political imaginary it offered had also been transformed from Fatah's vision of one democratic state that included Jews, Muslims and Christians, to accepting what became known as the 'two states solution', which implied a de facto recognition of the Israeli state and UN Resolution 242.[29] For Abu Iyad, becoming a revolutionary entailed an opening up of the horizon of possibilities, imagining ways of making the impossible possible; not only did he envision the path to national liberation for the Palestinians, but he also advocated, and indeed institutionalised with the PLO, a working democratic structure, which was unique in its regional context. However, the mid-1970s mark the significant shrinking of the horizon of possibility to clearly demarcate the possible from the impossible, as the PLO was institutionalising and promoted what its leaders, including Abu Iyad, believed to be a 'pragmatic' solution, even though they were challenged by Arafat's rivals.

Khalaf was old enough to remember life before the expulsion. He was a boy of fifteen when the collapse of the city of Jaffa prompted his father to leave for Gaza on a makeshift boat. In his autobiography Khalaf stresses that

[28] Chamberlin, *The Global Offensive*; Amal Jamal, *The Palestinian National Movement: Politics of Contention, 1967–2005* (Bloomington: Indiana University Press, 2005); William B. Quandt, Fuad Jaber and Ann Mosely Lesch, *The Politics of Palestinian Nationalism* (Berkeley: University of California Press, 1973).

[29] Resolution 242 of 22 November 1967 refers to the aftermath of the 1967 June war and the Israeli military conquest of the West Bank, the Gaza Strip and the Golan Heights. Among other stipulations, the resolution also requires the 'withdrawal of Israel armed forces from territories occupied in the recent conflict' (UN S/RES/242 (1967)). This unfortunate wording has produced conflicting interpretations, the minimalist of those, espoused by Israel, claims that the resolution does not, in fact, require that Israel withdraws from all the territories it had occupied. See, for instance, Shabtai Rosenne, 'On Multi-Lingual Interpretation – UN Security Council Resolution 242', *The Israel Law Review*, vol. 6, no. 3 (1971), pp. 360–6. The maximalist interpretation was espoused by Arab states but rejected by the PLO.

he had multiple social relations with Jews: his father, who owned a small shop in Hakarmel market, which back then was partially within Jaffa's municipal boundaries, had several Jewish customers and suppliers. Young Salah, who used to relieve his father at the store, also tended to these customers and learned to converse in Hebrew. Hakarmel market area and its surroundings – Manshiyyeh and Kerem Hateymanim, the Yemenite quarter – were contact zones where Jews and Palestinians interacted daily: some were neighbours, sharing crowded residential neighbourhoods, while others conducted business, selling foodstuff and household wares.[30] Khalaf also recalls that he and a few of his Palestinian friends used to socialise with Jewish boys and teens from his immediate area, since most of them were Yemenis with whom he conversed in Arabic.[31] These forms of everyday sociability started to sour when, shortly after the end of World War II, Khalaf was accused of assaulting Jewish boys even though he claims it was him who was attacked by an angry Jewish mob in Tel Aviv. His former Jewish friends bore false witness against him, leading to his conviction. The adult Abu Iyad, reflecting on that transformative experience, directs his sense of betrayal not at the Jews, but at the Zionist movement that drove a wedge between him and his former friends, and by extension, between Arabs and Jews.[32] As the title of his autobiography suggests, Abu Iyad, a Palestinian leader,[33] projected his personal story onto the collective narrative of national struggle: if Zionism, an alien colonial movement, poisoned social relations in Palestine and produced sectarian schism between Jews and

---

[30] One Palestinian woman I interviewed in Jaffa recalls her next-door neighbour, a girl her age, who was, until 1948, her best friend. The two in fact shared the same first name, 'Ayisha in Arabic and Haya in Hebrew, both mean 'life'. A Jewish couple that still resides in the area recall Palestinian men and women selling eggs and milk in their neighbourhood. Yet another Jewish man was born and raised in a house in the midst of Manshiyyeh, across from the local police station and the famed Baydas mansion. The neighbourhood was referred to in official British and Hebrew correspondence as 'Karton', in northern Manshiyyeh, and according to a 1945 census, it was home to 6,000 Jews and 3,000 Muslims. See Or Aleksandrowicz, 'Paper Boundaries: The Erased History of Neveh Shalom' [in Hebrew], *Theory and Criticism*, vol. 41 (Summer 2003), pp. 181–2.

[31] Abu Iyad with Eric Rouleau, *My Home, My Land: A Narrative of the Palestinian Struggle*, trans. Linda Butler Koseoglu (New York: Times Books, 1978), pp. 5–6.

[32] Ibid., p. 9.

[33] See ibid., p. 226.

their fellow Muslim and Christian countrymen, then liberation means the elimination of Zionism and creation of a democratic state for all.[34]

At the moment of inception, liberation struggle was conceptualised first and foremost as an armed struggle, which would override the 'sterile verbosity' of political ideologies and parties, and instead work as a 'catalyst of unity', critical under the conditions of dispersal and marginalisation in the context of the international political arena.[35] Armed struggle was thus not just a major component of the organisation, not even merely a liberation tactics; it was perceived in existential terms. Participating in armed anticolonial struggle was to exert Palestinianness against the consistent Israeli denial of its existence, and against Israel's attempt to reduce Palestinians to a 'refugee problem', to be settled vis-à-vis neighbouring Arab states.[36] This new phase of the resistance movement broke with the leadership of notable families that characterised the pre-Nakba nationalist movement; at the same time, the rise of Fatah throughout the 1960s also signified a new way of collective action that differed from previous armed formations of the 1950s, that were more individualistic and clandestine in nature, and from the tutelage of Arab states that stifled Palestinian armed struggle and subordinated its cause to their agenda. For Abu Iyad the founding of Fatah in 1958 was a watershed in Palestinian history, an expression of an essential Palestinian identity and a sense of collectivity that at that moment were not attached to a nation state, and that moreover,

---

[34] Ibid., p. 139. The notion of the one democratic state was the topic of a heated debate within the resistance movement; see Alain Gresh, *The PLO: The Struggle Within, Towards an Independent Palestinian State* (London: Zed Books, 1988), pp. 34–42. Thompson argued that his claim that Jews can be persuaded away from Zionism points to his naiveté and perhaps even ignorance about the collective psyche of Israeli society. See Thompson, *Justice Interrupted*.

[35] Gresh, *The PLO*, p. 35.

[36] I discussed Israel's insistence of negotiating the fate of the refugees over the heads of Palestinians in Chapter 2; for further discussion of the existential dimension of armed struggle, see Sayigh, *Armed Struggle*, pp. 88–91; on armed struggle as a liberation strategy and its shortcomings, see Jamal R. Nassar, *The Palestine Liberation Organization: From Armed Struggle to the Declaration of Independence* (Westport, CT: Praeger, 1991), pp. 98–106; Yasser Arafat addressed the link between the revolution and Israeli denial: 'PLO Chairman Yasir Arafat (Abu Ammar): An Interview (August 1969)', in Walter Laqueur and Barry Rubin (eds), *The Israel-Arab Reader: A Documentary History of the Middle East Conflict* (New York: Penguin Books, 2008), p. 138.

encompassed a population dispersed across multiple borders. Revolutionary violence was to provide Palestinians, both refugees and those under Israeli occupation, forward-looking means of expressing a new form of identity, one that is bound to their places of origin but also forges horizontal forms of attachment and belonging.

The revolutionary moment of post-1967 also represented potentiality: in 1968, Abu Iyad publicly spoke about Fatah's vision for a democratic state in all of historic Palestine, which would be shared by Muslims, Jews and Christians, just like Jaffa had been before Zionism. He acknowledged this vision necessitated 'a great deal of courage and boldness' to overcome the victimhood state of mind and open up utopian imagining that reject the political 'here and now' for a possible 'there and then'.[37] That same year, as Fatah took over the leadership of the PLO, the Palestine National Council (PNC) voted on and ratified its new charter.

However, the 1968 Palestinian National Charter is rife with its own problems and contradictions. For instance, its drafters constantly conflated Palestinianness and Arabness, stressing 'Arab unity' as a precondition for the liberation of Palestine, and attempting to define Palestinianness through ethnic forms of belonging, i.e. being Arabs.[38] This slippage, which on some levels excluded Jews, Armenians and other non-Arab people who reside in Palestine, and its potential conflict with the notion of the 'democratic state' was also picked up by the PLO's Israeli detractors as well as internally within the Palestinian resistance movement.[39] These contradictions and tensions demonstrate the precarity of imagined futures: that attempting to envision a future that overcomes the present can produce its own internal fissures and

---

[37] Abu Iyad, *My Home*, p. 139.
[38] 'Palestine National Council: The Palestinian National Charter (July 1968)', *The Israel-Arab Reader*, pp. 117–18.
[39] For an Israeli-Zionist critique of the Palestinian conceptualisation of the democratic state, see Y. Harkabi, 'The Meaning of "a Democratic Palestinian State"', in *The Israel-Arab Reader*, pp. 182–94; Harkabi also documented internal disputes within the Palestinian *fedayeen* organisations regarding the question of the future state's Arabness vis-à-vis a large Jewish minority and its implications for the participation of Jews in the Palestinian resistance movement which was advocated, among others, by Abu Iyad. For the internal debate as for the role of the Jews in the liberation movement and especially in the future state, see Gresh, *The PLO*, pp. 30–52.

contradictions. At the same time, it also points to the fluid and contingent nature of such a project. Thus, imagined futures can also transform over time, with the change of circumstances.

Such pivotal transformation occurred in the immediate aftermath of the cataclysmic events of September 1970 in Jordan, in what some in Fatah aptly identified as a 'point of no return' (borrowing from Frantz Fanon) in the history of Palestinian armed struggle.[40] With their prestige and confidence boosted following the battle of Karameh, Palestinian resistance fighters were on a collision course with King Hussayn of Jordan, whose authority was challenged by the PLO and their massive social and military base in the country. In a successful bid to reassert his sovereignty, Hussayn's army attacked and crushed the Palestinian resistance, with thousands of civilian casualties as 'collateral damage'.[41] What became known as 'Black September' resulted in the regrouping of the *fedayeen* in Lebanon and the beginning of a new phase in the armed struggle against Israel. The PLO's spectacular defeat, however, only enhanced the international support for the Palestinian cause among members of the non-aligned movement, anticolonial forces in Africa, Asia and Latin America and non-state actors, such as the Association of Arab-American University Graduates, where Hisham Sharabi (whose life history will be discussed below) was one of the leading luminaries. Ultimately, the ousting of the PLO fighters from Jordan resulted in Palestinians becoming 'a political fact', recasting the resistance as an important regional player that required political engagement.[42]

---

[40] Chamberlin, *The Global Offensive*, p. 141. For assessments of the legacy of the September 1970 crisis in Jordan and on Jordanian–Palestinian relations, see Nigel J. Ashton, 'Pulling the Strings: King Hussein's Role during the Crisis of 1970 in Jordan', *The International History Review*, vol. 28, no. 1 (2006), pp. 94–118; Laurie A. Brand, 'Palestinians and Jordanians: A Crisis of Identity', *Journal of Palestine Studies*, vol. 24, no. 4 (Summer 1995), pp. 46–61; Hussein Sirriyeh, 'Jordan and the Legacies of the Civil War, 1970–71', *Civil Wars*, vol. 3, no. 3 (2000), pp. 74–86.

[41] Abu Iyad, who was hiding among the civilian population in Amman with other PLO figures, was captured and interrogated by the Jordanian security apparatus before being allowed to depart.

[42] Not only did Western states such as the UK and France acknowledge the importance of the PLO, but there were even voices within the US security establishment that proposed to incorporate the more 'moderate' factions (notably Fatah) into the Middle East political process and encourage them to accept a negotiated solution to the Palestine problem, be it a 'ministate' in the West Bank or a Jordanian-Palestinian confederation. However, Kissinger

The 1973 October War shifted the power relations and diplomatic dynamics in the Middle East. With renewed confidence after relative military successes, the Sadat regime in Egypt[43] and the Hashemite kingdom of Jordan were leaning towards direct negotiations with Israel, as US Secretary of State Henry Kissinger attempted to lure them away from the USSR and into the American fold. Kissinger's containment strategy aspired to isolate the PLO from its potential allies in the Arab world and shut out the Palestinians from his planned Geneva peace conference. This spectre of marginalisation of the PLO was looming just as the organisation enjoyed respectability in and through the UN, reflected through the acceptance of the PLO in observer capacity, Arafat's first formal address to the General Assembly in 1974[44] and General Assembly Resolutions 3236 (22 November 1974) and 3379 (10 November 1975).[45] These diplomatic successes of the Palestinian resistance movement were, in hindsight, effects of the non-aligned movement and its third-worldist articulations in the UN, which Kissinger attempted, and, as the 1970s came to a close, succeeded to foreclose.[46]

A seasoned and perceptible leader, Abu Iyad sought to reconstitute the Palestinian revolution in light of what he thought was most feasible to achieve

---

was loathe to engage the PLO and opted instead for the maintenance of the status quo vis-à-vis Jordan and singling out Israel as US' closest ally in the region and the recipient of the most substantial military aid. See William B. Quandt, *Peace Process: American Diplomacy and the Arab-Israeli Conflict after 1967* (Washington, DC: Brookings Intitution Press, 2005 [1993]).

[43] Specifically, Egypt's willingness to negotiate with Israel the 1975 Sinai accords which eventually led to the Camp David peace treaty of 1978.

[44] The English translation of the speech has been fully reproduced here: Yasir Arafat, 'Address to the UN General Assembly (November 13, 1974)', in Laqueur and Rubin (eds), *The Israel-Arab Reader*, pp. 171–82; see also Shafiq al-Hout, *My Life in the PLO: The Inside Story of the Palestinian Struggle*, trans. Hader al-Hout and Laila Othman (New York: Pluto Press, 2011), pp. 119–30.

[45] Resolution 3236 'reaffirms the inalienable rights of the Palestinian people in Palestine', including their right to national independence and stressing their right to return, which, as I argued in Chapter 3, had been largely sidelined since 1967. See the text of the resolution A/RES/3236. Resolution 3379 determined that 'Zionism is a form of racism and racial discrimination'. See A/RES/3379. This resolution was revoked in 1991 as a pre-condition for the Israeli participation in the Madrid peace conference of that year.

[46] For discussions of Kissinger's containment strategy and the diminishing of the power of the General Assembly as a result, see Chamberlin, *The Global Offensive*, and Vijay Prashad, *The Poorer Nations: A Possible History of the Global South* (London: Verso, 2012).

rather than the radical pursuit of a maximalist vision. In his words, the PLO, and in particular Fatah, began focusing on what it perceived as 'pragmatic' or 'realistic', in order to assure the longevity of the Palestinian liberatory project.[47] In this context, Abu Iyad promoted the concept of a Palestinian 'ministate' on any part of Palestine to be liberated, ideally by diplomatic means. This was the emergence of what later became known as the 'two states solution', or a Palestinian entity in the West Bank and the Gaza Strip next to the state of Israel.

Abu Iyad, who considered himself a revolutionary leader, argued that his most important role was to inspire hope, which, for him, meant to abandon 'dangerous illusions' about the impossible, namely, the liberation of all of Palestine and the return of the refugees to their places of origin. Instead, he proposed:

> our people will bring forth a new revolution. They will engender a movement much more powerful than ours, better armed and thus more dangerous to the Zionists. There is no doubting the irrepressible will of the Palestinian people to pursue their struggle, come what may. It is the nature of things. We are determined to survive as a nation. And one day, we will have a country.[48]

Abu Iyad offered deferred hope: the present and the 'foreseeable' future merge to produce what is available, feasible and possible. A 'full' liberation committed to the larger goal of return and the formation of a democratic state over all of historic Palestine is here postponed to an unknown future, to be carried out by future generations. The hope that Abu Iyad offered Palestinians therefore inhabits an internal irreconcilable tension: between what is desired (full liberation and return to the homeland) and what is 'feasible', between the present and the future and finally – between the possible and the impossible.[49]

---

[47] See, for instance, Abu Iyad, *My Home*, p. 138.
[48] Abu Iyad, *My Home*, p. 226.
[49] In a twist of irony, in January 1991 Abu Iyad was assassinated by an operative sent by Abu Nidal (*nom de guerre* of Sabri Khalil al-Bana), a former PLO militant gone rogue, and the son of an affluent owner of citrus groves in the Jaffa area. See Patrick Seale, *Abu Nidal: A Gun for Hire* (London: Hutchinson, 1992).

From Quiet Exile to Public Intellectual

Hisham Sharabi (1927–2005) could not have led a more different life than Abu Iyad. Like Khalaf, he was born in Jaffa, with roots elsewhere: his mother hailed from an upper-class Acre family, while his father's family originated in Nablus. His privileged upbringing isolated him from those outside the boundaries of his social class, and unlike Khalaf, Sharabi did not socially engage with Jews, even though he too grew up in Manshiyyeh, and based on his description, in close proximity to Jews.[50] Moreover, it seems that Sharabi was less attached to Jaffa than to other places that he linked, in his memoirs, with formative experiences: his grandparents' lavish house in Acre, where the poor came for alms every Friday, and Beirut, the city of his youth and his early, but significant, political activism. Sharabi was attending the University of Chicago during the Nakba, and yearned to return – to Beirut, where his friends and party members were. His commitment to the Syrian Social Nationalist Party (SSNP) and especially its charismatic and authoritarian leader Antun Sa'deh ended in disappointment and detachment from politics, which Sharabi himself called 'quiet exile'. From 1949 until the 1967 June war, he deliberately avoided political engagement and dedicated himself to scholarship, which he considered 'apolitical'. Only in the wake of the 1967 'setback' and the rise of the Palestinian resistance, did Sharabi refashion himself as a Palestinian-American public intellectual, a noted proponent and critic of the PLO. He explained the rather abrupt transformation:

> We suddenly saw ourselves for what we were in the eyes of the 'civilized' world: another species of Third World sub-humanity, existing outside history – the new Red Indians, the blacks of Israel.[51]

---

[50] Based on an interview I conducted with Moshe Kashi, Feingold houses and Bella Vista, owned by his family, were across the street from the Baydas mansion and the police station that are also mentioned by Sharabi. On Feingold houses, see also Dalia Karpel, 'The House in Manta Ray, Corner of Banana Beach' [in Hebrew], *Haaretz*, 2 February 2012, http://www.haaretz.co.il/magazine/1.1631243 (last accessed 26 May 2016).

[51] Hisham Sharabi, 'Liberation or Settlement: The Dialectics of Palestinian Struggle', *Journal of Palestine Studies*, vol. 2, no. 2 (Winter 1973), p. 34.

Sharabi's years at the University of Chicago and Georgetown detached him from the immediacy of political action. But as the quote suggests, it did provide him with a comparative settler colonial framework and the analytical clarity to situate the Palestinian plight. The period of political detachment from the Palestinian struggle, then, allowed Sharabi to observe and form his own intellectual engagement with other liberation struggles, in the Third World and in the US itself, especially the civil rights movement and black liberation, prominent in American campuses in the 1960s.[52]

According to Sharabi, the Nakba left Palestinians 'outside of history', easy prey to forces that kept exploiting them: the Israeli occupiers, Arab states, Arab elites and political parties. The idea of return remained at the level of empty rhetoric, 'impotent anger, sad longing'[53] devoid of meaningful political action. It took the 1967 defeat for Palestinians to not only launch critiques of the status quo, but to actually engage in meaningful political action that catapulted them back into history; taking up armed struggle was formative of a new Palestinian identity that was at the same time divorced from Arab political rivalries and productive of the new 'revolutionary Arab man'.[54] Sharabi, who was inspired by the 1967 Arab defeat and the rise of armed struggle, was convinced that the Middle East needed to be reformed, but that the Arab intellectual culture was so profoundly flawed and lacking rigour and the ability to innovate, that the only productive source of transformation lay in the West itself, specifically in the liberal philosophical tradition.[55] This tension between a staunch anticolonial stance and a sharp critique of an Arab 'lack' is evident in the way in which Sharabi reminisced his years at the American University in Beirut as intellectually barren, arguing for a profound flaw in Arab culture that is self-reproducing and leaves student unable to critically engage with the world.[56]

[52] Keith Feldman, *A Shadow over Palestine: The Imperial Life of Race in America* (Minneapolis: University of Minnesota Press, 2015).
[53] Sharabi, 'Liberation', p. 34.
[54] Sharabi, 'Liberation', p. 35.
[55] Lawrence Davidson, 'Remembering Hisham Sharabi (1927–2005)', *Journal of Palestine Studies*, vol. 34, no. 3 (Spring 2005), p. 60.
[56] Sharabi reiterated the acute lack of scholarship and education in the Arab world, something that he had to overcome upon his arrival in Chicago. In fact, he frames his intellectual coming of age as being able to successfully overcoming the disadvantages of an Arab education; see

This inherent lack is the cause for the deficiencies of the Palestinian resistance, and the reason it had manifested in 'spontaneous, disorganized activity'.[57] One of the main problems that plagued the movement, postulates Sharabi, was the lagging behind on developing its own revolutionary theory, one that would overhaul exploitative class relations and that would inspire multiple progressive revolutions across the Arab world. His conceptualisation of liberation, and therefore hope, is that of a utopian process: continuous revolution until the refugees return to their homeland and society is made anew. In other words, the purpose of liberation struggle is more than just political; a postcolonial Middle East would be possible only with the refashioning of Arab selfhood and the emergence of the new revolutionary Arab, that did not lag behind the West and that abandoned oppressive cultural norms.[58]

This was also the reason for Sharabi's vocal opposition to Abu Iyad's pragmatic approach. Settling for a ministate was not merely about deferring liberation, but rather, it would work to normalise and cement the very social structure that needed to be overthrown. In fact, he argued, deferring liberation meant in practice abandoning it, since 'political settlement surrenders not only fundamental rights but kills the will to fight, putting off indefinitely the possibility of liberation'.[59] Promoting a political settlement, then, was a de facto acceptance of the status quo; since revolutionary consciousness was inherently oppositional to the status quo, settlement meant stunting the development of revolutionary consciousness among the Arab masses and keeping the Middle East behind the West.[60]

Yet, in 1998, in the wake of the Oslo Accords, Sharabi seemed to have warmed to the idea of a political settlement.

> I try to remind myself of what sustained all Palestinian refugees over the long years of exile: this land is not a memory, it is not lost, it is out there where it can be seen and touched, a patrimony that can never be given up or taken away.

Hisham Sharabi, *Embers and Ashes: Memoirs of an Arab Intellectual*, trans. Issa J. Boullata (Northampton, MA: Olive Branch Press, 2008), pp. 20–1.

[57] Sharabi, 'Liberation', p. 35.
[58] As opposed to the present, where the masses are 'rooted in medieval culture'. Ibid., p. 38.
[59] Ibid., p. 37. As indeed occurred after the Oslo Accords and the creation of the Palestinian National Authority.
[60] Ibid., p. 39.

Does this mean that there can be no peaceful solution to the conflict? Does the solution lie in the reversal of what happened 50 years ago and the destruction of Israel? No, the clock cannot be put back, the past cannot be redeemed, Israel's destruction cannot be the goal. The conflict's real solution cannot be a zero-sum outcome, but only a political compromise. The legitimate struggle of the Palestinians will seek a solution based on justice, international law, and the imperative need for mutual accommodation and survival.[61]

Despite his vocal advocacy for the Palestinian right of return, Sharabi imagined his return to his 'Arab homeland' of Beirut, a plan foiled by the outbreak of the Lebanese civil war. Perhaps his longing for Beirut represented his profound attachment to his formative years at the American University, and the passionate faith in the leader, as he kept referring to Sa'deh in his autobiography, and the idea of 'natural Syria', encompassing Palestine as its southern province.[62] But the longing for Beirut also demonstrates the centrality of the city in Palestinian collective memory as a hub of resistance and centre of knowledge production. Maintaining Palestinian archives and research centres, as well as the visibility of resistance leaders in Beirut, recast the Lebanese capital as the core of the Palestinian state-in-waiting. The prominence of Beirut also featured in Abu Iyad's autobiography, as the city where Israel could assassinate multiple PLO leaders in one assault.[63]

Sharabi did return to Jaffa, at least symbolically, to participate in the funeral of another intellectual giant, born and raised in Jaffa's Manshiyyeh quarter – Ibrahim Abu Lughod, whose own return to his homeland was enabled by the Oslo Accords and his American passport.[64] Just like Sharabi, Abu Lughod's

---

[61] Quoted in Davidson, 'Remembering', p. 63.
[62] See Sharabi, *Embers and Ashes*, pp. vi–vii.
[63] Abu Iyad specifically referred to the assassination of Yusuf al-Najjar, Kamal Adwan and Kamal Nasir (9 April 1973) by Israeli commandos of the elite IDF unit Sayeret Matkal, in their Beirut apartments in the same building. See Abu Iyad, *My Home*, pp. 114–18; On the activities of the PLO in Beirut up to the Israeli invasion of 1982, see Rashid Khalidi, *Under Siege: PLO Decisionmaking during the 1982 War* (New York: Columbia University Press, 1986), pp. 17–42.
[64] Abu Lughod's presence in Palestine was made possible only at the sufferance of the Israeli authorities. His burial in his home town of Jaffa was a result of a deal between the Palestinian Authority and Israel, with the latter threatening last minute cancellation. See Edward Said, 'My Guru', *London Review of Books*, vol. 23, no. 24 (13 December 2001), pp. 19–20.

forced departure from Jaffa, just a few days before the city fell, provided him with the opportunity to travel beyond Palestine. Abu Lughod's newly discovered mobility took him across the Arab world and finally to the US, where he pursued an academic career. Similar to Sharabi, the June 1967 war and spectacular Arab defeat had a profound impact on Abu Lughod: in retrospect, he claimed that he was politicised as a result of the overt racism he experienced in the US, and that the founding of the Association of Arab-American University Graduates (AAUG) was a direct response to the degradation of everything Arab in American public life.[65] After the 1970s and the death of Nasser, Abu Lughod traded his profound faith in Arab nationalism for commitment to Palestinian liberation, through his engagement with the PLO leadership in Beirut. Abu Lughod resettled in Palestine in the 1990s and, with his death, became Jaffa's first returnee. However, the indifference of the local Palestinians to the funeral procession appeared to reveal the cleavages within the Palestinian experience, between the politics of diasporic intellectuals and the mundane survival struggles of those who remained in the city after 1948.[66]

For all three men, their political coming-of-age occurred just as the Palestinians were becoming visible on the world's stage. Prior to 1967, they were reduced to 'Arab refugees' who constitute a 'problem' to be solved. Their homeland now globally recognised as Israel, their nationhood denied; indeed, as Sharabi acknowledged, John Foster Dulles, US Secretary of State in the Eisenhower administration, postulated that once their displacement recedes far enough to the past, presumably within a generation, the refugees will forget about Palestine and forge new national identities in their places of exile.[67]

---

[65] Hisham Ahmed-Farajeh, *Ibrahim Abu Lughod: Resistance, Exile and Return* (Birzeit: Ibrahim Abu Lughod Institute of International Studies, 2003), pp. 101–2.

[66] See Daniel Monterescu, *Jaffa Shared and Shattered: Contrived Coexistence in Israel/Palestine* (Bloomington: Indiana University Press, 2015), pp. 108–9.

[67] Hisham Sharabi, *Palestine Guerillas: Their Credibility and Effectiveness* (Washington, DC: The Center for Strategic and International Studies, 1970), p. vii; the overall policy focused on strengthening the US position in the Arab world vis-à-vis the Soviet Union, the regional incorporation of Israel, and economic development as a mean of pacification. The 'Arab refugees' were therefore to be absorbed into Arab states. See Deborah J. Gerner, 'Missed Opportunities and Roads not Taken: The Eisenhower Administration and the Palestinians', *Arab Studies Quarterly*, vol. 12, no. 1/2 (Winter/Spring 1990), pp. 67–100.

Yet even after 1967 and Karameh, Israel's diplomats stepped up their efforts to elide Palestinianness and instead insist that not only were the Palestinians generic Arabs, but that the guerillas were mere terrorists bent on killing Jews (thus invoking the spectre of antisemitism and the Holocaust). One such oft-quoted endeavour is a now-infamous 1970 interview of Gold Meir on British Thames television. Meir, a Ukraine-born American Jew who migrated to Mandatory Palestine and rose to prominence in Mapai (Land of Israel Worker's Party), made the claim that there is 'no such thing as a distinct Palestinian people'. Moreover, added Meir, she was a Palestinian herself, since she used to carry a Palestinian passport between 1921 and 1948 and lived in the territory controlled by the British 'between the Mediterranean and the Iraqi border'. Meir refers to Palestinian guerillas as 'these people' who are supported by Arab regimes and are hellbent on 'piracy' and 'murderous acts' against Israelis.[68]

However, these strenuous efforts by Israel and its allies to continue the denial of Palestinian nationhood were countered by the activities of the three exiles I discussed in this chapter. The rise of Palestinian guerillas to which both Kanafani and Abu Iyad contributed (albeit in very different forms) resulted in the elevation of the PLO and Arafat within the institutions of the international community. Sharabi, in tandem with fellow intellectual giants Abu Lughod and later Edward Said, introduced the study of Palestine and Palestinians into the bastion of Western academia. In other words, though still an uphill battle,[69] these men were vital to the formation of new visibilities for Palestinians, globalising and forging new enduring connections between various struggles for liberation, especially within the framework of empire.[70]

---

[68] The full interview is available here: https://youtu.be/w3FGvAMvYpc.

[69] The 1970s were an era in which, in some circles, Israel was still considered a 'heroic' force that emerged victorious from its military encounter with the Third World, unlike the US in Vietnam. See Melani McAlister, *Epic Encounters: Culture, Media, and U.S. Interests in the Middle East since 1945* (Berkeley: University of California Press, 2001), pp. 155–97.

[70] See, for instance, Paul Chamberlin, 'The Struggle against Oppression Everywhere: The Global Politics of Palestinian Liberation', *Middle Eastern Studies*, vol. 47, no. 1 (2011), pp. 24–41. On the enduring legacy of these connections, especially in the context of African Americans and other black diasporas, see Noura Erakat and Mark Lamont Hill, 'Black-Palestinian Transnational Solidarity: Renewals, Returns, and Practice', *Journal of Palestine Studies*, vol. 48, no. 4 (2019), pp. 7–16, and Nadine Naber, 'The US and Israel make the Connections for Us: Anti-Imperialism and Black-Palestinian Solidarity', *Critical Ethnic Studies*, vol. 3, no. 2 (Fall 2017), pp. 15–30.

Returning to Kanafani's 'man is a cause', my analysis of these three exiles demonstrates the dialectics of this phrase: on the one hand, humans are shaped by the circumstances in which they find themselves. Thus, Khaldun was erased and replaced by Dov not just as a result of his biological parents' terror-induced flight from Haifa, but also, perhaps mainly, because he was socialised to become a soldier, loyally serving the Jewish state. And yet, at the same time, Kanafani, Khalaf and Sharabi, displaced from their homeland, are not bereft of agency. Just like Khaled, Said and Safiyya's younger son, they reinvent themselves in the shadow of tremendous loss – but also a promising opportunity to forge new liberatory futures.

4

LIVING IN MEMORY: EXILE AND THE BURDEN OF THE FUTURE

What we share, no matter where God has placed us on this wretched earth, is the same corner we cry in when we are forced to look into ourselves. Suddenly the name brands drop off, the refugee IDs fade. When we are shoved into it, made to look at ourselves and at our past; when our future is at our back and our past is made into an angle so acute that every family has the same points leading to the same doom; when we hold onto that corner because we do not know how to build ourselves anymore, sustain our dialect, live our traditions, and be free, it is clear: we are running out of space.

Norah al-Bireh[1]

In a 1998 essay, Palestinian scholars Salim Tamari and Rema Hamami shared their impressions of multiple visits to Jaffa, the 'lost paradise' of their respective families' histories. The '*via dolorosa*' of pilgrimage to the ancestral place is literally a source of pain, anger and frustration: Hamami's aunt, upon recognising her childhood home in Jabbaliyeh, exhibits an outburst of emotions and refuses to proceed inside; Beshara, Tamari's son, expresses his anger and frustration at the ongoing displacement of the city's remaining Palestinians;

---

[1] Norah al-Bireh, 'Angular Identities of the Palestinian Diaspora', *Sixteen Minutes to Palestine*, 18 June 2015, https://web.archive.org/web/20150715034018/http://smpalestine.com/2015/06/18/the-angular-identities-of-the-palestinian-diaspora/ (last accessed 13 January 2022).

Tamari himself, however, responds with sarcasm when he meets Shlomo, a Moroccan Jewish man who settled in the city in the wake of the Nakba and the ethnic cleansing of Jaffa's Palestinians. Although Shlomo inhabits a complex liminal position of being both a coloniser and, as a Mizrahi Jew, a subaltern, in the final analysis, for displaced Palestinians, his presence, despite his self-identification as an Arab, represents his status as a settler and theirs – as refugees. Tamari and Hamami dub their repeated pilgrimages to Jaffa 'virtual returns', denoting the illusory aspect of the journey: their trip only has the temporary effect of return, in both the temporal and geographical sense, yet by the end of the visit, the phantasmagoria of return dissipates and the reality of refugeehood creeps back.

Tamari, who is Jaffa-born and Hamami, a second-generation *Yafawiya*, navigate through memories of urban past and present-day realities of rapid gentrification and de-Arabisation. Both share a sense of 'being burdened by Jaffa', forced to carry it around, 'weighed down by its past and [their] duty to that past'.[2] The repeated 'virtual return' pilgrimages are reminiscent of Sisyphean attempts to reconcile fantasies about a golden past and the pain of irrevocable loss.

The discussion below continues to follow the Jaffa refugees along their routes of displacement by way of a few exemplary life stories. In Chapter 3 we saw how for some first-generation refugees, exile offered opportunities and opened up, rather than foreclosed, potential for self-refashioning and meaningful political engagement. This chapter, however, focuses on the second- and third-generation refugees whose itineraries of exile represent spatial contraction that led refugees into decrepit camps and decades of confinement that produced the effect of 'running out of space'.

Hamami argues that there are no 'former Jaffaites'. Since Palestinians carried their memories of the city everywhere they went, one remains a *Yafawi*. Over the decades, their descendants, who inherited this burden, have devised creative ways to redefine their relationship to Jaffa and find meaningful ways to call themselves *Yafawiin*.[3] Embarking on 'virtual returns' as a form of

---

[2] Salim Tamari and Rema Hamami, 'Virtual Returns to Jaffa', *Journal of Palestine Studies*, vol. 27, no. 4 (Summer 1998), p. 67.

[3] Ibid., p. 67.

emplacement, identity-endowing strategy is one of the salient ways of negotiating family histories of trauma and displacement.

The final section highlights what is new in contemporary expressions of resistance. Based on ethnographic fieldwork and interviews with Jaffa refugees in Nablus-area refugee camps and second-generation Palestinian exiles, I explore how these refugees envisioned their future Palestine, carved out their own horizons of expectations and framed hope (or lack thereof) in relation to the foregone tradition.

Between Jaffa and Ramallah, Past and Present

Unlike Khalaf, Sharabi and Kanafani, Raja Shehadeh never experienced life in Jaffa before the Nakba. Born to an affluent Palestinian family three years after they were forced to flee the city to Ramallah, Shehadeh was raised on his grandmother's memories of Jaffa, and his father's silent rage at his displacement, dominating his sense of self:

> The elders held the keys to that lost world, the world that gave my life its meaning. Their reminiscences, their evocative descriptions, and nothing else. It was within that narrative of the lost world that I placed myself, defined myself, and assessed where I stood in the world. To be a man was to be the way my father was in Jaffa. The good life was the night life of Tel Aviv.[4]

During his formative years, the Shehadeh family not only invoked memories of Jaffa among themselves and with friends but insisted on centring their lives around their lost city. His grandmother, Julia, replicated her old routine of visiting the same former neighbours and friends who also ended up in Ramallah.[5] The family was in fact living in memory: Julia could 'hear' the waves of the Mediterranean and 'sense' the familiar breeze on her skin, while Aziz Shehadeh kept staring westward, searching for the urban landscapes and lights.

Living in memory also meant that Shehadeh grew up with an acute sense of uprootedness, of being in the 'wrong place'. Ramallah was just a temporary place of residence, a (rather indefinite) interlude before returning to the

---

[4] Raja Shehadeh, *Strangers in the House: Coming of Age in Occupied Palestine* (South Royalton: Steerforth Press, 2002), p. 31.
[5] Ibid., p. 20.

'real' place of belonging, Jaffa; for a long time, the Shehadehs were staying at the family's summerhouse, clinging to the hope of returning to their Jaffa home. The refugees' gaze, fixated on the west in the general direction of Jaffa, symbolically reorganised space: the physical location of the refugees was relegated to the periphery while the object of their gazes, not even visible to them (although they could 'sense' its existence) became the core of their being and, as Shehadeh noted, their sole source of self-identification.

Shehadeh's masculine ideal revolved around his father, Aziz, a Palestinian self-made man whose identity straddled both cities, Jaffa and Tel Aviv: although both his residence and law office were located in Jaffa, Tel Aviv's night life beckoned with the promise of revelry and forms of sociability unavailable in Jaffa. Daytime Jaffa offered Aziz the respectability of family, law and the nation while night-time Tel Aviv undermined the colonial and ethnic divide that positioned it as the 'quintessential Jewish town' rival to the Arab city nearby. Aziz's memories of Tel Aviv's night life clearly challenge the post-Nakba revisionist histories, both official and popular, that constituted social, ethnic and political boundaries between the two cities, where the paths of Arabs and Jews had never crossed other than in battle.

Twice Aziz Shehadeh returned to Jaffa; the first time, shortly before the fall of the city. His mother-in-law sent him to fetch her expensive furniture, but instead, he spent his brief visit in the nearly empty city regretting ever leaving it. We get a glimpse of what a deserted, once bustling city looks like through the eyes of the refugee: streets lose their familiarity with the people gone, stores shuttered and gardens left untended. In the days before its occupation, Jaffa was suspended between its former animated self and the transformations I described in my second chapter. In the meantime, the city was populated with the ghosts of its departed inhabitants. When Aziz opens the door of his own house, there is a sense of eeriness, and he immediately invokes the ghost-like images of his wife, 'in her pink satin dressing gown', moving, almost floating, in his imagination, 'from room to room'.[6] This poignant absence led him to decide against removing anything from the house, other than a small decorative Buddha statue; the house should remain as it is, ready to be repopulated after the family's brief sojourn in Ramallah ends and they are able to return

[6] Ibid., p. 15.

and resume their lives. He returned to Ramallah empty handed, to the chagrin of Julia, and spent the next two decades standing on the hilltops, his gaze fixated in the direction of the city he longed for and the life he wished to resume.

In his son's account, Aziz Shehadeh's second visit to Jaffa occurred in the aftermath of the 1967 war, in a manner reminiscent of Kanafani's fictional refugees seizing the opportunity to make the journey back. He was driven by an old Jewish colleague who served in the occupying army beyond the 1949 armistice lines, and into a territory that had existed in refugees' memory for twenty years, 'traversing abandoned space and regaining lost time, going back through the darkness to where the lights shone every night'.[7] For the former *Yafawi* attorney, then, the journey was to undo political, spatial and temporal boundaries: while the Nakba resulted in two decades of living in a memory and political inaction for Palestinian refugees like Aziz, the Naksa opened a new horizon of futurity and avenues of political engagement. Aziz's journey from the hilltops to the coastal plane, previously blocked to him, symbolised the dissolution of a mental barrier between despair and hope.

This poignant journey made visible all those landscapes that were meticulously preserved in the refugees' memory. Aziz recognizes every village along the way, and once they enter the city, its landscapes are painfully familiar, but Jaffa is 'ruined'; without its people, the city is 'but a mere ghost of herself with pale crumpled skin, dead silent'.[8] The former bustling Palestinian port city is now teeming with ghosts, as his gaze oscillated between past and present, fantasy and reality. In one afternoon, Aziz Shehadeh transgressed the boundaries between his Ramallah present, Jaffa past and the future, symbolised by the glittering lights of Tel Aviv. Ironically, Aziz realises that the lights he used to longingly gaze upon from his Ramallah exile were not those of Jaffa. As darkness descended on Jaffa, Tel Aviv's night-lights invited him to visit the 'living town', forever abandoning his ghosts.

The present, he realised, belongs to those who replaced the Palestinians, Judaicised and modernised the city and left Arab Jaffa behind in the darkness. In the meantime, the *jil Filastin*, the generation that experienced the expulsion, had robbed the young of its future, forcing them to live in memory as they have,

[7] Ibid., p. 57.
[8] Ibid., p. 61.

impressing them with a life of inaction. The journey to Jaffa was a transformative experience for Aziz Shehadeh and marked a break with the past:

> If in the past we were a lamenting people, now we would become dynamic, taking our fate in our own hands. We must begin a new way of life, a new social and spatial organization of our society, not cramped but spread out, using the empty hills to establish new communities where those living in refugee camps could move, where the new Palestinian would be created: a forward-looking, bold, assertive citizen able to come to terms with his history, who would challenge the enemy to make peace on the basis of a new division of the land between the two states living side by side in peace together.[9]

Aziz Shehadeh had made the journey from Ramallah to Jaffa and Tel Aviv, but coming back to his hilltop home in the West Bank was not returning to his point of departure; the trip remade Ramallah from a temporary shelter, a mere vantage point to gaze upon one's 'true' home, to a living and livable city, a launching pad for a new modern existence for Palestinians, modelled after Tel Aviv but made in their own image. Instead of living in memories populated by ghosts, Palestinians were to take control of their destiny, and abandon illusions of liberation marketed by both the Arab states and the resistance, both of which he considered futile, dangerous even.

These realisations propelled Aziz Shehadeh into peace activism; days after his trip he collaborated with men from the Israeli intelligence apparatus to produce a document charting out a vision for post-1967 Palestine, which would be partitioned into two states, Jewish and Palestinian. Palestinians would abandon their demand to return to their former homes in exchange for independence and peace. This idea, which he continued to advocate until his assassination in 1985, was visionary for its time, when Israelis basked in the post-victory euphoria and the Fatah-led PLO was just beginning to garner popularity among the Palestinian masses. The document also preceded UN Resolution 242, as well as later proposals for two states, including those discussed in my introduction, and the 'ministate' promoted by Abu Iyad and others within the PLO leadership. Although for a while, Shehadeh became a

[9] Ibid., p. 66.

popular speaker among a certain section of the Israeli (Ashkenazi) left, the document was utterly ignored by Israel's political leadership.[10] Over time, Israel has also taken over the reorganisation of space in the West Bank, except instead of new Palestinian communities for the uprooted, the occupation erected countless strategically positioned, exclusively Jewish settlements, which dot the hills surrounding Ramallah and other urban centres and control connecting roads. This, in addition to the separation barrier and the checkpoints, eviscerating the territory Shehadeh envisioned as the core of the nation state.[11] Contrary to Aziz Shehadeh's hopes, the decades following the June 1967 war only saw the West-Bank Palestinians running out of space, as the territory on which they were allowed to live kept contracting with each settlement and military incursion.

For Raja Shehadeh, the 'setback' which motivated his father's peace activism marked the beginning of his own disavowal of politics at all costs, deferring to his father in all things even at the price of social marginality. His profound faith in the universality of human rights and the rule of law constitute the basis for his political engagement with the Israeli military occupation. With the founding of al-Haq (1979), the first Palestinian human rights organisation, Raja Shehadeh promoted/expressed the hope that appealing to the rule of law by publicly shaming the occupiers would force them to redress injustice.[12] Shehadeh is representative of a generation of Palestinian activists who, since the late 1970s, have worked within the ever-expanding framework of NGOs, depending on and accountable to transnational networks of similar organisations. The NGOisation of the West Bank and the Gaza Strip, which swelled

---

[10] Ibid., pp. 49–52. See also Raja Shehadeh, 'My Father's Peace Proposal', *The Daily Beast*, 11 September 2012, http://www.thedailybeast.com/articles/2012/11/09/my-father-s-peace-proposal.html and Akiva Eldar, 'In 14 June 1967 They Already Drafted an Agreement' [in Hebrew], *Haaretz*, 4 June 2007, http://www.haaretz.co.il/misc/1.1415076 (last accessed 26 May 2016).

[11] For an analysis of the spatial dimension of the Israeli military control of the West Bank, see Eyal Weizman, *Hollow Land: Israel's Architecture of Occupation* (New York: Verso, 2012).

[12] For an in-depth discussion of the founding of al-Haq, see Lori Allen, *The Rise and Fall of Human Rights: Cynicism and Politics in Occupied Palestine* (Stanford: Stanford University Press, 2013), pp. 33–64.

during the Oslo years, has come under fire in the wake of the Second Intifada and NGOs are often the objects of cynicism and distrust.[13]

'Running out of Space' in Nablus-area Refugee Camps

For the majority of Palestinians displaced from territories that became part of Israel in 1948, refugeehood meant coming under the control of international aid regimes, in particular the UNRWA. The ability of men like Hisham Sharabi and Abu Iyad to develop political consciousness and engage in meaningful action was constituted, significantly, by their access to resources unavailable to most camp refugees, such as higher education, and especially the ability to travel. Mobility played an important part in their self-fashioning as political agents, as revolutionaries and thinkers.

Since the vast majority of Palestinian refugees cannot afford the luxury of extensive travel and acquiring advanced academic degrees abroad, it is vital to consider the effects of continuous displacement and the ways in which these refugees have been engaging with the idea of return. These are the very people whose available space has been contracting rather than expanding, and who have been languishing in cramped, dilapidated camps for seven decades. With the Israeli 1967 occupation and the brutal suppression of political activity, as well as various forms of popular resistance, these West Bank camp Palestinians have been 'running out of space'.

A segment of this population resides in three refugee camps within the Nablus city limits: Balata, 'Askar and Camp no. 1, locally known as al-'Ayn. The majority of the refugees in these three camps originated from the Jaffa, Lydd and Haifa districts. Today, they number around 50,000, and are forced to live in makeshift structures, built haphazardly as families expanded, with inadequate infrastructure.[14] In Balata, where I was based, during the summer, there is running water only four days of the week and sewage flows freely through

---

[13] Moreover, human rights NGOs are often critiqued for enabling colonial violence; see Nicola Perugini and Neve Gordon, *The Human Right to Dominate* (New York: Oxford University Press, 2015).

[14] Based on data available on UNRWA's website, http://www.unrwa.org/where-we-work/west-bank, as well as Erni Gustafson and Nabil Nabil Alawi, 'Aliens, but Friends: Practice Placement at Balata Refugee Camp, Palestine', *European Journal of Social Work*, vol. 18, no. 3 (2015), pp. 398–9.

the narrow alleyways, which, in the absence of playgrounds, are also where the camp's children spend most of their time, when they are not studying in UNRWA's overcrowded classrooms.[15] All three of these camps are extremely cramped, but Balata, which was established in 1950, is infamous for being the most crowded of them, with about 28,000 people living in 0.25 square kilometres.

What drew me to these camps specifically was the relatively high number of refugees from the Jaffa district. As it turned out, the people I spoke with, either in the form of semi-formal interviews or casual conversations in the marketplace or at the Yafa Cultural Centre (established 1996), repeatedly articulated their unquestionable attachment to Jaffa, but also stressed that the urbanites 'fled to Jordan and left us here in the camp'. For these camp dwellers, being *Yafawi* did not necessarily mean tracing one's origin to the city of Jaffa; rather, urban authenticity was linked to their suffering as camp refugees and forming communities that are based on a shared sense of belonging: being both 'from here' and 'from over there'.

I interviewed 'Adel at his home in the 'new' 'Askar camp, surrounded by family members. 'Adel's home is a rarity in the camps' landscape: the house was relatively large, surrounded by a greenery-covered fence, allowing its occupants to enjoy privacy, another rare commodity in a refugee camp. He greeted us at the door, leading us to his garden, unheard of in the context of the cramped West Bank camps. 'Adel proudly walked us through the garden, among the fig trees, grapevines and tomato flowerbed, pointing to the chicken coop – 'everything my family needs is here', he exclaimed. He proceeded to lead us back into the house and we all congregated in the living room. 'Adel is the maternal uncle of a Balata friend, whose family graciously invited me to stay in their meager home as long as I conducted my research. It was 'Adel's sister who suggested I pay a visit to her brother, and made sure I was warmly received. His niece volunteers to translate for a British activist and myself, even

---

[15] For more on the effects of camp life on Balata's children, see Alice Rothchild, 'In Balata, the Occupation is not just of Body, but of Mind', *Mondoweiss*, 21 June 2013, http://mondoweiss.net/2013/06/balata-occupation-body (last accessed 26 May 2016); for a comprehensive study of Balata's youth in the post-Intifada (the first one) era, see John Collins, *Occupied by Memory: The Intifada Generation and the Palestinian State of Emergency* (New York: New York University Press, 2004).

Figure 4.1 'Football with the martyrs': children playing football in the narrow alleys of Balata refugee camp. On the wall behind them there are posters commemorating a local *shahid* (Arabic, martyr, often referring to fallen resistance fighters); the top of the mural reads *awda*, 'return' in Arabic. (Photo by the author.)

Figure 4.2 A mural inside the Yafa Cultural Centre, Balata refugee camp, depicting a baffled Israeli soldier uncovering the return key and the inscription 'but we will return to Jaffa, Balata [refugee] camp'. Opposite the soldier stands Handhala, the popular drawing by the late Naji al-Ali, symbolising both the catastrophe of expulsion and the hope of return. (Photo by the author.)

though I understand the Arabic. As 'Adel tells his story, his daughters-in-law listen attentively, trying to hush an impatient toddler.

'Adel was born in Abu Kabir, which, in those years, was a suburb of Jaffa, still drowning in the lush greenery and seductive scent of its orange groves, or *bayarat* in Arabic. In fact, although 'Adel spoke Arabic, whenever he referred to the orange groves he used the Hebrew word, *pardes* (singular) or *pardesim* (plural). 'Life was good at the beginning,' he sighed, 'everyone who was [in Abu Kabir's groves] were Arab. We were the owners and not the Jews. The problems began when the Jews who came from abroad, from Europe ... not the local ['original', *asasiin*]. They attacked and fired at us.' The 'trouble' 'Adel was referring to was the rapidly growing fire exchanges in early 1948,[16] mainly in the borderland areas, between the Hagana and local Palestinian militias. The deterioration of the situation was particularly taxing for the local population, the owners and labourers of the groves, and like many others, 'Adel's family left for Lydd, where they remained for six months, until 'problems started between the Jews and the [Palestinian] resistance'. He was referring to what is known in Israeli military history as 'Operation Dani', the IDF offensive designed to 'cleanse' (read ethnically cleanse) the areas southeast of Tel Aviv, especially the road to Jerusalem,[17] although both Lydd and Ramleh were designated to be part of the UN-proposed Arab state. Nevertheless, once they were abandoned by the Arab Legion, the Palestinian defenders were unable to prevent its fall to Israeli forces on 11 July 1948. Though a young boy of twelve at the time, 'Adel clearly remembered the IDF jeeps and armoured vehicles pouring into town, and the widespread devastation in their wake.

Soon after the conquest of Lydd, the IDF concentrated the civilian population inside a mosque, soon releasing the elderly, women and children. 'Adel recalls that the older boys and the men had to remain inside the mosque (*misgad*, he tells me in Hebrew) and that they were massacred. The rest of the

---

[16] See Chapter 1.
[17] Arnon Golan, 'From Palestinian-Arab to Israeli Towns, 1948–1967', *Middle Eastern Studies*, vol. 39, no. 4 (October 2003), pp. 121–39; Alon Kadish and Avraham Sela, 'Myths and Historiography of the 1948 Palestine War Revisited: The Case of Lydda', *The Middle East Journal*, vol. 59, no. 4 (October 2005), pp. 616–34; Benny Morris, 'Operation Dani and the Palestinian Exodus from Lydda and Ramle in 1948', *Middle East Journal*, vol. 40, no. 1 (Winter 1986), pp. 82–109.

population was told to flee.[18] 'Adel recalls how, at a checkpoint erected by the Israeli army, soldiers ordered his mother to hand over her golden jewellery. 'They robbed us; we were afraid', he summed up. From there, civilians were forced to march, in the scorching summer heat, several kilometres, first to the Beit Shemesh (Jewish settlement) area, and from there to Ni'lin, right across what eventually became the 1949 armistice line. Many of the most vulnerable refugees died along the way, while others camped under olive trees and in agricultural lands ('not in houses', 'Adel said), exposed to the elements. After a brief stay in Bir Zeit (a town near Ramallah), 'Adel's family relocated to Nablus ('we lived on the mountain') and was finally directed to the newly created refugee camp. After a few years in a tent, they moved into a more permanent shelter, 'four of us in one small room'.

Like many other Palestinian men in the West Bank and the Gaza Strip, the 1967 Israeli occupation offered opportunities for low-paying menial jobs, especially in construction and maintenance. This is also the reason why so many men of that generation speak Hebrew so fluently. As 'Adel shifts the conversation to tell me about his post-1967 fortunes, he also switches to Hebrew. I also change roles with his niece, since, like most of her generation (except for those who spent many years in Israeli prisons), she does not understand a word of Hebrew; I now find myself in the role of Hebrew-to-English translator, for the benefit of the niece and the British visitor. The daughters-in-law, however, who speak no English, quickly lose interest in the conversation, but remain seated out of politeness.

'Adel had also made a 'virtual return' of sorts thanks to the Israeli permits regime that allows those Palestinians thoroughly scrutinised by the

---

[18] For more on the massacre inside the Dahamash mosque and the expulsion of the population, see Walid Khalidi, 'Introduction to Spiro Munayyer's *The Fall of Lydda*', *Journal of Palestine Studies*, vol. 27, no. 4 (1988), pp. 80–98; Benny Morris, *The Birth of the Palestinian Refugee Problem, 1947–1949* [in Hebrew] (Tel Aviv: Am Oved, 1991), pp. 274–82; Morris, 'Operation Dani'; *Zochrot et al-Lydd* (Tel Aviv: Zochrot, 2012). For Israeli-Zionist historians' counter-claims that the events of Lydd resulted from dynamics on the ground rather than ordered by the highest political and military echelons, see Kadish and Sela, 'Myths and Historiography'. The Lydd massacre was immortalised in a famous poem by Natan Alterman, an Israeli and avid Zionist: see Yair Auron, 'Breaking the Silence: The Poem that Exposed Israeli War Crimes in 1948', *Haaretz*, 18 March 2016, http://www.haaretz.com/israel-news/.premium-1.709439 (last accessed 18 March 2016).

state's security apparatus to seek employment inside Israel as day and seasonal labourers in menial jobs rejected by most Israelis. Ironically, 'Adel managed to obtained long-term employment with the Tel Aviv-Jaffa municipality as a parks maintenance worker and even, he added, was made a 'boss' (*ba'al bayit*, in colloquial Hebrew) in charge of his own small crew of Palestinian low-waged labourers. The two decades in this position provided him the time and the means to re-acquaint himself with his childhood urban landscapes, occupied and radically transformed by the influx of Jewish migrants. He asked me where I lived, and I name the street. He responds with a smile: 'I know, it is right by a city park. Very good neighbourhood.'

His work also produced a few poignant encounters. One of those occurred in recent years, when the IDF placed the camp under curfew. 'Adel and his family were sitting on the roof when a group of soldiers suddenly appeared, demanding them to retreat into the house. Then, a young soldier looked at 'Adel and asked him: 'Is your name 'Adel and you used to work in Hayarkon park in Tel Aviv?' 'Adel realised the stern uniformed man ordering him around used to work in his crew as a teen during the summer holidays.

Just before the beginning of the Second Intifada (2000–5) which terminated his employment, 'Adel decided to take his elderly father, now deceased, to visit Abu Kabir:

> He could not remember a thing. They built a beer factory and a garage for buses near the house. We stood together outside the house and I asked him: where is our house? He answered: not here. I told him this is the house. He could not recognize the place because of the orange groves [they were gone]. They built a second floor. A woman upstairs asked: what are you doing here? We said this was our house. She responded: take me back to Libya and come and have your house.

This anecdote illustrates an intimate knowledge of place: though expelled from Abu Kabir as a young boy, 'Adel is instantly able to recognise his home, even though the immediate surrounding is transformed and urbanised. Unlike his father, 'Adel's work permit provided him with the opportunity to observe not only the process of rapid urbanisation but also the intra-Jewish dynamics that undergirded it. He is acutely aware that Abu Kabir is part of Tel Aviv's 'black city', that is, that part of the capital that is relegated to the destitute and working class and therefore has remained underdeveloped.[19] When he talked about present-day Abu Kabir, he mentioned its residents were all Mizrahi Jews, like the woman from Libya, and that it was a mixed residential-commercial area, dotted with small factories and auto body shops. This bittersweet story of 'virtual return' also provides insight into the fraught encounter between the refugee and the person occupying his home, which we have already seen in Kanafani's story. This anecdote offers a possibility to consider the implementation of the right of return without expelling the current occupants. In fact, here, the Palestinian refugee himself articulated affinity, if not sympathy, to the Jewish settler who inhabits his home, opening up a possibility to imagine a resolution that does not result in another displacement. I will return to this question in Chapter 7.

Finally, before we parted ways, I asked him whether he had ever considered an actual return. 'I don't know,' he sighed. 'Only God can say. There is trouble between Jews and Arabs, so I don't believe [it would happen]. God willing [*In sha' Allah*] there will not be [trouble]. There are many Palestinians in Syria, Jordan, Egypt, America, Europe. Maybe our neighbour from abroad will return as well.' I discovered a similar sense of resignation among other refugees. Decades of poverty and displacement, and the constant threat of violence from the Israeli occupation elicited melancholia. Thus, for instance, when I asked acquaintances at the camp how they were, some responded *zift* (bad, Arabic colloquial). Nevertheless, refugees welcomed my inquiries even when it required them to dredge up painful memories of uprooting.

Most of the refugees who agreed to semi-formal interviews were male. But on occasion, I chanced upon women who were willing to share their stories. One of those women was Ibtisam, a resident of al 'Ayn camp, originally from Khayriyya, a village located just 7.5 kilometres east of Jaffa. Though a young girl by the time of her family's forced departure, Ibtisam vividly remembered the citrus groves surrounding their house, and her happy childhood: 'See we were young, but we were attached to it, just like the adults were.' That happiness abruptly ended when Hagana forces conquered the village during operation Hametz, in the last days of April, designed to cut off Jaffa from

---

[19] The term 'black city' was coined and widely circulated after the publication of Sharon Rotbard, *White City, Black City* [in Hebrew] (Tel Aviv: Bavel, 2005).

its hinterland and blockade the city.[20] Ibtisam remembered exchange of fire between the raiding Zionist forces and a few local defenders, even though the Israeli military archives have recorded no resistance in the village when it was overtaken by the Hagana.[21]

Ibtisam proceeds to speak about life at the camp where she is virtually confined – 'I do not go places.' Unlike many of the men, she has never been back to her village, as Palestinian women did not become part of the workforce in Israel after 1967, and therefore have had less opportunity for 'virtual returns'. Her husband, however, worked in Israel for three years, and reported back to her that her father's house was demolished, as was the majority of the built area of the village, save for one of the schools, and a few houses.[22] Her speech is steeped in melancholia: 'such is the life of refugees ... I don't go to places, and I don't want to. I'm in pain from this whole world.' Not even the thought of return eases this existential pain; rather, it reminded her of her father, who once said that all he wished for was to die in his own town, even if it meant he would return for one last night. Instead, he was fated to live in squalor as a refugee, and watch his sons and grandchildren brutalised and imprisoned. Like her father, Ibtisam would rather die in her lost village, but since she knows this is impossible, she suffers the pain of refugeehood. At the same time though, that same pain is a marker of 'authenticity': most of her relatives left Palestine for Jordan. She complains that exile dissolved the intimacy of kinship ('the younger generation, they don't know each other'). Ibtisam finishes with an indirect criticism of those Palestinians who left: her

---

[20] *Hametz* is the Hebrew word for leavened bread and its byproducts, forbidden for consumption for Jews during the holiday of Passover. Hagana's nomenclature indicates the Zionist military leadership's attitude towards the Palestinians as obstacles to be removed, like *Hametz*.

[21] See Morris, *Palestinian Refugees*, p. 141. Ibtisam may have remembered an earlier episode when Palestinian resistance fighters were forced to retreat from Abu Kabir to Khayriyya. Around that time, Palestinian snipers were firing on Ef'al, a Jewish settlement adjacent to Khayriyya.

[22] Some of the remaining structures are inhabited while others remain deserted. For decades, Tel Aviv area municipalities used the village's agricultural lands as a landfill until recently, when it was rehabilitated and turned into a national park, named after Ariel Sharon, infamous for his role in the Qibiya (1953) and Sabra and Shatila (1982) massacres. See Walid Khalidi, *All that Remains: The Palestinian Villages Occupied and Depopulated by Israel in 1948* (Washington, DC: Institute for Palestine Studies, 1992), p. 249.

grandson, upon his return from a visit in Jordan, told her 'grandma, we've stayed in Palestine and it's better for us'.

Diasporic Silences

I have known Daniel for several years now. We both travel in similar circles and have several friends in common. However, for several years, he had been rather reluctant to share his life story with me. I knew both his parents were refugees from Jaffa and that they did not wish to discuss their early lives. Daniel himself shared that attitude as well. And then something happened. Daniel made his first 'virtual return' to Jaffa, and ever since, he has been trying to redefine his relationship to the city.

Both his parents' forced departure from Jaffa occurred at a young age. His paternal grandfather, a resident of 'Ajami and a low-level employee of the British Mandate, coaxed a fisherman to give up his only boat (and the means of escape for the family) for a handsome amount of money, and Daniel's father, then a small child, sailed to Lebanon with his parents. The realisation that this last-minute escape depended on his grandmother's meager funds only dawned on Daniel when a distant relative in Jaffa told him that only those who could afford to flee did while the poor were left to their fate. 'They really thought they were about to be massacred,' Daniel explained to me.

Daniel's mother, however, was born in the now-obliterated Manshiyyeh quarter to a Lebanese mother who still had relatives in Beirut. The family connection proved to be useful during the mass flight from Jaffa. Although neither of Daniel's parents were camp refugees, for the first decade or so after the Nakba, their fortunes could not have been more dissimilar. Daniel's mother, who was merely a child, and her family continued their middle-class existence in Beirut, largely thanks to their existing social network and her father's education. At the same time, his father's family experienced tragedies and squalor. Soon after their arrival in Lebanon, his mother gave birth and then passed away, probably because her husband could not afford proper health care. Then Daniel's paternal grandfather died as well, and his children were literally left to fend for themselves on the streets of Beirut. They never registered as refugees with UNRWA, largely due to pride rather than actual need. In those first years, it was Daniel's uncle who supported his two younger siblings, making sure they received a proper education. It is perhaps the bitter memories of these tragedies that he traced back to the family's expulsion from Jaffa that prompted Daniel's father's self-imposed silence. In fact, the only thing he was adamant about was stressing that they were the only branch of the family left alive, and that everyone else had perished.

Living through the Lebanese civil war (1975–90) may have exacerbated this silence on the earlier trauma of the Nakba, given that Palestinians, whose status had already been precarious even before the war were scapegoated by various factions.[23] These multiple traumatic experiences were probably what prompted Daniel's parents to migrate to Canada, 'literally in the middle of the night', in 1989, before the end of the civil war. By that time, they already had meaningful support networks in Canada in the form of other relatives who had exited Lebanon before.

Daniel himself refers to his refugeeness as a sort of burden, in a similar fashion to Rema Hamami: 'it was constantly thrown on you as a child. Continuously victim, victim, victim, the world is terrible and unfair place.' For someone who grew up with the horrors of a civil war, his strangeness always thrown in his face ('you are not really from here') and the persistent silence of his parents, no wonder Daniel rejected the 'Palestinian within' and stayed away from the topic of his lost ancestral land and adopted a Lebanese identity in its stead.

Only a few years ago, Daniel decided he was ready to visit Jaffa. He defines his journey not as 'root-searching' but rather as an act born out of the necessity to 'fill the gap in my head' and 'break the barrier of fear' of

---

[23] The Phalangists, of course, considered the Palestinians obstacles to Lebanese internal peace and security and vowed to 'remove' them by any means possible, especially violence. Their alliance with the Israeli army, which invaded in 1982, culminated in the Sabra and Shatila massacres. Thereafter, other groups targeted Palestinians, such as Shiite militant Amal and the Syrians, who, Daniel remembered, dropped barrel bombs on their neighbourhood in 1989. For more on Palestinians during the Lebanese civil war, see Julie Peteet, *Landscape of Hope and Despair: Palestinian Refugee Camps* (Philadelphia: University of Pennsylvania Press, 2005); Rosemary Sayigh, *Too Many Enemies* (Atlantic Highlands: Zed Books, 1994); Diana Allen, *Refugees of the Revolution: Experiences of Palestinian Exile* (Stanford: Stanford University Press, 2014); Michael Hudson, 'The Palestinian Factor in the Lebanese Civil War', *Middle East Journal*, vol. 32, no. 3 (Summer 1978), pp. 261–78; Robert Fisk, *Pity the Nation: Lebanon at War* (Oxford: Oxford University Press, 2001); Rami Siklawi, 'The Dynamics of Palestinian Political Endurance in Lebanon', *The Middle East Journal*, vol. 64, no. 4 (Autumn 2010), pp. 597–611; Marvine Howe, 'Palestinians in Lebanon', *Middle East Policy*, vol. 12, no. 4 (December 2005), pp. 145–55.

confronting one's silenced past. In hindsight, he argues that he was ready for the possibility of finding 'nothing' or not being able to connect with anything, because the city had changed so much since the day his parents left it. Moreover, he was repeatedly told by family members that there was 'nothing left' and that Jaffa was completely destroyed under the Israeli occupation. This type of mental effacement of a lost place is not uncommon among diasporic *Yafawiin*; the destruction of Jaffa represents for them a break with trauma and an attempt to make sense of their refugeehood, in a similar manner to Daniel's parents' insistence that they were the only surviving family members. The problem, of course, is that these discourses of erasure, in fact, play into the hands of Israeli state propaganda that seeks to sever Palestinians' affective attachment to lost places of origin. In addition, these discourses also efface the existence of a viable Palestinian community in the city, and in Daniel's case, of the many relatives that never left, whom he discovered when he began visiting.

Daniel found a cousin within ten minutes of being left alone to explore the city, and from that moment, he argues, the past just came very close to the surface 'so I could look at a place and see something else'. He managed to trace the route his Alzheimer's-ridden uncle used to take from the family's home to school, even though the uncle's markers were no longer there – but Palestinians who are intimately familiar with their city were. This practice of counter-mapping, of excavating places through a form of visual archaeology is a form of spatial resistance; against the state's multiple erasures, de-Arabisation and ongoing Judaisation-cum-gentrification, whose roots Chapter 2 traced to the post-Nakba 'new normal',[24] Palestinians resort to strategies of remaking space back into the intimately familiar.[25] Based on his uncle's sensory memories, of having to orient oneself towards the sea from the house's balcony through a particular bodily movement, he was able to locate the house. Moreover, his uncle's detailed account of what it felt like to play football on a *ramleh* (a mound) enabled Daniel to find the particular

---

[24] See Chapter 2.
[25] Ibrahim Abu Lughod went through a similar process when he returned to his city of birth. See Lila Abu Lughod, 'Return to Half-Ruins: Memory, Postmemory, and Living History in Palestine', in Ahmad H. Sa'di and Lila Abu-Lughod (eds), *Nakba: Palestine, 1948, and the Claims of Memory* (New York: Columbia University Press, 2007), pp. 77–104.

playground, complete with the same embodied sensation of stepping and running on it.

The mixture of exhilaration and shock involved in the emotional process of (re)discovery in the company of a newly found cousin were complicated further when Daniel attempted to show his father a video that he made documenting his journey. Rather than share his son's enthusiasm, his father remained obstinate that the city was indeed in ruin and nothing was left, regardless of the mounting evidence to the contrary and his son's passionate pleas. Finally, he just left the table and refused to even look at the computer's screen.

Daniel's parents lost hope of ever returning to Jaffa, he posits, because their entire identity is based on loss and mourning and commitment to the memory of place that 'literally, they would lose themselves. They don't know how to be any other way.' Holding on to deep injury is also a way to restate their commitment to Palestine and address their regret and shame at having left. At the same time, they keep reiterating their faith that their descendants return in their stead. Daniel himself has only considered the possibility of buying property in Jaffa as a form of more concrete (rather than virtual) return before he discarded the thought when he considered the political realities of occupation and 'Jewish-only and whatever only', as he puts it.

> There is something hopeful about seeing that there are people there, that they remember my grandfather, there's family and there are kids that are there and there are things that are familiar … there's something hopeful about the fact that it doesn't matter how big the effort is, or how big the state is, there are certain things they cannot erase. They cannot erase me.

For Daniel, then, it is the present that is meaningful and to which he formed an attachment, rather than following a trail of memories of loss and mourning. His Palestinianness is therefore tied more to what is there than to what was destroyed or lost. On a certain level, Daniel's notion of return is delinked from political formations; this is not a question of what kind of a state is currently in charge of things, but a question of how Palestinians find new and meaningful ways to reattach themselves to place, even as refugees who can only come as virtual returnees at the suffrage of the Israeli state.

Conclusion

When I was working in one of Israel's military archives, collecting documentation on the expulsion from Jaffa and its environs, I met an older Jewish man, who turned out to be a veteran Hagana fighter, who boasted active participation in several military operations in 1948 that resulted in the depopulation of villages and towns. 'Would you like to know how to make the Arabs run?' he once asked me. His crassness notwithstanding, I wanted to hear the answer. 'You surround a village on three sides, leaving one wide open in the direction you wish them to flee, and then you begin firing your gun in the air, to scare them.'

I was reminded of this anecdote as I was writing about itineraries and routes taken by Palestinians in 1948; with so many being forced to flee on foot, their path was prescribed for them as the Zionist forces opened a single escape route (often eastward). Those who left Jaffa by sea did not have multiple options either: with many on overcrowded ships, fishing boats and dinghies, they could only make it safely as far as Lebanon in the north or Gaza in the south.

And yet, the routes ahead were less than predictable. Many Palestinians ended up confined in UNRWA-administered refugee camps, fighting to overcome trauma and survive, running out of space with each violent convulsion of military occupation, civil wars and state counter-insurgency. Others, however, seized opportunities offered by the opening up of new routes to carve new horizons for themselves and for the Palestinian collective, newly imagined. The 1967 Naksa marked a fleeting moment for Palestinians to redefine the meaning of homeland and their relation to it; that was the moment, to return to a quote that opened the previous chapter, of radicalisation of thought and of political action.

As popular understandings of liberation evolved, so did the meaning of refugeehood: some sought to disavow it, step back into history and reclaim the future. Conversely, for others, refugeehood became a marker of authenticity and a means to heap criticism on those who abandoned them in the camps. At the same time, we would be wise to avoid romanticising either refugeehood or revolutionary action; Palestinians were forced into 'angular' existence through occupation and mass expulsion, hence their insistence on the sanctity of the right of return as a core issue for ending the 'conflict'. What this chapter attempted to highlight is some of the myriad ways by which Palestinians make their exilic existence meaningful while reconfiguring their affective relationship with their place of origin.

5

BROKEN TILES AND PHANTOM HOUSES: URBAN INTERVENTION IN TEL AVIV-JAFFA NOW

I am walking in their way
Lowering my gaze
Towards the lost village
Leaving a dusty past
Of a ghost city
A city of ruins
Replete with bleeding stones
Grieving stones
A mark to remember
The people of Jaffa.[1]

In the short film *Rosetta*, first screened at the 2013 Nakba and Return film festival organised by Zochrot,[2] a dream-like sequence is showing a young

---

[1] Sama Shaqra, 'I Was With Them' [in Hebrew], in Yossi Granovsky, Yonatan Kunda and Roman Vater (eds), *Jaffa's Language* (Jerusalem: Carmel, 2009), p. 158.

[2] Zochrot (Hebrew, 'remembering') is an Israeli NGO, founded in 2002 to promote 'acknowledgement and accountability' for the mass expulsion of Palestinians and advocate for the right of return. The organisation purposefully targets the Israeli public and has, over the years, launched several educational initiatives to engage Israelis as a means to 'generate processes in which Israeli Jews will reflect on and review their identity, history, future' and claim moral responsibility for the Palestinian plight. See the organisation's mission statement: http://zochrot.org/en/content/17. I will return to Zochrot's activities in the next chapter.

keffiyeh-clad Palestinian girl walking along the Jaffa beach, among the ruins of Irshid (Arabic for Rosetta), a small neighbourhood that once stood just north of the clock tower square area. As the girl recovers a shard of an arabesque-style floor tile, she carefully wraps it in her keffiyeh, only to use it as the base for a small makeshift model of an Arab home, which she then leaves on a rock nearby.[3]

The arabesque-style floor tiles are making a comeback these days. Home décor 'experts' trace their roots to mid-nineteenth century Europe, another commodity exported to the Middle East via merchants, diplomats and mercenaries that arrived to the region in droves as the Ottoman Empire was rapidly growing weaker and unable to resist these incursions.[4] Today, although these tiles are in high demand, the geometrical and floral patterns are no more than mass-produced adhesives, custom designed to match the tastes of buyers, as much as they are made to mimic and resemble the famed 'Jaffa style' tiles (see Figure 5.1). Conversely, Jewish artisans settled in and around the old city of Jaffa, which serves as an 'artist colony', offer their own, high end, similar products for those who can afford them.[5] Unlike the mimicry, the flooring tiles that adorned Jaffa's modern houses were hand-painted by local artisans, a craft that, against the claims of latter-day 'experts', has a long history in the Levant.

While the renewed interest in these 'Jaffa tiles' as a colonial and neoliberal commodity attempts to strip them of their Arab history and rootedness in Palestine (and the region), the short film *Rosetta* reclaimed these tiles and reinscribed them into the history of Jaffa: unlike the mass-produced Israeli mimicry, the tiles in *Rosetta* tell a story of loss and trauma. Found in pieces, buried under the rubble of a demolished Palestinian neighbourhood, they are reclaimed as authentically Arab, wrapped in a keffiyeh, a symbol of resistance and steadfastness, and used to symbolically rebuild the homeland.[6]

---

[3] The four-minute film can be viewed here: https://youtu.be/-yY6xMZCtLc.
[4] A typical example of 'expertise' on these tiles attributing them to European import: Avi Levi, 'Everything on Tel Aviv's beautifully adorned tiles' [in Hebrew], *Xnet*, 21 April 2013, http://xnet.ynet.co.il/design/articles/0,14563,L-3100596,00.html; Yonat Nahmani, 'Draw me a Floor' [in Hebrew], *Calcalist*, 5 November 2014, http://www.calcalist.co.il/real_estate/articles/0,7340,L-3644034,00.html (last accessed 26 May 2016).
[5] https://nogatiles.co.il/.
[6] Ted Swedenburg, '12 The Kufiya', in Asef Bayat (ed.), *Global Middle East: Into the Twenty-First Century* (Berkeley: University of California Press, 2021), pp. 162–74. https://doi.org/10.1525/9780520968127-015.

Figure 5.1   A screenshot from an Israeli manufacturer of 'Jaffa style' decorative tiles. The city here is invoked as quintessential oriental and 'mysterious', and the product is described as imbuing any space with a sense of 'time travel' and 'a bit of mystery'.

The creator of this short film is Gil Mualem-Doron, an Israeli scholar, teacher and artist who resided in Jaffa when we first met in 2011. His deep connection to the city, evident in his artistic work, manifested through his activism within local working-class communities, both Jewish and Palestinian, most affected by the housing crisis. In the past decade, Jaffa has become the playground for out-of-town Jewish developers, land speculators and gentrifiers, whose extensive incursion into the city has gradually pushed the more vulnerable groups out and into the peripheries.[7] Palestinians in particular have less choices; they are unable to relocate to Jewish-only neighbouring cities like Holon and Bat Yam in large numbers, and the option of moving even farther, to southern development towns or to West Bank settlements, is completely blocked to them.

This transformation of Jaffa was, and still is, particularly evident in Yehuda Hayamit Street, where Mualem-Doron lived at the time. Just across the street from the military radio station building, a huge structure was up for auction,

---

[7] See, for instance Daniel Monterescu, 'The "Housing Intifada" and its Aftermath: Ethno-Gentrification and the Politics of Communal Existence in Jaffa', *Anthropology News*, December 2008, p. 21 and his 'Identity without Community, Community in Search of Identity: Spatial Politics in Jaffa' [in Hebrew], *Megamot*, vol. 47, no. 3–4 (2011), pp. 484–517.

slated for redevelopment, designed for affluent Jewish buyers, while the street's residents, both Palestinians and Jews, were struggling to keep up with the rapidly increasing cost of living. Mualem-Doron's affective attachment to his street went beyond his involvement in spontaneous and planned acts of protest against redevelopment and gentrification; until 1948, the street was named after King Faisal, the Hashemite monarch to whom the British awarded Iraq to rule over after their failure to secure his Greater Syria kingdom. Ironically, the street reconnected Mualem-Doron to his own Arabness, as his father, who migrated from Iraq following the deterioration of the status of Jews after the Nakba, Hebraicised his Arab-sounding surname, Mualem (teacher), to Doron: 'it's a pity. There aren't many streets in Israel named after Iraqis, not even Iraqi-Jews.'[8]

Spatial Resistance

While this chapter focuses on Mualem-Doron's artistic projects, it is also noteworthy that he does not operate in a political and creative vacuum. In the wake of the Second Intifada, which broke out in 2000, and Israeli police violence targeting Palestinian citizens of the state, a young generation of Palestinian activists has made its presence known. Some organised in or alongside institutional NGOs, like al-Rabita (The League for Jaffa's Arabs, established 1979), while others opted for more loosely organised collective action in informal associations such as al-Shabiba al Yafiyya (Jaffa youth) or Darna (The Popular Committee for Land and Housing Rights, est. 2007).[9]

This new generation of activists has been working to contextualise ongoing challenges of housing, demolitions and evictions that Palestinians in Jaffa (and in Israel in general) face. In particular, the surge of neoliberalisation of

---

[8] Gil Mualem-Doron, *Mind the Gap: Transgressive Art and Social Practices* (artist's independent publication).
[9] For more on the Rabita, see Daniel Monterescu, *Jaffa Shared and Shattered: Contrived Coexistence in Israel/Palestine* (Bloomington: Indiana University Press, 2015), pp. 115–17. For a Hebrew-language discussion of the rising tide of Palestinian activism in Jaffa and other bi-national cities in Israel, see Rona Sela, 'Weaving the Change: Activism and Transformation from 2000 in Israel's Bi-national Cities' [in Arabic and Hebrew], in *Effervescence: Housing, Language, History, A New Generation in Jewish-Arab Cities* (Tel Aviv: Nahum Gutman Museum of Art, 2013), pp. 214–33. Over the course of the last few years, Darna has focused on providing legal counsel to Jaffa residents whose homes are slated for demolition, thus moving from the realm of the informal to become more institutionalised.

real estate and the continuous displacement of Palestinians in and from Jaffa have prompted these activists to creatively link the current urban transformation, its acquisitive motivations and the enduring Nakba. In other words, sedimented collective memories of ethnic cleansing, expropriations and intensive Judaicisation of the city, what I called 'the new normal' (see Chapter 2), have been unearthed and invoked in public, as a means of challenging and undermining the state's efforts at marginalising Palestinians and eliding their histories from public spaces.[10]

Part of this new surge of Palestinian activism is also articulated through creative interventions in urban landscapes. In Jaffa, for instance, the artistic collective Parrhesia (from the Greek, 'free speech' or 'daring to speak the truth'),[11] in which there were both Jewish and Palestinian members, launched *Derekh Hasafa* ('through language', also literally 'the language's path' in Hebrew), a visual bilingual dictionary that literally reinscribed Arabic in public, through graffiti. Each stencil presented an Arabic word alongside its Hebrew transliteration translation. The words chosen by local communities and stencilled by Parrhesia artists/activists reflected a keen sense of urban and political consciousness: language, border, education, tree, Nakba. The project was designed to mark particular urban paths that narrate local histories and bring the Palestinian presence from the margins to the core of Israeli public consciousness, especially in 'mixed' cities like Jerusalem and Jaffa.[12]

A different form of public was imagined by the Jaffa-based Ayam collective that created *The Jaffa Project – an Autobiography of a City*, an interactive website, now defunct, that curated audio and video testimonies from Palestinian elderly about pre-1948 Jaffa, categorised by themes. This remarkable website allowed visitors to produce countless different narratives about

---

[10] Sela, 'Weaving the Change', pp. 218–19.

[11] See Michel Foucault, *Fearless Speech* [in Hebrew], ed. Joseph Pearson (Los Angeles: Semiotext(e), 2001).

[12] https://osnatbaror.wordpress.com/ (last accessed 13 January 2022). Originally, the municipality agreed to fund materials needed for the project, provided the artists use erasable spraypaint. In other words, the establishment allowed critique as long as it can be erased just as the Arabic has been. See Hadas Kedar, 'The Colour of Money (Washes in Water)' [in Hebrew], *Hagadah Hasmalit*, 29 June 2014, http://hagada.org.il/2014/06/29/בעקבות-בוריס-גרויס-במכניזם-ההשמדה-של-ה/ (last accessed 4 January 2022).

Figure 5.2 *Derekh Hasafa*, a visual dictionary: Jaffa, Yefet street, December 2009. (Photo by Vered Navon.)

the city's Palestinian past by changing the order of key words they chose to click on. In 2012, the Ayam collective also launched *Jaffa 2030*, an ambitious project that aspired to encourage public forms of imagination about the future of the city beyond, and in spite of, the limitations of the colonial present. The launch party consisted of artistic installations that narrated Jaffa's pre-Nakba history alongside other works that teased the audience about the potentialities for transformations within and outside Jaffa: reclaiming the city from colonial and neoliberal powers as a form of celebration of new liberatory formations of urban binationalism and at the same time, expanding the audience's horizons of the possible to include the entire region. Against the Israeli state's ambitions to project its powers and reshuffle populations throughout the Middle East, these artists defiantly proposed to reconnect Jaffa with Beirut, Damascus and Baghdad, imagining a new postcolonial Middle East.[13] Just like *Autobiography*

---

[13] Even though the *Autobiography of a City* website is now defunct, the *Jaffa 2030* visitors centre is still online: http://thejaffaproject.com/jaffa-visitor-center/ (last accessed 4 January 2022).

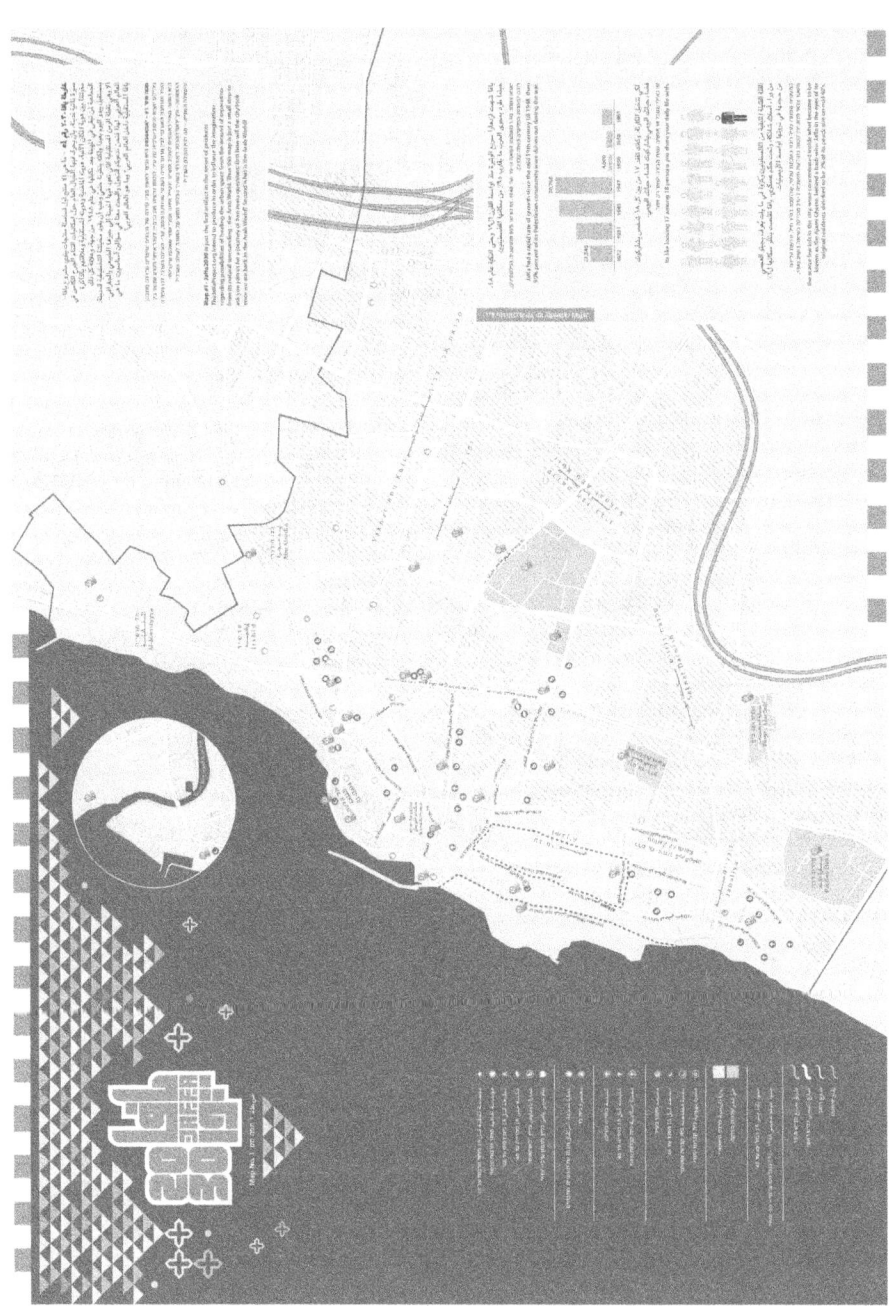

Figure 5.3 Jaffa 2030 'Map no. 1' showcasing Palestinian Jaffa.

of a City, Jaffa 2030 reimagined public as the virtual realm, where both images and information can circulate in defiance of the Israeli state and its security apparatus that still maintains its control over the Arab education system, media and artistic expression, but is far more limited in its ability to hinder online critiques.[14]

I interpret Gil Mualem-Doron's work within these contexts of emerging forms of local, young and creative forms of resistance against the 'new normal'. The mere fact that they are defying the state of things attests to the failures of the 'new normal' as a state project: born into a colonial reality that was produced in the aftermath of the Nakba and the Judaicisation of the city, this generation challenges the political status quo by 'dredging up' that which is no longer conscious as well as publicly articulating their desire to transgress and overturn the normalised realities of ethnonationalism, occupation and de-Arabisation of the urban space. Mualem-Doron's work, then, joins a host of other, similar-minded utopian projects that actively negate the here and now and open up horizons of possibility through the work of urban intervention.

This form of intervention, which can be traced back to the 1960s Situationists, encompasses different modes of creative engagement with urban landscapes designed to critique the architectural establishment and its complicity in global capitalist and neoliberalism that have shaped the modern city.

---

[14] State control over Palestinian cultural production has manifested in numerous ways over the years. Recent examples are defunding Haifa's al-Midan, the only Arabic-language theatre (Hasan Masri, 'For Palestinian Artists, the Freedom of Speech is Anything but Guaranteed', *+972 Magazine*, 20 June 2015, http://972mag.com/for-palestinian-artists-freedom-of-speech-is-anything-but-guaranteed/107997/ (last accessed 26 May 2016)); the Prime Minister's threat to close down the only television station for Palestinian citizens of Israel (Haggai Matar, 'Netanyahu Threatens New TV Station for Palestinian Citizens of Israel', *+972 Magazine*, 19 June 2015. http://972mag.com/netanyahu-threatens-new-tv-station-for-palestinian-citizens-of-israel/107971/ (last accessed 26 May 2016)); and the continuous surveillance over Arabic book production and importation (see Ayman Sikseck's report from 11 June 2015, http://www.i24news.tv/en/tv/replay/i24newsen/4289682474001 (last accessed 26 May 2016)). Acknowledging its relative weakness vis-à-vis online social media, Israeli lawmakers have resorted to legislation and other forms of exerting pressure in order to combat Palestinian online critique: see Sue Surkes, 'Facebook, Twitter, Removing 70% of Harmful Posts', *The Times of Israel*, 7 June 2016, http://www.timesofisrael.com/70-of-harmful-facebook-twitter-posts-said-removed/ (last accessed 26 June 2016), and AFP, 'Israel Plans Law against Using Facebook for "Terror"', *Yahoo News*, 22 June 2016 (last accessed 26 June 2016).

Urban intervention works directly on the terrain and landscapes of the city, strives to alter them and radically democratise public spaces and existing power relations.[15] In the context of Palestine, architecture and urban planning have been implicated in municipal and state efforts at creating and maintaining the 'new normal', and have actively participated in processes of eliding the Palestinian past of the city of Jaffa.[16]

My discussion of Mualem-Doron's work highlights the dimension of spatial resistance through acts of artistic urban intervention. Specifically, I focus on those projects that defy decades of Judaicisation and marginalisation of Palestinian urban histories by publicly confronting Israeli Jews with the uncomfortable truth of ethnic cleansing and provoking his audience with imaginaries about the possible future of the return of the Palestinian refugees. These provocations, I argue, are not simply designed to make Israeli Jews feel bad about their complicity in settler colonialism. Reinscribing Palestinian Jaffa in colonised and gentrified urban spaces creates the effect of haunting, the eeriness of recognising the presence of what is seemingly not there. The work of Gil Mualem-Doron actively produces what Gil Hochberg recently called 'visible invisibility', that is, forces the Palestinian history of Jaffa into Israeli Jews' line of sight despite decades of deliberate elisions and forgetfulness.[17]

---

[15] Gil Mualem-Doron, 'Urban Interventions and the Possibility of Radical Democratic Space', in City Mine(d), *Generalized Empowerment: Uneven Development and Urban interventions*, see http://www.citymined.org/index.php and http://www.generalizedempowerment.org/; see also Saskia Sassen, 'Making Public Interventions in Today's Massive Cities' posted on *Generalized Empowerment*'s website. On urban interventions, also see Ron Griffiths, 'Cultural Strategies and New Modes of Urban Intervention', *Cities*, vol. 12, no. 4 (August 1995), pp. 253–65; Thea Brejzek, ' From Social Network to Urban Intervention: On the Scenographies of Flash Mobs and Urban Swarms', *International Journal of Performance Arts and Digital Media*, vol. 6, no. 1 (2010), pp. 109–22; on the Situationists, see D. Pinder, 'Subverting Cartography: The Situationists and Maps of the City', *Environment and Planning A*, vol. 98 (1996), pp. 405–27; Martin Puchner, 'Society of the Counter-Spectacle: Debord and the Theatre of the Situationists', *Theatre Research International*, vol. 29, no. 1 (March 2004), pp. 4–15; Simon Sadler, *The Situationist City* (Cambridge, MA: MIT Press, 1998).

[16] Sharon Rotbard, *White City, Black City* [in Hebrew] (Tel Aviv: Babel, 2005).

[17] Gil Hochberg, *Visual Occupations: Violence and Visibility in a Conflict Zone* (Durham, NC: Duke University Press, 2015). Hochberg argues that 'something happens' to create the effect of the visible invisibility. In this chapter, I argue that it is the public artistic performance of Mualem-Doron that produces this effect for his audiences or at least aims to.

Many Israeli Jews accept and reproduce official state narratives about the events of 1948, for instance, arguing that Palestinians were never expelled but fled during wartime. In recent years, Zionist right-wing activists have been vocally denying the Nakba ever occurred and have actively attempted to disrupt and block commemoration events.[18] The haunting that Mualem-Doron's artistic projects effect challenge vocal denial and forceful attempts to suppress public rituals of Nakba commemoration; the specters of Palestinian Jaffa not only force Israeli Jews to acknowledge their presence, but undermine what has become, over the past several decades, a sense of the familiar or the 'homely'. This particular kind of haunting is productive of the uncanny, that which reveals itself to be frightening, even menacing, despite the fact it was 'something long known to us, once very familiar'.[19]

But this haunting is not designed simply to unearth suppressed colonial anxieties and make Israeli Jews uncomfortable; for Mualem-Doron, the significance of his work is its futurity dimension: once the invisible becomes visible again, the process cannot be reversed and the ghosts cannot simply be laid to rest and suppressed back into the collective sub-consciousness. This encounter, between the Israeli Jew and Mualem-Doron's haunting artwork is productive of political agency; it compels a response, even if unpredictable and contingent. Mualem-Doron cannot force his audience to embrace his form of political engagement, yet his work inhabits the hope, or subtle promise, that Israeli Jews are capable of overcoming colonialism and challenging the 'new normal' alongside Palestinians. The ghostly possession of Tel Aviv and Jaffa, then, are also symbolic ways of repossession and decolonisation of space.

---

[18] For instance, the 'Nakba Kharta' ('Nakba nonsense') booklet, available for download in multiple languages on the *Im Tirtzu* website, has become increasingly popular and widely referenced by young Israelis; https://imti.org.il/publications/booklets/ and a short video accompanying the booklet https://www.youtube.com/watch?v=5g818VNH1uM [in Hebrew, English subtitles].

[19] Sigmund Freud, 'The Uncanny, 1919', in David Sandner (ed.), *Fantastic Literature: A Critical Reader* (Westport: Praeger, 2004), p. 76. See also Yael Navaro-Yashin, *The Make-Believe Space: Affective Geography in a Postwar Polity* (Durham, NC: Duke University Press, 2012), pp. 181–4.

Bibi's House and Other Phantoms

Mualem-Doron's forms of urban intervention are rooted in place and its concrete sedimented histories. His 2010 retrospective exhibition 'Bibi's House' curated projects he led in his double role as a teacher, in both the (now defunct) Arab Democratic School for Science and Technology and the Community Architecture Studio[20] that his students, both elementary-school and college age created. In the context of the exhibition, its location – the school – temporarily became a transhistorical microcosm of the city: what otherwise might be considered another forlorn Ottoman-era ruin out of many, turned into the point of departure for the manifold stories the exhibition narrated, as well as its conclusion.[21]

At the time, the Arab Democratic School inhabited Bibi's House, on 13 Gaza Street, east of al-Nuzha (also known as Jamal Pasha, King George and Jerusalem) Boulevard. At the time of its construction by Haj Ali Bibi, one of the most affluent men in Jaffa, it was known as a *bayara* (Arabic, 'well') house, surrounded by lush greenery and orange groves. In the first few decades of the twentieth century, this area was Jaffa's ever-moving frontier, where modern urbanity met the hinterland, and the city's booming economy was largely dependent on orange growing and exporting. During the siege of Jaffa, the Bibi family fled the city, in the hope to return shortly after hostilities cease. But as I showed in my second chapter, the vast majority of the city's inhabitants were never allowed to return, and their properties, including the Bibis' estate were confiscated by the state of Israel and

---

[20] The Arab Democratic school was founded in 2004 by al-Rabita, but was forced to change course and focus on science and technology due to a sharp decrease in enrolment, which finally resulted in its closing the school in the autumn of 2011. On the short history of the school, see Gal Levi and Muhammad Massalha, 'Yaffa: A School of their Choice?', *British Journal of Sociology of Education*, vol. 31, no. 12 (2010), pp. 171–83; on the circumstances of the school's closure, see Gil Mualem-Doron, 'Closing the Gate' [in Hebrew], *Jaffa Portal*, 20 October 2011, http://www.yaffo.co.il/article_g.asp?id=2818 (last accessed 4 January 2022).

[21] On the figure of the ruin, see Walter Benjamin, 'Paris, the Capital of the Nineteenth Century (1935)', in W. Benjamin, *The Arcades Project*, trans. Howard Eiland and Kevin McLaughlin (Cambridge, MA: The Belknap Press of Harvard University, 1999), pp. 3–13. On the place of the Arab ruins in Israeli popular culture, see, for instance, Larry Abramson, 'What does Landscape Want? A Walk with W.J.T Mitchell's Holy Landscape', *Culture, Theory & Critique*, vol. 50, no. 2–3 (2009), pp. 275–8.

Figure 5.4 The Bibi family house on Gaza Street, Jaffa, April 2016. Currently it is used as an art studio and gallery for Tel Aviv-Based Ankori high school. (Photo by Haim Schwarczenberg.)

leased out for multiple uses. The Arab Democratic School was one of the house's recent tenants.

The exhibition symbolically rearranged the urban space by shifting the location of Bibi's house from the urban margins to its centre. Instead of the commonplace images of the port and the clock tower square, which have largely been occupied and claimed by the dual process of Judaicisation and gentrification, the exhibition consciously focused on the urban peripheries and former borderlands: Bibi's house (and adjacent area) and the northern, now demolished, suburb of Manshiyyeh. A large suburb at the periphery of Jaffa by the end of the British Mandate, Manshiyyeh was utterly depopulated during the April 1948 onslaught by the Irgun, finally demolished by the 1970s by the municipality to make room for several high-risers and parking lots.

The materiality of the house itself became an artifact to be gazed at and considered rather than an empty 'neutral' space where art is exhibited. As part of the larger exhibition, Mualem-Doron created a sound installation, in which speakers hidden in the house's walls and well were playing carefully selected parts of an interview with Walid Bibi, who grew up in the house and is currently an exile in Jordan. Those sections of the interview selected for this installation (which was titled 'Walls Talk') focused on Walid Bibi's bittersweet memories of his childhood and the daily life of his family in the house.

In the context of gentrification and repurposing of Arab homes and refugee properties, the forgotten and silenced history of the house as a site of familial intimacy surface once again, temporarily drowning the outside noises of the Judaicising city, which, by 2010, had long swallowed and taken over the orange groves. Visitors to the installation are invited to ponder the Nakba not just as a story of collective calamity and the destruction of a unique form of Palestinian urbanity, but as a deeply personal loss saturated in affect and a sense of belonging to a place that exists only in memory. Walid Bibi cannot physically embody his house and tell his story to visitors, but his disembodied recorded voice haunts the room, his phantom-like presence hovers through the walls. Visitors who wandered into the house through the Open House Tel Aviv festival,[22] and who were mainly Israeli Jews, were forced to confront Bibi's anger and pain, as the room's walls closed in on them, symbolically trapping them in, imposing Bibi's presence and the history of Nakba, against denial and deliberate forgetfulness. Moreover, Mualem-Doron opted to leave the original recording in Arabic without dubbing it into Hebrew, even though his target audience were Israelis.[23] This conscious decision reinscribed Arabic into the soundscapes in the part of the city which had been largely Judaicised and reinforced the Arab identity of its owners and architectural style. For Israeli Jews, most of whom are not Arabic speakers, the experience was designed to elicit a sense of disorientation, as the house and the city's Arab past were conjured to remind the Jewish visitors of their tenuous sense of strangeness. The longing in Bibi's voice and the happy childhood memories he recounted reminded the Israeli visitors of that which is no longer

---

[22] Open House is a local variant of a global architecture and design festival, which entails public visits in private spaces or 'heritage sites'; https://www.batim-il.org/en/ (last accessed 4 January 2022).

[23] Selected parts of the recorded interview were translated into Hebrew and hung to read on the bare walls. In this way, Mualem-Doron reverses the politico-linguistic order: it is the Hebrew that is rendered silent while Arabic is foregrounded and dominated the soundscape.

conscious: the expulsion of the Palestinians, the military occupation of the city and the subsequent de-Arabisation of the city; the visitors are there, in the house, because he, Walid Bibi, is not.

Palestinian visitors, on the other hand, are reminded of their own personal histories of displacement and marginalisation, as the haunting phantom of Walid Bibi narrates his own. As I mentioned in my second chapter, most of the families that remained in Jaffa after the Nakba were forced to relocate into what became the Ajami ghetto, losing their houses and becoming internally displaced persons. Moreover, many have relatives who remain in exile, in the Gaza Strip, the West Bank or abroad, including Jordan, and have grown accustomed to communicating with them through the telephone or the internet, often only able to hear their disembodied voices. The experience of 'Walls Talk' then, elicited a sense of commonality, intimacy even, with the absent Bibi, recreating the now-disparate urban community across borders. In this sense, Bibi's 'haunted house' was a reflection of the global Palestinian experience that transcends place and affectively links together those who reside in disparate locations, even if they are not able to physically meet.

Another sound installation in a different room maintains the sense of 'haunting'. Visitors were sonically accosted by what sounded at first like a cacophony of sounds and an incomprehensible mixture of languages. After a few moments of listening, one could discern two distinct soundtracks playing on top of each other: one was a recording of the school's sixth-graders singing the famous song *Yafa* (Arabic for Jaffa) by Fairuz and Joseph Azar, spontaneously translating it to Hebrew; the other soundtrack was the original recording of the song, drawn out to fit the length of the children's singing, until it loses its coherence, 'just like a fading memory', described Mualem-Doron. This installation, just like the one I described earlier, produced a 'haunting' feeling of a disembodied presence. However, this time, the dual soundtrack elicited contradictory, if complementing responses: on the one hand, the song's original recording was automatically replaying in the background, the lyrics repeating ad nauseum until they lost meaning and the song's affective intensity subsided. The Jaffa that existed in the song had faded away, like memories of life in the city before the Nakba, and like the Israelis' refusal to remember the violent occupation of the city. In this sense, the first soundtrack represented that which was lost to time and which is no longer conscious. Fairuz sings of longing for places that are no longer there, are beyond reach or that have transformed beyond recognition: Jaffa, Bissan and Jerusalem. The second soundtrack though, begins incoherently: a group of six-grade art class students attempting to sing in unison. When they finally managed to catch up with one another, each student was tasked with attempting simultaneous translation of the song, which, once again, resulted in jumbled singing, giggling and correcting one another. Unlike most Israeli Jews, the Palestinians of Jaffa are, by and large, bilingual: they are forced to communicate in Hebrew in addition to their first language. The children's fledgling attempts to translate a beloved Arabic song reflected the alienation of the majority of Israel's Jews from the rich tapestry of Arabic culture produced in the region around them. Most Israelis today cannot communicate in Arabic, even if in the case of many, their parents spoke the language. The extent of Arabic, for most Israelis my age, usually does not progress beyond what some call 'occupation Arabic', or the few phrases IDF soldiers commonly use in their daily encounters with Palestinians in the West Bank.

Yet, these children's haphazard translation re-concretise the song that is 'fading' in the background, refocuses the listener who attempts to make sense of the lyrics. The voices of the singing children anchor the image of Jaffa in the present; Jaffa is no longer a 'fading memory' of tragedy and loss, but a lively urban community. The phantom presence of the students reminded listeners of the survival of the Palestinian community, and moreover, elicited hope for a better future. The aspect of futurity was present through the lack: the empty room and the sounds of children singing and giggling were designed to produce a sense of potentiality, or what could or might occur if one strips the layers of deliberate forgetfulness and denial. The previous 'Walls Talk' installation exhumed a silenced past; this sound recording represented 'working through' a past of individual and communal catastrophe for Palestinians, and a sense of guilt for Israeli Jews. Finally, the students' bilinguality, just like Jaffa's Ana Lou Lou bar or Café Yafa analysed by Monterescu as 'binational spaces',[24] represents potentiality, a moment that allows us to consider that which is not yet here, another way of being in the world that is decolonial.

[24] Monterescu, *Jaffa*, pp. 88–94, 273–8.

Lived Spaces and 'Haunting'

In complete contrast to commonplace focus on Jaffa's familiar landmarks, such as the port, old city and the clock tower square, or the hyper gentrified flea market, the exhibition at Bibi's house highlighted the familiar and intimate for the school's students. Mualem-Doron's project 'My Jaffa' featured in the exhibition forced the visiting Israelis to confront the daily realities in Jaffa, experienced by young Palestinians. Instead of sites expropriated from the community by developers, municipality strongmen and the tourism ministry,[25] the Palestinians showcased those places they deemed 'their own', far from the tourists' beaten path and the prying eyes of Israelis searching to consume their 'backyard orient'. The candid photographs, taken by students and selected for the event, reflect everyday experiences of urban marginalisation in Jaffa: decrepit houses, under- and de-development, results of decades of deliberate neglect by the municipality; rapid gentrification – new and expensive condominiums, marketed for affluent Jews, next to a patchwork of small shacks, which the state considers 'illegal' and earmarks for demolition.

Yehudit Ilani, a longtime anti-demolition activist and a member of al-Rabita, explains to me the city's deceptive policies that are designed to gradually remove Jaffa's Palestinian residents through a strategy of declaring Ottoman- and Mandate-era buildings 'architectural heritage sites'. As a result, the municipality prohibits residents from altering them, despite the population's natural growth and families' need to expand their dwellings. The official proscription over renovations forces Palestinians to either alter their houses by adding new rooms or another floor (and risk demolition) or let their properties become so neglected until the municipality's engineering department declares them unfit for human habitation and forces their eviction. In any case, most of the Palestinians cannot afford purchasing units in new developments and are forced out of the city, often to Ramleh or Lydd.

The photographs are displayed on placards wedged into blocks, like those used to build the new gated communities but also like the blocks that make

---

[25] Natasha Roth, 'Wiping Palestinian History off the Map in Jaffa', *+972 Magazine*, 4 June 2016, http://972mag.com/wiping-palestinian-history-off-the-map-in-jaffa/119688/ (last accessed 26 June 2016).

up many of the illegal house extensions and, unlike the new condominiums, remain exposed, bereft of the layers of colour and other ornamental elements adorning the recent additions to the city's skyline. The illegal structures, in fact, are easily recognised by the presence of a mishmash of makeshift building materials: exposed bricks, asbestos and rusted metal slabs that do not shelter their owners from the winter's dampness or summer's scorching heat, and on the other hand, carry everyday intimate household sounds into the public spheres. In this installation, Palestinian children, many of them living in or adjacent to these illegal structures displayed them as lived spaces rather than the 'eyesore' Jewish newcomers to Jaffa call them or abstract constructs such as 'legality' (or lack thereof) obstructs from view.

The choice of placards was designed to remind visitors of banners and signs held by protesters. The installation, therefore, should be read as a silent protest, displaying Jaffa as a lived city, undermining the colour chrome brochures available through the municipal tourism bureau that depict pristine oriental urban spaces bereft of human presence. This silent protest foregrounded Jaffa as the victim of recent urban renewal processes, turning the neoliberal logic on its head by aestheticising the quotidian 'ugliness' of illegal structures and positioning gentrification as disruptive of the everyday.

Figure 5.5 Bibi's house, 'My Jaffa' installation. (Photo by the artist.)

Moreover, this installation also addressed a broader audience, physically absent from the room: the global Palestinian diaspora that posits Jaffa as a 'museum of the Nakba' that merely inhabits the ghosts of past residents. The exhibit defied the elision of the current Palestinian community, insisting on telling stories of survival and struggle, of both *sumud* and everyday hardships. In this way, the students of the Arab Democratic School mitigate their marginalised position both against Israeli Jews in general and their counterparts in Tel Aviv in particular, as well as diaspora Palestinians for whom Jaffa had become an Arab 'paradise lost'.[26]

Defying marginalisation and elision, from both Israeli-Zionist and diasporic Palestinian discourses, the students reinscribed Arabness back into urban spaces. 'Pedagogic Acts', a series of short videos screening in another room of the house, documented urban intervention acts that Mualem-Doron initiated and led, primarily in the area that used to be Manshiyyeh. In a series of direct actions, the students positioned models of buildings typical of turn of the twentieth-century Arab architecture, glued to shards of arabesque-style tiles. These buildings, the likeness of those once dotting the Manshiyyeh skyline, have not only been demolished by the municipality, but their remains were eventually buried under the Charles Clore Park created along the beach, together with the memory of the Arab neighbourhood that once stood there. Manshiyyeh was erased and annexed to Tel Aviv as its 'natural' appendage of modernity. Arab architecture was permitted to survive in Ajami and parts of Jabbaliyeh, where it is marketed for tourists as 'quaint' and 'oriental' and worse – diluted and selectively reproduced in the mansions overlooking the Mediterranean built for affluent Jews.

The reinscription of Arab architecture in Manshiyyeh, albeit in miniature form, was an action of reclamation of the place's Arab past, salvaging Manshiyyeh from Tel Aviv and wresting it back to Jaffa; this was a demand to be seen, a refusal to be denied existence or be relegated to the periphery. Gesturing towards reversing the process of dispossession and displacement, this act of urban intervention reclaimed space in the name of the 'ghosts' the miniatures represented, but for the living Palestinians and for those who will return.

[26] Monterescu, *Jaffa*, pp. 103–4.

Figure 5.6 'Pedagogic Acts': miniature Arab architecture in Charles Clore Park, formerly Manshiyyeh. (Photo by the artist.)

The miniature houses did more than physically reappropriate Palestinian-Arab urbanity from the Jewish city; they literally worked to 'haunt' people who happened to pass by. The students who planted these ghost houses in Manshiyyeh also interviewed passersby, most of them Jewish, interrogating them about their knowledge of the area and its history, confronting them with a silenced and buried past of forced expulsions and demolitions. The raw footage clearly reflects a certain sense of awkwardness and confusion visible on the faces of random interviewees. The surprise element aside, those interviewed by the students are visibly uncomfortable when confronted by young Palestinians with a camera who pose difficult questions. The forced recognition of catastrophe is also bookended by attempts to justify violence: 'it was wartime', 'they attacked us', 'we had no other choice'.

After exploring other marginalised urban spaces in Jaffa, the exhibition ended with a final installation that brought visitors full circle, back to the home of the Bibis. Yet, if an earlier installation endeavoured to tell the history of the house and its now-exiled owners, the final exhibit put the future on display: Mualem-Doron's architecture students were tasked to redesign the house for the post-return era, when Walid Bibi and his family return to Jaffa from their decades of exile in Jordan. Cleverly titled 'We Returned to the Land to Build and be Rebuilt', a reversal of the iconic Zionist anthem that replaced one word 'came' with 'returned', the project epitomises the exhibition. Just like in the earlier installation, the Bibis were not physically present in the room, nor were they available for consultations as the project's purported 'clients'. The house was indeed redesigned for them and on their behalf, yet the family had been absent throughout the entire process, and since the actual return of the refugees has not yet occurred, they are still absent and unable to opine about the variety of design options created for them. Even when, after several attempts of persuasion, Walid Bibi agreed to teleconference with the school's students just before the exhibition opened, he refused to directly engage with this installation, and only said he would return when 'Israel is wiped off the map'.

For both visitors and the students, the Bibis are ghosts inhabiting the house-turned-school confronting them with the uncomfortable history of ethnic cleansing and expropriation. The architecture students themselves, who had no prior knowledge about the Bibis, Jaffa or even the Nakba, were torn between 'acting professionally' (i.e. depoliticising the meaning of return and treating this assignment like all their other academic tasks) or seriously considering the political valence of return/planning for the return of the Bibis. As far as the students were concerned, the assignment was to redesign an existing house that would serve as a residence and a place of business. They were provided minimal instructions, in order to encourage diversity of imaginative responses. Thus, for instance, they were not told what kind of family-owned business would be operated on the premises, nor were they informed what part of the Bibi family was expected to resettle in the house.

One of these designs assumed a return of the extended family: Walid Bibi, his wife, son and his family, three generations under one roof. This model (see Figure 5.7) imagined the Bibi family taking residence in the house, while an underground passage from the well and cistern leads to a gallery that narrates the history of Jaffa and the family, a tale of loss, exile and return. The gallery was designed to resemble a minaret, an element the (Jewish) student figured would be culturally familiar to the family returning to a completely alien city. From the minaret's top visitors to the gallery would have a view of post-return Jaffa, thus connecting the city's past with its transformative present. Another student proposed a dwelling that focuses on the house's immediate outdoors. This model focused on a football field adjacent to the house, where the Bibi

Figure 5.7 A student's design for Bibi's house after the return. The minaret-like addition would serve as a gallery. (Photo by the artist.)

family could watch Arab and Jewish children play from the comfort of their balcony. The football field is partially covered by keffiyeh-shaped white shades, which remind the viewers of a tent, symbolising the years of wandering and exile that ended with the family's return to their home.[27]

Just like Mualem-Doron's 'pedagogic acts', this project was also designed to turn both visitors and students into political agents. The students approached this task with an air of utter depoliticisation. But as they admitted later, merely having to think about the return of the Palestinian refugees forced them to (re)consider their role as colonisers. This process confronted one student with the silenced past of her *moshav* as a Jewish settlement built atop of an ethnically cleansed Palestinian village. Other students openly articulated their discomfort; two even complained to the college's administration. A right-wing Zionist student grappled with the assignment by imagining a childless yuppie couple inhabiting the house and operating a trendy bathhouse for women of

[27] For more on the students' projects, see http://zochrot.org/en/article/53177 (last accessed 4 January 2022).

all religions, thus stripping the project from the political context of return and mitigating discomfort.

Many of those who came to view the exhibition were drawn to it by its title 'Bibi's House', erroneously thinking it was an event about Israel's then-prime minister, Benjamin Netanyahu, who owns multiple properties, one of them coincidentally located on Gaza Street in Jerusalem. Once inside, some 700 people, the bulk of them Jewish, wandered between the different installations. Mualem-Doron later reported that many had never heard about the Nakba before, let alone considered the possibility of the return of the Palestinian refugees.

The exhibition was one of the final events at the Arab Democratic School, which closed its doors the following year. The fact that the school explicitly highlighted its Palestinianness and was actively striving to reconstitute and empower the embattled Palestinian community in Jaffa may have played a role in the process that led to its closure, admitted Mualem-Doron. It is also a reflection of the municipality and the state's continuous attempts to reinforce the 'new normal', suppress any manifestation of Palestinian nationalism and keep rendering the Arabs voiceless and invisible.

Arab Homes for Sale

On a hot summer night, I left my apartment at the heart of Ajami, heading to Jaffa's historical port. The dark alleyways and narrow, almost nonexistent, sidewalks forced me to slow down, wary of the hurdles on my way, broken pavements and holes in the asphalt the municipality rarely tends to. As I reached the cusp of the Maronite quarter, near the immensely popular Abu-Hassan hummus restaurant, now shuttered for the night, I stopped in my tracks and gazed at the sight unfolding to the north, at the bottom of the hill, where Yehuda Hayamit (formerly Faisal) Street curves just past the crumbling walls of the old Jewish cemetery. Contrasting, almost taunting, the dark solitude of Ajami was the port, draped in blinding bright lights, the loudness of crowds of revellers drowning the distant hums of the waves. As I made my slow approach, I noticed people promenading about, in and out of the newly refurbished port area, between the immense hangers, which, until 1948, housed inbound and exported commodities – among the latter were Jaffa's famed oranges. These hangers had been renovated by the Tel

Aviv municipality in order to serve as commercial spaces, hubs of urban leisure culture for the Jewish residents of Tel Aviv and tourists. Trendy restaurants and cafes, alongside seafood and grill houses bearing Arab names, claiming 'authenticity' now resided in these large spaces, primarily marketed for Israeli Jews and tourists. This new and improved port was modelled after its now-defunct counterpart in Tel Aviv's north, which has become in recent years a popular commercial and entertainment district, a favourite on warm summer nights.

As I neared the crowds, the sound of people conversing was drowned in loud music played through speakers installed in various locations overhead. This was Platform, a municipally sponsored art fair, featuring craft-makers from all over the country, presenting their wares: children's toys made out of recycled metals, paper lampshades, and scented candles alongside booths offering magazine subscriptions. Then, among the sweaty fair-goers and tired parents chasing after small ice-cream-eating children, I noticed Gil Mualem-Doron's booth. Mualem-Doron was seated on a bar stool behind a small table, dressed all in white, a round straw hat on his head. Behind him – a large white banner, partially hiding a gigantic colourful mural. The banner featured only two inscriptions: on the right, 'Home-Land, home/estate' and a phone number; but what really caught my eye was a curious logo on the upper left-hand side. The logo was made out of two distinct images: an arabesque pattern common in old Arab houses and a silhouette of the old city and the port. At the bottom of the logo the city's name appeared in three languages (Arabic, Hebrew and English) in a font reminiscent of Arabic calligraphy. This was the only location in the entire event that invoked a distinct Arab presence, despite the recent history of Jaffa as an Arab city and cultural centre, and in spite of a visible Palestinian community living nearby, within walking distance. Indeed, the whole event was very much an Israeli-Jewish affair, catering to residents of Tel Aviv strolling around in shorts and tank tops, tilting their heads to the rhythm of the rock n' roll music in the background.

The small table in front of Mualem-Doron showcased several handmade models of old Palestinian homes and plastic gun-toting soldiers, each model and soldier glued to a shard of arabesque-patterned tile. A small plain sign at the foot of the table stated the ostensible purpose of this display:

BROKEN TILES AND PHANTOM HOUSES | 141

Figure 5.8 'Arab Homes for Sale' at Platform art fair: Gil Mualem Doron making an announcement to the audience. (Photo by the artist.)

'Arab Houses for Sale'. He greeted me hurriedly, in order to tend to a middle-aged couple slowly approaching the display. 'What is the meaning of this?' asked the man, a suspicious expression on his face. 'Arab homes for sale,' replied Mualem-Doron and with the air of a skilled salesman continued: 'Who does not wish to live in an Arab home? The high ceilings, the large windows bringing in the sea breeze ... why, it is the essence of the Israeli dream!' The man still seemed suspicious, but his wife exhibited some interest. She nodded at the sales pitch and approached even closer to inspect the models up close. Mualem-Doron, observing her, carried on with his performance: 'These are models of real houses. If you purchase one, I will also

Figure 5.9 Miniature Arab houses, glued to a piece of broken arabesque-style floor tile. (Photo by the artist.)

provide you with the address so you can go and inspect it yourself. I'm sure it will be to your liking. Then, if you are interested to move ahead with the sale, call this number on the banner behind me.' The couple inquired whether these properties were in the city of Jaffa, and whether they would need serious renovations, since, 'as we all know, these are old structures and the Arabs haven't been taking good care of them'. Mualem-Doron assured them the houses indeed needed 'some' work, but they are utterly habitable. The couple departed, promising to think about it, not before they grabbed a business card with the 'agency's number'.

After they left, Mualem-Doron explained the conceit: the models represented Palestinian houses in Manshiyyeh, the northern suburb of Jaffa which was mostly destroyed during the Irgun's assault and heavy shelling in late April 1948. The surviving structures were later repopulated, often squatted, by Jewish migrants (many of whom were from North Africa) and Jewish 'refugees', those residents of the former frontier areas affected most by the borderland warfare of winter 1947–8. The Tel Aviv municipality, that had plans for the area, incrementally evicted these Jewish squatters during the

1950s by declaring these structures 'dangerous for habitation'. The addresses provided to potential 'customers' no longer existed; when the Tel Aviv municipality finally demolished the remaining structures and pushed the rubble to the beach, it made sure to completely obliterate any remnants of the street layout, in order to avoid ownership claims by displaced Palestinians. Should Mualem-Doron's 'potential customers' actually attempt to locate one of those houses, they would find themselves unable to navigate through streets that are no longer there.

This act of conjuring phantom-like houses and streets denotes the poignancy of this settler colonial context: on the one hand, there is the Israeli desire to own an Arab house that Mualem-Doron mentioned to his would-be 'customers' – not just in the physical sense of actually inhabiting one, but also through claiming legitimate ownership. These claims have been made through eliding the land's Arab history and recasting an ancient Jewish or Canaanite culture on depopulated buildings, as had been done in 'Ayn Hawd/Ein Hod after the Nakba in the process of creating Marcel Janco's artists colony.[28] Another way Israel has claimed ownership was by invoking the 'return' of the Jews to 'their' homeland and place of origin,[29] from which they were once displaced.

But there is another layer to this act: Israelis may claim their right to the land, but the unexpected reappearance of the phantom houses (like those designed by Mualem-Doron), aimed to elicit the coloniser's anxiety, pangs of guilt or fear of engulfment. Moreover – the sudden disorientation in the colonial city, the momentary appearance of the familiar as unfamiliar, and the inability to navigate in space and locate the object of desire (the Arab house) highlight the colonisers' foreignness, their inability to claim intimate knowledge of the place. Organised denial and elision of the Jaffa's Palestinian-Arab history, and Israeli-Jewish wilful ignorance of conquest and displacement render the colonisers' familiarity with urban landscapes shallow. Mualem-Doron's phantom houses expose the city as a palimpsest of histories, and work to de-familiarise these spaces by the performance of alternative memory. The coloniser's disorientation stands in contrast with the familiarity of Palestinians

---

[28] Susan Slyomovics, *The Object of Memory: Arab and Jew Narrate the Palestinian Village* (Philadelphia: University of Pennsylvania Press, 1998).

[29] In this sense, Mualem-Doron's choice of 'Home-Land' as his fictitious real estate agency is quite astute.

with space, in the face of destruction and loss. Thus, for instance, Ibrahim Abu Lughod was able to lead his daughter through Manshiyyeh, orienting himself in haunted space and clearly identifying specific locations with which he had been intimately familiar.[30]

Mualem-Doron's careful choice of naming his fictitious real estate agency Home-Land[31] reflects a certain tension between the two sections split by the hyphen: a forced separation between the two, as 'home' denotes an object of desire, a loss of place that nonetheless is constantly invoked. Palestine as a place of belonging is more than particular plots of land, Arab architecture or orange groves; Palestine's multi-valence as a 'home' is refracted through one's specific position. For refugees, especially stateless ones, the idea of return to whence one belongs is, in many ways, a means of survival and projects of world-making. For the internally displaced, Palestine as a 'home' may denote hope of liberation from settler colonial rule and its concomitant status of second-class citizens. For Palestinians, therefore, the current separation of the abstract idea of home from the concreteness of land is the very thing that needs to be overturned.

For Israeli Jews, however, the hyphen represents a different kind of lack. Not only do most Israeli Jews trace their familial histories to elsewhere, but attachment to place is framed as a 'return' to the land of mythical ancestors, but that sense of 'home' is produced through the acquisition of land by way of colonial conquest. The settler, disoriented by the unfamiliar landscapes, remakes place in his own image in order to stake his claim to it. The lack denoted by the hyphen represents these efforts to elide traces of another presence – in this case, of the colonised and absent Palestinian – through continuous attempts to reproduce the national place. In this context, Jaffa is a prime example of this process: the creation and maintenance of the 'new normal' I described in Chapter 2 have intensified in the previous two decades as more boutique hotels and gated communities for affluent Jews popped up in the city, increasingly displacing the local Palestinian population. The event's

---

[30] Lila Abu Lughod, 'Return to Half-Ruins: Memory, Postmemory and Living History in Palestine', in Ahmed H. Sa'di and Lila Abu Lughod (eds), *Nakba: Palestine 1948 and the Claims of Memory* (New York: Columbia University Press, 2007), pp. 77–104.

[31] Although an actual agency (Homeland) with a similar logo does exist and is prominently featured in the current phase of Judaicisation/gentrification of Jaffa.

venue, the old Jaffa port, is a case in point; as fishermen are displaced for more cafés, restaurants and artistic fairs, the port is rapidly expropriated and repurposed primarily for the benefit of Israeli-Jewish developers, entrepreneurs and their clientele.

The tensions of home/land were also powerfully invoked by another subterfuge: when prospective 'clients' called the number on the banner behind Mualem-Doron (and on his business card), they heard an Arabic rendition of a famous Israeli song, 'I have no other country':

> I have no other country
> Even if my land is burning.
> A mere word in Hebrew
> Penetrates my veins, my soul,
> With an aching body, a hungry heart,
> This is my home.
> I will not be silent, because my country
> Has changed its face.
> I will not give it up,
> I will remind her,
> I will sing in her ears,
> Until she opens her eyes.[32]

The background to this song, penned by Ehud Manor (1941–2005), which has become an Israeli classic, is itself not bereft of internal contradictions. Originally penned as an anti-war hymn, the song became popular nationwide in the 1980s and was considered a protest against the invasion of Lebanon. Twenty years later it was appropriated by right-wing settlers opposed to the 'pullout' from the Gaza Strip (which also entailed the removal of several small outposts). Yet Palestinians are conspicuously absent from both interpretations. The liberal Zionist understanding of the song laments a disagreeable transformation of the country; Manor belonged to a generation of Ashkenazi Jews who came of age in the years following the Nakba, under the rule of Ben Gurion's Mapai. For him, and other artists, politicians and writers of that generation, those years are commonly referred to as 'the good old Eretz

---

[32] Lyrics, Ehud Manor, music by Coreen Alal.

Israel', code for the absolute hegemony of the Ashkenazim, the subjugation of the Mizrahi Jews and the military rule that kept the Palestinian minority in check.[33] This Ashkenazi elite laments 1967 as a year of profound transformation, with the occupation of the West Bank, the Gaza Strip and the Golan Heights, that altered the Israeli self-image from perpetual victim ('surrounded by enemies') to a fierce regional military power. The victory of the Likud party in 1977 with the help of the Mizrahim brought the era of the Mapai regime to an end, and challenged the hegemony of the old cultural and political elites associated with it. For Manor and his generation, that 'change' is the cause for the 'aching body' and the desire to restore the old order.[34]

However, when callers listened to a recording of the Arabic rendition, the familiar and relatable lyrics suddenly became incomprehensible, eliciting a sense of disorientation and menacing unfamiliarity similar to that felt by 'customers' who sought out the addresses of the phantom houses in Manshiyyeh. So if, according to the song 'a mere word in Hebrew' makes an Israeli literally feel 'at home', listening to the same words in Arabic was designed to elicit the opposite feelings, of being 'out of place', inhabiting someone else's home. Thus Mualem-Doron undermines the settler colonial project by turning the table on the Israelis; just like in Manshiyyeh, where the state attempted to transform Palestinian landscapes into Jewish ones by obliterating identifiable traces of Arab presence and manufacturing the national home/land in its stead, Mualem-Doron's performance in 'Arab homes for sale' seeks to symbolically overturn this process, not only by reminding Israelis of the 'no longer conscious' but also by alienating and disorienting the settler in what is otherwise familiar space.

While the majority of fair-goers were Israeli Jews, most of them from outside of Jaffa, one Palestinian family stood out in the crowd; a hijabi wife, her imposing husband and their small children approached Mualem-Doron's table, carefully eyeing the banner and the model houses. Mualem-Doron, who noticed them, carried on with the charade, explaining the process of

---

[33] See Yehouda Shenhav, *Beyond the Two State Solution: A Jewish Political Essay* (Cambridge, MA: Polity Press, 2012).

[34] The right-wing appropriation of the song, naturally, ignores the Palestinian plight, in particularly in the Gaza Strip, where settlers exploited the labour of locals under the heavy guard of the IDF.

'purchasing' an Arab house, 'the dream of every Israeli'. At first, the man listened silently, but upon the invocation of the 'Israeli dream' he was unable to hold back his anger: 'What is the meaning of this?' he asked. 'My family has been living in this city for generations, and now you intend to displace us for profit?' he raised his voice. A small crowd of Israelis gathered around us, eager to witness the exchange. Mualem-Doron never lost his composure, and explained to the man that he, too, can share the 'Israeli dream' and consider buying a house large enough for his family. At this point, the man and his family hurriedly stepped away from the table, his rage visible to the small audience. Mualem-Doron rushed after him, and quietly explained the subterfuge, to which the man and his wife reacted with a burst of laughter as they returned to the table. For a native *Yafawi* family, watching the transformation of the old port, a symbol of the city's economic flourishing prior to the Nakba, into an art fair for Israelis must be a disorienting experience. Other Palestinians, including my neighbours in Ajami refrained from taking part in this and other similar events. Everyday markers of Judaicisation-cum-gentrification are evident throughout the city, including in Ajami (where, a few years ago, a national religious Jewish settlement popped up) and in Jabbaliyeh (where the construction of the Peres Centre for Peace displaced several families).

Just like many of Mualem-Doron's artistic performances, the political work of 'Arab homes for sale' goes beyond the display of the models, or the act of public presentation. On a deeper level, the performance merely begins during and after the artist's interaction with his audience. The phantom houses and recorded song, as well as Mualem-Doron's 'sales pitch' itself are designed to solicit a reaction from spectators, yet at the same time, these responses are unexpected and contingent upon the position of the spectator: the Palestinian man reacted with anger, whereas dozens of Israeli Jews responded with curiosity and genuine interest. Even after it ends, the performance lingers in the kind of work it does – turning people into political agents. In this sense, Mualem-Doron's performance in itself is an articulation of futurity, because it opens the door for deliberation, political action and intervention in the here and now of settler colonialism. Unsettling the settler's sense of 'home' also challenges the impasse of present realities of Judaicisation, gentrification and ongoing displacement. At the very least, it undermines the claims for certainty of the present colonial order and calls to question the premise of this certainty; the state's project of creating the national space, a homeland, is unsettled, as traces of another presence – that which is no longer conscious – become visible through the invocation of tensions inherent to the hyphenated home/land. The phantom houses were designed to have a lingering effect in the minds of spectators that continues to yield unexpected consequences – for both performer (who wishes to undermine the present) and for the current political order (that wishes to reproduce itself).

Conclusion: Between Jaffa and Gaza

In December of 2014, Mualem-Doron participated in Intervals, an art festival and a fundraiser for legal expenses of anti-occupation activists, with a new series of collages titled 'For Sand thou are and unto Dust shalt thou Return'. This series, consisting of eight separate pieces, was created in the aftermath of operation Protective Edge, which was the official name given to the extensive Israeli military offensive in the Gaza Strip in the summer of 2014, and resulted in over 2,000 dead Palestinians, the vast majority civilians.[35] Each collage in this series refers to one of the eight villages and suburbs that were ethnically cleansed during the Nakba and eventually incorporated into Tel Aviv.[36] The series reinforces the haunting effect present in Mualem-Doron's work I discussed in this chapter: the pieces invoked the spectral presence of Palestinian villages that have been buried under Tel Aviv. In fact, he teases a reversal: urban landscapes of cement buildings and high-rises are symbolically buried, covered by shards of colourful arabesque-style floor tiles, where a lone witness to the horror casts a shadow. At the same time, the ghosts conjured in this series are also of Palestinians in Gaza, besieged and starved by Israel, and those killed by air raids, drones and artillery fire. Mualem-Doron explained that he explicitly wanted to represent the 'unbroken connection' between the Nakba of 1948 and the catastrophe in present-day Gaza, where many of Jaffa's

---

[35] A recent OCHA report puts the total number of dead at 2,220, with 1,492 of them civilians: http://reliefweb.int/sites/reliefweb.int/files/resources/annual_humanitarian_overview_2014_english_final.pdf.

[36] Those villages and suburbs are: Abu Kabir, the Fishermen's village, al-Shaykh Muwanis, Manshiyyeh, Irshid, Jamasin, Salameh and Sumeil.

Figure 5.10 'For Sand thou art, and unto Dust shalt thou Return': fishermen village/Tel Aviv-Gaza, 1948–2014. (Photo by artist.)

refugees reside. The sand invokes the commonplace myth of origin that claims Tel Aviv was 'born of the sand dunes' while the dust is a reference to Israelis online calling to 'grind Gaza into dust'.[37]

In the context of this chapter, the artistic acts of urban intervention of Mualem-Doron and his interlocutors were designed to elicit a sense of discomfort and disorientation among Israeli Jews. Through art, colonised urban spaces in Tel Aviv and Jaffa become haunted by spectres of Palestinians, those who are absent and those who live nearby but are marginalised, neglected and relegated to oblivion.

The ghosts of Jaffa's past (and present), invisible to the Israeli eye trained to see only that which has been normalised to become familiar, need to be summoned into visibility. The work that Mualem-Doron's art does is exactly that: making the spectral visible, the hidden and forgotten – known. Under these conditions, the artistic encounter is also a form of conversation: the audience is summoned to acknowledge the uncomfortable presence of what has been

---

[37] See http://intervals.exiguo.us/artist/99.

normalised as invisible, recognise the existence of that which had been suppressed and made subconscious; this recognition also compels the audience to be possessed, respond, and forge new forms of political agency.

Finally, 'haunting' is not a spontaneous thing. Ghosts need to be summoned; their presence must be made known. Artists like Mualem-Doron, the Parrhesia group and Ayam collective, and activists who call upon these spectres to come forth and *re-possess* public spaces, challenging settler colonialism, reveal the cleavages of the 'new normal'. Despite conscious efforts by the state, the municipality and the neoliberal market forces, the colonial present is negated, undermined, becoming undone. Tel Aviv haunted by Jaffa is the failure of the 'new normal', and this failure reveals the potential for its overthrow.

6

FEELING PALESTINE IN SOUTH AFRICA

Recognizing the historic injustice committed in 1948 and afterwards, Hoping for a better, cooperative future, We, Jews who live here, in Israel Call for the return of the Palestinian refugees to their homeland, which is also our homeland. The return of the Palestinian refugees does not mean that others will be uprooted and destroyed. It is a shared vision of a just, egalitarian future that will be better for us all. Nor is the return only a dream or a hope, but a right recognized in UN Resolution 194. The Cape Town documents, which were prepared jointly by Jews and Palestinians, define the preconditions for the practical implementation of the return, based on the following principles: 1. Our shared land has enough room and sufficient resources to resettle and compensate those of its inhabitants who were exiled, without evicting anyone from their home. 2. The actual return will be preceded by a process of winning over all the communities affected. The process of healing past wounds will continue after the return begins, through ongoing community work. 3. After the return, the country will really and truly act according to principles of freedom, justice and peace. All its inhabitants will have equal rights. The country will ensure freedom of religion, education, conscience, language and culture and will protect the holy sites of all religions. After the refugees were exiled from their land they kept faith with it in all their diasporas, never ceasing to pray and hope to return to their homeland. We entreat the Palestinian refugees in the refugee camps and everywhere else: Return!

We will join you to build the land. Come home!
'Proclamation of Return', Zochrot, read in Tel Aviv, 23 December 2012[1]

In August and September 2013, Israeli media, pundits of all political colours, and keyboard activists on social media were embroiled in a public debate surrounding the planned Zochrot conference titled 'From Truth to Redress: Realizing the Return of the Palestinian refugees'. The event, first of its kind in Israel, was to be held, strategically, in the Eretz-Israel museum in Tel Aviv, on the lands of Shaykh Muwannis, a Palestinian village depopulated in 1948. Indeed, the official invitation reclaimed the village's lands and its elided history by identifying the museum's location as Shaykh Muwannis. An extremist Zionist nationalist NGO, Im Tirtzu ('if you will'), launched a public campaign to pressure the museum to rescind its agreement with Zochrot, resulting in a legal battle of sorts between both parties. When it became evident that the event was to go on as planned, Im Tirtzu attempted to revoke the legal status of Zochrot as an NGO. In the end, the detractors of the conference merely contributed to widen the circulation of the right of return as a concept that required serious consideration. The conference's organisers, on their part, reported the event was attended to capacity.

This chapter studies a shared Zochrot-Badil project called 'Envisioning the Return of the Refugees'. Zochrot is a Tel Aviv-based NGO, which, as its name implies (Hebrew, 'remembering'), focuses on preserving the memory of pre-1948 Palestine, its lost life-worlds, cultures and demolished landscapes, and educating the Israeli-Jewish public about the Nakba, or the ethnic cleansing of the country's Palestinian population, an act that enabled the establishment of the Jewish state. Established in 2002, Zochrot's trademark is its Saturdays' guided tours of depopulated villages, towns and urban neighbourhoods, often in the company of internally displaced persons (IDPs) from that particular locale who share their memories of violent uprooting. This format of 'memory activism' is not a coincidence, as it corresponds with ideologically imbued, state-sponsored pedagogical tools. The Zochrot tours fuse the pre-state Zionist practice of 'knowing the land' through hiking[2] and the post-1960

---

[1] https://zochrot.org/en/activity/54550 (last accessed 6 January 2022).
[2] Nadia Abu el-Haj, *Facts on the Ground: Archaeological Practice and Territorial Self-Fashioning in Israeli Society* (Chicago: University of Chicago Press, 2001); Yifat Gutman,

phenomenon of the rise of the witness testimonial, which can be traced to the Eichmann trial.[3]

More recently, however, Zochrot has been making an important shift: although still committed to the work of memory, Zochrot is increasingly involved in open discussions about the future of Palestine. More significantly, this shift is also a dramatic turning point from speaking about the right of return (of Palestinian refugees) as an abstract legal concept, to actively envisioning the realities and practicabilities of such a return.

Badil (Arabic, 'alternative'), a Bethlehem-based Palestinian refugee rights advocacy group, was founded in 1998. Its mandate is far broader than Zochrot's; Badil consciously frames its publications in international law, but its activities far surpass the boundaries of the legal realm. The NGO maintains an impressive resource centre and engages in knowledge-production, primarily through its flagship publication *al-Majdal*, as well as periodic thematic reports. Citing Palestinian identity as the core of the organisation's mandate, Badil recruits its staff and activists from the different segments of Palestinians society in the West Bank, Israel and the diaspora, thus making an explicit transnational – rather than local – claim.

Zochrot and Badil launched a joint project aiming to plan and render the return practical, imaginable and even tangible. I was invited to join the working group and thus became a participant in this project and a co-author of the subsequent 'Cape Town document', which will be discussed in detail

---

'Past before Future: Memory Activism in Israel-Palestine', PhD dissertation, The New School, 2011.

[3] Michael Rothberg, *Multidirectional Memory: Remembering the Holocaust in the Age of Decolonization* (Stanford: Stanford University Press, 2009). Significantly, though, as Gutman correctly observed, this format serves to highlight the asymmetrical authority of the Nakba tour ritual: the Palestinian story is mediated and its claim to veracity conferred under the aegis of Israeli Jews. It is Zochrot, an Israeli NGO, that determines the authenticity of testimonies (by carefully selecting the survivor-witness), leads memory tourists through the site, produces knowledge about it (in the form of a booklet), and finally – holds a ceremony of placing signage identifying key locations (mosques, churches, cemeteries) at the site. This asymmetry enhances the tension inherent in the politics of knowledge production in settler colonial projects. Zochrot indeed works to undermine the state's systematic silencing and erasure of the country's Palestinian-Arab past, thus dislocating its effort at Judaicising landscapes. But at the same time, the format selected for this work reflects the political order and the fact that Palestinians are granted 'permission to narrate' under Israeli-Jewish supervision.

in Chapter 7. 'Envisioning the return of the Palestinian refugees' ambitiously aspired to shift the discourse about the return from a 'right' to 'practice' by asking its participants, Israeli Jews and Palestinians, to plan and imagine everyday life in a post-return polity on multiple scales, from state administrative, symbolic and legal apparatuses to micro levels of urban landscapes in Tel Aviv and Jaffa. This year-long joint project yielded a few unexpected twists and turns, taking the group to Cape Town, South Africa, on a study tour of post-apartheid society, and back to Palestine to dilapidated refugee camps.

This chapter will offer a discussion of the tensions inherent in, and particular to, projects of 'imagining futures' such as this one. On the one hand, participants are required to make a temporal leap to a future that is 'not yet here', a 'horizon imbued with potentiality'.[4] On the other hand, the documents produced through this project, and the visions they entail, are temporally and spatially situated. They are rooted at the multiple encounters and interactions between people and the engagements of people with landscapes, places as well as itineraries and the affective processes they engender. Fantasy and the imagination are steeped in affect; visceral processes are both implicated with and constitutive of the imaginary as well as elicited by it. By 'fantasy' I mean to denote those imaginaries which are on the one hand rooted in tangible realities but also push towards the horizons of possibility. The fantasies of participants in the Cape Town visit were guided by the histories of settler colonialism both in Palestine and South Africa, and the visceral ways they experienced post-apartheid realities. I wish to explore how these imaginaries were articulated through affect, or the ways in which individual participants, as well as the group as a whole, processed affective reactions as they engaged with each other, multiple sites, itineraries and routes.

The Commensurability of Apartheid

The choice of South Africa as a springboard to imagine Palestine's future was not a foregone conclusion. Other options were considered, in particular Rwanda and Guatemala, where in both cases, an ethnic minority fled genocide,

---

[4] Jose Esteban Munoz, *Cruising Utopia: The Then and There of Queer Futurity* (New York: New York University Press, 2009).

endured refugeehood but eventually returned to a process of reconciliation.[5] Organisers finally opted for South Africa for three main reasons. First, the other cases of refugee return and reconciliation represented internal ethnic conflicts that emanated from particular sociopolitical contexts that were less relevant for the Palestinian case, where mass expulsion and displacement were results of settler colonial policies. Unlike Guatemala and Rwanda, South Africa is a prominent example of settler colonialism, even though, arguably, the colonial question was largely muted (or downplayed) in post-apartheid public deliberation and legal arrangements. Second, in recent years, the apartheid analogy, by which I mean pointing out the similarities between Israeli state policies and those of the apartheid regime, has become salient in global activist (and some academic) circles. Exploring this analogy, and its application to the case of Palestine, appealed to both Zochrot and Badil (the latter had already conducted their own fact-finding mission to South Africa). Finally, funding and guidance for this project dictated the logistics of the tour. The joint delegation's hosts and local interlocutors in Cape Town were members of KAIROS, a local chapter of a global Christian movement enmeshed in several social justice struggles around the world, in particular Palestine. The leadership of KAIROS in this tour also meant that our itineraries were carefully planned by our local interlocutors to reflect their faith-based form of activism. Significantly, these itineraries and pre-arranged meetings with selected individuals were to perform as meaning-making moments that would produce certain understandings and responses, but potentially foreclose others. For instance, had it not been for the KAIROS- and African National Congress (ANC)-affiliated meeting convenors, we might have heard more critical voices about the Truth and Reconciliation Commission (TRC) as a tool of nation-building that produced its own set of silences.[6]

---

[5] Mahmood Mamdani, *When Victims Become Killers: Colonialism, Nativism, and the Genocide in Rwanda* (Princeton, NJ: Princeton University Press, 2002); Patricia Pessar, 'Women's Political Consciousness and Empowerment in Local, National and Transnational Contexts: Guatemalan Refugees and Returnees', *Identities: Global Studies in Culture and Power*, vol. 7, no. 4 (2001), pp. 461–500.

[6] This critique of the TRC as a way to forestall black anger and as a tool of nation-building has been articulated by scholars and activists early on. See for instance Lekoko Kenosi, 'Records, National Identity, and Post-Apartheid South Africa: The Role of Truth Commission Records in Nation-Building', *Archives and Manuscripts*, vol. 36, no. 2 (2008), pp. 76–87;

Recently, anthropologist Julie Peteet has taken a closer look at the apartheid analogy and its political effectiveness, arguing that such a comparison situates particular histories within broader contexts and frameworks of analysis, and thus works to 'de-exceptionalize' and 'de-nationalize' histories.⁷ In the case of Israel, as I demonstrated in Chapter 2, the state has made a claim to be an exception in the region, the 'only democracy in the Middle East'. Its practices of mass expulsions and especially blocking the return of the refugee fly in the face of such claims. This chapter, then, adds to that earlier discussion by broadening the analysis of Israel's practices vis-à-vis the Palestinians and locating it within a specific set of settler colonial 'family resemblance' while still accommodating specificities and differences. The apartheid analogy is linked to the rise of the Boycott, Divestment and Sanctions (BDS) movement in 2005. This recent juxtaposition of Israel and South Africa has yielded important political lessons in terms of strategies and potential trajectories for the Palestinian struggle.⁸ But the analogy has a much longer history than its current phase, in the kind of arguments produced by proponents of the apartheid analogy, from Maxime Rodinson in the early 1970s to Peteet's recent intervention.⁹ Generally speaking, these comparisons focused on structural

---

Tanya Goodman, 'Performing a 'New' Nation: The Role of the TRC in South Africa', in Jeffrey C. Alexander *et al.* (eds), *Social Performance: Symbolic Action, Cultural Pragmatics, and Ritual* (Cambridge: Cambridge University Press, 2006), pp. 169–92; Akin Akinwumi, 'The Will to Transform: Nation-Building and the Strategic State in South Africa', *Space and Polity*, vol. 17, no. 2 (2013), pp. 145–63.

⁷ Julie Peteet, 'The Work of Comparison: Israel/Palestine and Apartheid', *Anthropological Quarterly*, vol. 89, no. 1 (Winter 2016), pp. 247–81.

⁸ On this, see Jon Soske and Sean Jacobs (eds), *Apartheid Israel: The Politics of an Analogy* (Chicago: Haymarket Books, 2015), especially Mahmood Mandani's intervention, relevant to the discussion here, about the role anti-apartheid Israeli-Jewish activists should take.

⁹ Maxime Rodinson, *Israel: A Colonial-Settler State?*, trans. David Thorstad (New York: Monad Press, 1973). Other notable contributions to the rather long history of this comparison are: Uri Davis, *Israel, an Apartheid State* (Atlantic Highlands: Zed Books, 1987) and his *Apartheid Israel: Possibilities for the Struggle Within* (London: Zed Books, 2003); Ilan Pappé (ed.), *Israel and South Africa: The Many Faces of Apartheid* (London: Zed Books, 2015); Amneh Daoud Badran, *Zionist Israel and Apartheid South Africa: Civil Society and Peace Building in Ethnic-National States* (London: Routledge, 2010); Marwan Bishara, *Palestine/Israel: Peace or Apartheid – Occupation, Terrorism and the Future* (London: Zed Books, 2002); Jimmy Carter, *Palestine: Peace, Not Apartheid* (New York: Simon & Schuster, 2006); Virgina Tilley (ed.), *Beyond Occupation: Apartheid, Colonialism and International Law in the Occupied Palestinian Territories* (London: Pluto, 2012); John Quigley, 'Apartheid Outside

similarities between apartheid South Africa and Israel (either within its internationally recognised borders or the 1967 occupied territories alone) in terms of legal discrimination, restrictions on mobility and access to resources, or highlighted the moral and racial aspects of these two settler colonial formations. Although analyses often diverge, these arguments offer a comparison 'from above', emphasising ideological and state-formation that underscore two comparable sets of legal and political systems.

In this chapter, I offer an addendum to this volume of scholarship, by suggesting an analysis of commensurability (rather than comparison) that is rooted in affect. In what follows, I will retrace the groups' journey through post-apartheid urban landscapes in the greater Cape Town area, explicitly focusing on the encounters between group members and local interlocutors, the sites they visited and were led through, as well as the intra-group interactions and tensions. The commensurability that is at the heart of this chapter does not emanate from a structural comparison, but rather from the subjective ways Palestinians and Israeli Jews experience a sense of what Freud called 'the uncanny' and Navaro-Yashin called 'eeriness', or a sudden realisation of unexpected similarities: as commensurability unfolds, lived spaces intersect and partially merge with other sites – Jaffa is reimagined as a refugee camp in the West Bank or, as I will demonstrate below, as a Cape Town neighbourhood razed by the apartheid regime.[10] The work of commensurability exceeds shared grief and expressions of solidarity. Turning our attention to the ways commensurability is experienced and embodied and to the realm of affect makes the work of hope visible. Put differently: the politics of comparison opens up opportunities for a trans-regional approach to collective resistance, embracing strategies that have been effective elsewhere. Commensurability, by contrast, is rooted in experience and affect and elicits a sense of hopefulness that emanates from successful struggles and human solidarities.

Africa: The Case of Israel', *Indiana International & Comparative Law Review*, vol. 2, no. 1 (1991), pp. 221–51; Mark Marshal, 'Rethinking the Apartheid Paradigm', *Journal of Palestine Studies*, vol. 25, no. 1 (Autumn 1995), pp. 15–22.

[10] Sigmund Freud, 'The Uncanny, 1919', in David Sandner (ed.), *Fantastic Literature: A Critical Reader* (Westport: Praeger, 2004), pp. 71–101; Yael Navaro-Yashin, *The Make-Believe Space: Affective Geography in a Postwar Polity* (Durham, NC: Duke University Press, 2012).

This emerging hope generates new imaginaries, political activism and subjectivities that revolve around the tangibility and practicability of return.

Planning as Resistance

Participants in this project are not merely engaging in symbolic and/or discursive acts of reclamation or provocation, such as Mualem-Doron's artwork from the previous chapter. Rather, planning goes beyond critique of the status quo towards imagining into being a radical alternative. Planning for a reversal of history and for redress of injustice concretises an alternative to state and municipality authority, as well as to nationalist and colonial histories. In Chapter 2, I described the process that had begotten the 'new normal', or normalising the occupation of Jaffa and the deliberate shattering of hope for repatriation. Planning the return of the refugees means dislocating that false sense of normalcy by pointing in another, and opposite, direction, as well as undermining the state's project of foreclosure of hope. This project of planning, then, works to undo decades of violent erasures, from collective memory, from official histories and from the urban landscapes.

The object of desire, the return of the 1948 refugees of Jaffa, has been all but rendered impossible by the 'new normal' of life under occupation and the absorption into the municipality of Tel Aviv (see Chapter 2). As many of my interlocutors revealed, both in Jaffa and in forced exile, the mere notion of return became a hollow idea that, with the passage of time, lost a sense of concreteness or immediacy. Life under occupation, either as second-degree citizens or subjects of military rule has become the only thing many know or remember. Refugees in Balata refugee camp, for instance, kept telling me 'it's normal (Arabic, *'adi*) for us' when I asked about living in a dilapidated refugee camp, with running water only four days of the week, or about night raids and arrests of young men. Over time and under the 'new normal', return has become a wish, a desire for a place familiar through fading personal histories; it is, as I said, hollow, because of the acute and painful acknowledgement that the past is irrevocable, that one cannot magically turn back the clock as if the last seven decades never happened. Indeed, this is also the argument I hear from many Zionist Israeli Jews: 'do you honestly think history can be undone?' The act of imagining and planning the return, then, is a radical shift from invoking a wish, and a step towards making the object of desire more tangible, grounded in both the traumas of the past and the realities of the present. This chapter is therefore about 'in-betweeness': the interaction between human beings, on many roads between places, and between moments of despair and visions of futurity.

The journey to South Africa that this chapter focuses on ran concurrently with other, less ambitious return-related projects. One such project that also involved Zochrot through a coalition group by the name of 'Udna (Arabic, 'we have returned'). However, these projects were localised and focused on smaller, agrarian communities, such as Ma'loul near Nazareth, and were actively run by displaced persons from that village. In addition to planning, upper Galilee communities such as Iqrith and Bir'im actively reclaimed their lands, resettling and maintaining a continuous presence on the ruins of their villages despite adverse responses from the state, in particular the Land Administration Authority that has made several attempts to forcibly remove them.[11]

A more symbolic form of reclamation and 'return' is the 'March of Return', organised by the Committee of the Internally Displaced Persons since the late 1990s. This march, usually with many thousands in attendance, occurs annually on the Israeli 'Independence Day' as a direct challenge to the state-sanctioned celebrations, and is often staged on sites of destroyed Palestinian villages.[12] Although the right of return has been the core of Palestinian claims since 1948, it is no coincidence that its transformation into forms of practice emerged only in the last two decades. While the 1950s and 1960s were marked by silencing any form of Palestinian dissent through Israel's military rule, the pressing issue in the two decades following 1967 was the struggle over the ever-growing rapid land annexation and the governmental 'Judaicising' projects, particularly in Galilee. Since the Oslo Accords there emerged what

[11] Samera Esmeir, 'A Guide for the Perplexed: On the Return of the Refugees', *Middle East Research and Information Project*, 28 April 2014, https://merip.org/2014/04/a-guide-for-the-perplexed/; Patrick O. Strickland, 'Palestinian Refugees Mark One Year of Return to Destroyed Village', *Electronic Intifada*, 15 August 2014, http://electronicintifada.net/content/palestinian-refugees-mark-one-year-return-destroyed-village/13757 (last accessed 26 May 2016).

[12] Dan Cohen, 'Thousands of Palestinians Mark Nakba Day at March of Return', *Mondoweiss*, 8 May 2014, http://mondoweiss.net/2014/05/thousands-palestinian-citizens.html (last accessed 26 May 2016).

is commonly known as the 'stand-tall generation', younger cadres of activists who defied attempts to silence them – by both the Israeli state and the Palestinian old guard.[13] Moreover, the rapid marginalisation of Palestinian citizens of Israel from peace negotiations and the mainstreaming (and subsequent decline) of the two-states model motivated these young activists to stake their claim to alternative nationalist narratives of displacement and return as opposed to state-building.

'Joint Action' across the Colonial Divide

The 'envisioning' project under scrutiny here was born out of previous experiences of what Zochrot and Badil members called 'joint action', a study tour in the former Yugoslavia (2009) followed by a workshop in Istanbul (2010) out of which emerged preliminary documents of principles of unity.[14] The concept of joint action was put to the test soon after the two organisations agreed on moving forward from abstract concepts and into the realm of planning and fleshing out a reality of return. Thus, in autumn of 2011, both NGOs formed their core groups that became a part of this current, much more ambitious, undertaking. But what did it mean for coloniser and colonised to jointly imagine a mutual post-liberation terrain? Is it even possible to jointly feel and articulate hope in a reality that is the radical other from that which we envision and that, furthermore, constantly reconstitute geographical, racial and ethnic boundaries?

Naji 'Owdeh (Arabic, 'return'), then-director of al-Fineiq (Arabic, 'Phoenix') centre at the Deheishe refugee camp, explained to me that joining this action was not easy for him. 'We need to work a lot to break the ice,' he explained, as we were sitting his office in the Lilac centre, which he founded after leaving al-Fineiq. '[This type of idea] is difficult for the majority of both sides ... and needs a lot of planning.' Indeed, mutual suspicion between the groups was voiced during and after the first encounter. While the Zochrot

[13] Dan Rabinowitz and Khawla Abu Baker, *Coffins on our Shoulders: The Experience of the Palestinian Citizens of Israel* (Berkeley: University of California Press, 2005).
[14] See Akram Salhab, 'Badil-Zochrot Joint Action: Practical Approaches to Refugee Return', *The Struggle for Palestinian Rights: New Strategies in a Changing Middle East*, No. 46 (Summer 2011), https://www.badil.org/publications/al-majdal/issues/items/1401.html (last accessed 6 January 2022).

members were told that our Badil counterparts have formed a rather sizeable working group akin to ours (at the time we numbered about twenty participants), only five of them attended the first meeting in Bethlehem and were more interested in a presentation rather than an open discussion. Back in Tel Aviv, members of Zochrot voiced their disappointment: Yoav, for instance, claimed that 'he had never felt so unwelcome' and that he felt 'the people did not want us there'. Perhaps, mused Janet, a Palestinian from Jaffa, 'Jews represent the occupation for Palestinians in the '67 territories. I also represent the occupation for them. This is, after all, a Jewish group.' Lital, another Zochrot member immediately and emphatically corrected her: 'it's an Israeli group'. This sense of unbridgeable gap between the two groups was then addressed by Manal, who explained Badil's delicate position and its membership's collaboration with Zochrot. The NGOisation of the West Bank in the post-Oslo era, funded by American and European organisations, and the brutality of the Second Intifada, contributed to the absolute rejection of the 'coexistence' model (*Du-Kiyum* in Hebrew, derogatively referred to as 'Duki' by anti-normalisation activists) and general suspicion of Israeli activists and NGOs attempting to operate there.[15] A glimmer of hope was offered by Salah, a refugee from the village of 'Ajur and a member of Badil, who also participated in previous encounters. Salah was impressed by Zochrot's commitment for the right of return and refugee rights, and argued for ameliorating communications between the two groups. 'We should meet more often,' he proposed. However, arranging meetings between occupier and occupied proved a challenging task, on more than one level.

The realities of occupation and spatial segregation enforced through complex networks of military checkpoints, walls, fences and travel permits dictated Zochrot's working schedule and modes of operation. Thus, the NGO's members' privileges as Israeli citizens also prescribed mobility whereas our counterparts were forced to stay in place; the result was that each meeting necessitated detailed planning of the drive from Tel Aviv to Bethlehem, located in area A and therefore officially banned for Israeli citizens, by-passing the heavily policed checkpoints. The road from Tel Aviv to Bethlehem and back, and,

---

[15] Lori Allen, *The Rise and Fall of Human Rights: Cynicism and Politics in Occupied Palestine* (Stanford: Stanford University Press, 2013).

as I discuss later, from Palestine to South Africa, traversed more than checkpoints, national borders and geographies of occupation; it also forced a temporal porosity, the ability to envision a future that is radically different from the status quo.

But if we override the linearity of time, and create a point of encounter between the present and an uncertain distant future, can 'landscapes of hope of despair'[16] or real places that are geographically distant from each other actually meet as well? Badil, in collaboration with DAAR (Decolonizing Architecture Art Residency, located in Beit Sahour, on the outskirts of Bethlehem) introduced us to the concept of 'stereoscopic vision', which means exploring the interconnectedness between what they called the 'extra-territorial space of refuge and the destroyed site of origin'. Stereoscopic vision, then, was a concept developed to recreate the urban landscapes of Jaffa in ways that would incorporate the right and practice of return to what was lost with what communities built over time elsewhere, especially in refugee camps. This approach, explains Alessandro, an architect working closely with Badil, forced Zochrot to take into account refugees' complex relationships with their surroundings: both the 'places of origin' and all their places of exile. In fact, he insisted, we must also think about itineraries of multiple displacements and returns, which situate Jaffa and the refugee camps in regional and global contexts. What would happen to Beirut or Balata when refugees go back to Jaffa, and in what ways would the latter be affected and transformed by the cultural encounters produced by returnees from different places in the globe? Alessandro attempted to ground this radical and rather abstract approach in a particular example.

Based on his experiences in the Deheishe refugee camp and the creation of al-Feneiq cultural centre, Alessandro and Naji (then the centre's director) argued that al-Feneiq could be used as a model for what they call 'present returns', by which they meant a culturally centred return rooted in camp experiences. In this model, they suggested, a similar centre can be established in Jaffa by returnees, for instance, from Balata and 'Askar camps; their branch of al-Feneiq would reflect and be attuned with their specific experiences of camp life.

[16] Julie Peteet, *Landscape of Hope and Despair: Palestinian Refugee Camps* (Philadelphia: University of Pennsylvania Press, 2005).

They located this centre at the site of a surviving old city complex, which, among other things, used to house the famed Damiani soap factory during the late Ottoman era.

Their presentation encountered unexpected opposition from the visiting Zochrot members. Sivan, a Jewish resident of Jaffa, wondered whether the planners even considered the present population of the city or the current use of the old building, which houses al-Saraya, the Arabic-Hebrew theatre. 'The building you imagine as vacant or abandoned,' she argued, 'is in fact home to a lively existing cultural centre' that embodies the city's current spirit and human geographies; it is a place of encounter for young Palestinian and radical Jewish artists, writers, actors and activists. In fact, the very existence of a place like al-Saraya or nearby Ana Loulou (a bar popular among a similar crowd) challenges the notion of Jaffa and its place in Palestinian national memory as the quintessential Arab city. Sites like al-Saraya and Ana Loulou represent present-day attempts to create a shared urban culture that transcends racial and ethnic boundaries. Both of these spaces already serve as Jaffa's 'spaces of hope', loci of revolt against the state's prescribed racial segregation and microcosms of what the city might become. Sivan's intervention, in effect, exposed cleavages in Alessandro and Naji's stereoscopic vision. She reminded them that although planning the return of the refugees required taking into account places of origin (a notion that should be complicated and unpacked) and sites of exile, the 'Envisioning' project could not afford to overlook the cultures, people and places that have developed in the city since Palestinians were expelled. In other words, 'present returns' needed to also include those *in situ*, Palestinians who are internally displaced, those who never left, and the Jews that are now rooted in place as well. Back in Tel Aviv, Sivan was reflecting on the intense first meeting with our Badil counterparts and potential challenges ahead. While Zochrot explored and debated the political implications of the 'Envisioning' project, questions like 'do we, who possess colonial privileges, have the right to plan for those who are absent from these discussions', it seemed that Badil and their allies at DAAR never reflected on such questions. Moreover, added Ari,

> Their model completely overlooked my living environment, what I consider my hometown – and my place in it. Perhaps we have been speaking of return

almost like a figment of our imagination, an unlikely occurrence, because, let's face it, for us, if the return doesn't actually happen it would not be a great disaster. But that is not the case for them, of course.

This uneasy acknowledgement of fundamental differences between the two groups lingered as the delegations headed to Cape Town, South Africa, for a study tour of post-apartheid society and its challenges.

Israel's system of colonial segregation dictated separate itineraries to South Africa. While the Zochrot delegation, coming from Tel Aviv, boarded a plane at Ben Gurion international airport at Lyd, our Palestinian counterparts were forced to travel to 'Amman, Jordan, traverse several military checkpoints and the Allenby bridge, which prolonged the journey by another day. The separate routes taken to our next site of encounter clearly affected the ways in which we came to think about the kind of future we desire for Palestine.

Optimism and Melancholia in Cape Town

On the joint delegation's first day in Cape Town, we awoke early in the morning, and wearing our Sunday best, rushed to nearby St George Cathedral for a mass led by Archbishop Desmond Tutu, followed by breakfast with him at the church's cafeteria. Excited to meet this world-renowned figure, several members of the delegation tried to crowd behind him and at his side. Mr Tutu shared his experience of humiliation by a young female Israeli soldier when he was detained at the airport in 1989, but at the same time, made light of the situation in an attempt to elicit our amused laughs. When asked about the possibility of reconciliation between the formerly colonised and the perpetrators he answered:

> In South Africa we couldn't know with certainty that people would want to forgive, but I think people possess a wonderful capacity for forgiveness, perhaps even a disposition. You have to risk it and change the regime ... most people don't enjoy harming others ... the day will come when people look back and won't understand why they did the terrible things they're doing today.

And like many other anti-apartheid activists, the archbishop also added that we must tell ourselves the same thing they did in the heyday of struggle:

'in our lifetime'. Tutu's profound sense of optimism, not just about the situation in Palestine but also about human nature (which, no doubt, emanated from his deep religious convictions) infected us all. When we left the cathedral, we were elated, chatting enthusiastically among ourselves about the work we came to do. It felt like endless possibilities were out there, waiting for us to dream of and share with the world. The encounter with the South African archbishop elicited a sense of optimism that the seemingly bleak situation in Palestine can be transformed into hope, liberation and reconciliation.

The mood changed entirely when the group arrived at the next site, the black township Gugulethu, which was a 'dumping site' for 'surplus people', as non-whites were sometimes called, from the Cape Town area.[17] After we assembled in what seemed like a central open-air shopping centre and were introduced to Mbongeni and Mcedisi Twaloand from the local anti-eviction campaign we were led through streets of vast residential areas. These streets were lined with modest-looking small houses, occasionally surrounded by dry and yellowing shrubbery. Local residents came out and gazed at us curiously; children waved hello. It was only later, once we learned more of the local race relations and politics, that a few members of the delegation realised that the attention we undoubtedly attracted during our visit in Gugulethu and elsewhere was largely due to the fact that onlookers 'read' us as a racially mixed group of whites and coloureds, a rare sight in South Africa, especially in the townships. Later, Janet, a Palestinian from Jaffa, shared her daunting experience with the rest of the group. She recalled a local woman approached her and asked whether she is looking for a maid, since she happens to be quite good

---

[17] Gugulethu, located about 15 kilometres outside of Cape Town, was founded when Langa, another area strictly designated for blacks only, was deemed overcrowded. Gugulethu, like many other townships outside the Bantustans, was established for those non-whites employed in European-only areas and were economically dependent on Cape Town. For a more comprehensive analysis of forced removals and the formations of townships and Bantustans, see Desmond Cosmas, *The Discarded People: An Account of African Resettlement in South Africa* (Harmondsworth: Penguin, 1971); Laurine Platzky and Cherryl Walker, *The Surplus People: Forced Removals in South Africa* (Johannesburg: Ravan Press, 1985). Two decades after the abolition of the apartheid regime, though, Gugulethu is still economically depressed and largely dependent on Cape Town, see Annika Teppo and Myriam Houssay-Holzschuch, 'Gugulethu™: Revolution for Neoliberalism in a South African Township', *Canadian Journal of African Studies*, vol. 47, no. 1 (2013), pp. 51–74.

at cleaning houses. That moment, she concluded, was when she realised the relativity of whiteness. She, who has been identified as the nonwhite 'other' of the Jews her entire life, was suddenly read as white in a different context. The whole experience at the township (and later on at the refugee camp) made her feel uneasy, even angry.

> I feel we experience everything from the perspective of poverty and wretchedness; we are made to see how poor these people are instead of focusing on anti-poverty action. I am experiencing all this from the perspective of a white person which means self-righteousness and self-flagellation.

Sivan remembered how passers-by in Cape Town's city centre used to curiously gaze at her whenever she went out with the Palestinian members of the group. At first, she had not realised the reason for that unwarranted attention, until

> I was shocked to find out that people look on and made comments because I happen to be white in the company of dark-skinned people ... it happened to me repeatedly. There were comments and gazes all the time. Once, a woman asked me how I relate to them [the Palestinians] and I realised I am the only white woman in the street accompanied by brown people.

The question of race, and the differences between South Africa and Palestine in that respect first emerged during that first day in Gugulethu. The local activists led us to a dilapidated windowless house where we were graciously welcomed by 'Noma' China, a middle-aged heavy-set woman. The house felt stifling in the oppressive afternoon heat, and countless flies were buzzing about, occasionally perching themselves on two infants sleeping soundly on the floor. Noma explained that twenty-nine people lived in this two-room dwelling, and that they all faced forced eviction. She was speaking in one of South Africa's many native languages, her speech translated for us by one of the local activists who accompanied us. Like millions other blacks and South Africans of colour, Noma was uprooted from her original community and ended up transferred to this racially segregated township during the apartheid era. She explained she had no desire to return, because her original community was long gone and, in the meantime, a new one had sprung up there, in Gugulethu, one with a powerful sense of mutual responsibility, local pride and social cohesion. Noma's rejection of the idea of a 'return' to a 'place of origin' points to the ways in which such notions could be complicated: is the place in which one (or one's ancestors) was born a marker of 'origin' that should be retrieved by all means? What does it mean to 'return' to a place that is lost in the present and that has become 'alien'? Noma's insistence on the primacy of community and forms of solidarity crafted out of experiences of displacement indicate, then, the importance of considering present attachments and social ties, in a manner that is similar to members of Zochrot's critique of Alessandro's plan for Jaffa I quoted above.

When I stepped outside for a breath of fresh air, Eitan whispered to me that he overheard the Palestinian members comparing the scene at the township to their own refugee camp existence. 'It's like looking at the mirror,' they said, 'except here is far worse.' The Palestinians in the group identified with both the histories of uprootedness they share with township dwellers, as well as the consequent emerging of new forms of solidarity and community, but they were also taken aback by (what seemed like) lack of rage and collective struggle. Instead, they interpreted the scene as one of acceptance of the current situation and a general sense of resignation. By the end of the visit, the Palestinian group, inhabiting a history of mutual assistance, collected donations on behalf of the family in order to get their windows fixed. This sense of recognition by Palestinians seemed to dwell on past experiences of displacement, framed as similar to their own. Yet, as we shall witness below, later discussions of return reverted to an uncomplicated notion of a 'place of origin', largely glossing over Noma's emphasis on present communal ties.

The next day the delegation visited a refugee camp located at Mandela Park.[18] Driving through green hills and majestic trees, the landscapes suddenly shifted as the camp appeared over a ridge. As we approached, we could make out a few miniscule brick houses amidst a mishmash of rusty steel freight containers.

---

[18] According to the UN Refugee Agency (UNHCR), there are over 900,000 refugees and asylum seekers currently in South Africa from countries such as the Democratic Republic of Congo, Burundi, Zimbabwe, Ethiopia and Somalia. This already vulnerable population has been under periodic threat of xenophobic violence from South Africans; see Michael Neocosmos, 'The Politics of Fear and the Fear of Politics: Reflections on Xenophobic Violence in South Africa', *Journal of Asian and African Studies*, vol. 43, no. 6 (December 2008), pp. 586–94, as well as the UNHCR website for figures: http://www.unhcr.org/pages/49e485aa6.html.

We were first led to a building that housed what seemed to be modest offices and a meeting room. There, we were given a presentation by Braam Hanekom of PASSOP (People Against Suffering, Oppression and Poverty) and a local activist, a migrant from Nigeria, who explained the camp was now home to persons displaced internally as well as from neighbouring countries, and that cohabitation has produced waves of intra-camp violence. Naji, the prominent activist at the Deheishe refugee camp in Bethlehem, keenly interrogated our hosts about communal activism. He later admitted to me it was an 'emotional moment' for him exactly because he suddenly identified certain similarities between the refugees and IDPs of Mandela Park and Deheishe, where he had also served on the local popular committee.

Although Palestinian refugees in particular (and in a different way, the rest of us) acknowledged familiarity in the status of refugeeness, they also articulated an acute sense of difference. Naji, for instance, described their situation as 'much harder' than the refugees in Deheishe and the rest of the camps in the West Bank. During a later meeting, he also explained that whereas all camp dwellers in Palestine and elsewhere in the region are Palestinians, in South Africa it seems refugee camps are much more ethnically diverse and therefore lacked social cohesion. As an organiser in his own camp, he also noted the absence of a system that works with refugees, like UNRWA, which, among other things, established schools in Palestinian refugee camps.

As we were walking through the camp, occasionally stopping to photograph the dilapidated shipping containers-cum-dwellings, we all agreed the living conditions at the camp are beyond wretched. Clothes hung on makeshift laundry lines outside, in the streets and between houses, sometimes on the barbed wire fence surrounding the camp. A child locked behind steel bars that separate his container-home from the dusty alley; a young woman, who introduced herself as Fortunate, invited me into her home, which was a windowless boiling-hot container, where she lived with her young son. I asked her how long she has been staying at the camp, and she answered: five years. I hurry back outside to the unpaved street to escape the stifling interior, ashamed at my bodily reaction. We keep walking around; some of us are having their photographs taken with local children, who smile at the strangers' cameras. I suddenly felt like a colonial tourist, voyeur and consumer of third world misery, my whiteness as a marker of self-congratulatory benevolence.

I returned my camera to my backpack and kept looking around. This tour and the performance of poverty echoed Janet's critique of the particular framework which was imposed by the local organisers. Leading the group through 'landscapes of despair' was designed to elicit certain kinds of reaction, and, as I learned later, to enhance the liberatory narrative of the ANC, which many of our interlocutors, active in the camp, were affiliated with (at the time unbeknownst to members of the delegation).

Months later, after the Zochrot members' first visit to Deheishe refugee camp and my own sojourn in Balata, I was able to reflect more on the differences between these sites. During an interview in her university office, on a hot summer day, Sivan articulated my thoughts:

> The differences are striking. At the Palestinian refugee camps one constantly senses the spirit of resistance with the [anti-occupation] graffiti, the look in people's eyes when they notice a Jewish visitor at the camp, powerful pride and dignity. Here [in South Africa] people have given up.

What Sivan (and others) interpreted as the absence of resistance was apparently filled with the hope of receiving charitable donations from Western NGOs. Some of the small brick structures at the Mandela camp were donated by Dutch and other European philanthropic societies. Local activists doubled as agents of the state, as they were also members of the ANC and towed the party line rather than voice an opposition. One cannot help but ponder the difference between the ANC, revered as the 'liberation party', voted into power through general election, and the feeble Palestinian Authority, still doing the bidding of its colonial occupier and whose nominal president is forced to obtain special permits from Israeli authorities whenever he wishes to cross the separation barrier.[19]

District Six Seen through Palestinian Eyes

On one particularly hot summer day, our joint delegation was driven to District Six, which used to be a residential area at the heart of Cape Town, until its 60,000

---

[19] Yet, at the same time, the ANC has been the focus of intense criticism for its neoliberal policies, lack of transparency and ample corruption. See, for instance Olivia Lannegren and Hiroshi Ito, 'The End of the ANC Era: An Analysis of Corruption and Inequality in South Africa', *Journal of Politics and Law*, vol. 10, no. 4 (2017), pp. 55–9.

ethnically and socially diverse inhabitants were forcibly removed following the 1966 Group Areas Act.[20] This brutal expulsion was followed by the razing of the majority of the structures, with the exception of houses of worship.[21] One of them, a former church, is now home to the District Six Museum.[22] As soon as we walked in, we were overwhelmed by a plethora of images, exhibits and printed data that fill the place. We found ourselves walking aimlessly, trying, in vain, to absorb as much as possible. Despite the valiant efforts of the museum's curator, who did her best to impose some semblance of order and coherence onto the museum and the ways we experienced it, most of us felt disoriented.

Climbing to the gallery, I noticed the museum's floor was covered by a map depicting a network of roads, streets and alleyways. The map was adorned by quotes on its edges, written with colourful markers by community members and visitors. Significantly, countless markers of places were also handwritten on the map: locations of stores, schools, playgrounds and lost homes. This elaborate memory map was prominently located at the heart of the museum, where all visitors had to pass. Most other exhibits, such as street signs, maps and blow-up images, were hanging on the walls, arranged by certain organisational logic (thematic or chronological); other smaller items, such as house keys, children's toys and silverware, carefully selected by professional curators, were exhibited in glass cases. The memory map, however, was handwritten by multiple lay-people, eschewing stylistic conventions, hierarchies of taste and of importance and curatorial commonsense. Furthermore, whereas exhibits were commanding respect and distance, the memory map was asking, demanding even, to be

---

[20] District Six was one of forty-two areas where populations were forcibly removed around the Cape Peninsula along the Table Mountain range. See John Western, *Outcast Cape Town* (Cape Town: Human & Rousseau, 1981); on the group areas act, see Alan Mabin, 'Comprehensive Segregation: the Origins of the Group Areas Act and its Planning Apparatuses', *Journal of Southern African Studies*, vol. 18, no. 2 (1992), pp. 405–29.

[21] Deborah M. Hart, 'Political Manipulation of Urban Space: The Razing of District Six, Cape Town', *Urban Geography*, vol. 9, no. 6 (1988), pp. 603–28.

[22] Charmaine McEachern, 'Mapping the Memories: Politics, Place and Identity in the District Six Museum, Cape Town', *Social Identities: Journal for the Study of Race, Nation and Culture*, vol. 1, no. 3 (1998), pp. 499–521; Ciraj Rassool, 'Memory and the Politics of History: in the District Six Museum', in N. Murray, N. Shepherd and M. Hall (eds), *Desire Lines: Space, Memory & Identity in the Post-Apartheid City* (London: Routledge, 2007), pp. 113–28.

Figure 6.1 District Six memory map covering the floor of the museum. (Photo by the author.)

defiled and stepped on by visitors. The small space was inhabiting shreds of past lives, frozen in time, rearranged according to professional conventions; the floor memory map was, perhaps, District Six's way of defying that process of museumisation, a way of making itself once again visible, rematerialising through its own rubble. For Palestinians, the creation of the District Six Museum as a project by a displaced community that insists on preserving the memory of everyday living in a working-class urban neighbourhood was understood as the display of *sumud* (Arabic, 'steadfastness'). One form of *sumud* is the production, often using meager resources and amateur work, of memorial books dedicated to specific ethnically cleansed communities, displaced during the Nakba. The commemoration of the everyday, both by Palestinians and former residents of District Six, not only preserves fond memories of communal solidarities, but also symbolically reconstitutes these communities despite their dispersion.[23]

[23] On Palestinian memorial books, see Rochelle A. Davis, *Palestinian Village Histories: Geographies of the Displaced* (Stanford: Stanford University Press, 2011). The District Six Museum, much like the Palestinian memorial books, was very much a community project

Blown-up portraits of former residents adorned the gallery, facing the inner central space of the museum, and haunted us with their powerful phantasmic presence. A shiver went down my spine; I felt their eyes on my back whenever I turned away, pleading to be acknowledged, demanding their tragedy remembered. A quote on a wall above an array of black and white photographs caught my eye. I scribbled it hurriedly in my notebook: 'It struck me that our history is contained in the homes we live in, that we are shaped by the ability of these simple structures to resist being defiled.' Raed, a Palestinian citizen of Israel and a member of the Zochrot group, who was eyeing the same exhibit offered an explanation: 'I think it means no matter where they exile us to, we carry memories of home with us, even if we are forced to leave over and over again.' The question of attachment to one's home was one that kept resurfacing throughout our entire stay in South Africa. As I discuss in Chapter 7, during the heated debate over the drafting of the 'Cape Town documents', it was the question of 'the second occupant' that flared up repeatedly in the debate and elicited the most passionate reactions. This question of multiple attachment and the translocality of diasporics and refugees will come up again in the final chapter, as I discuss the engagement of Palestinians with the question of return to Jaffa after decades of urban transformations.

At the same time, this inscription also echoed a sentiment similar to the one articulated by Noma, who defined 'home' relationally rather than through the rigid linearity of 'a place of origin'; home, after all, is where 'our' community resides. This communal sense of belonging, though, inhabits contradictions: one can sense and articulate a deep affective attachment to one's lived spaces and those who inhabit them as a shared communal form of identification. At the same time, one can also articulate belonging to an abstract cross-border and generation community, by invoking shared histories of displacement and violence. Raed himself embodies this complexity: as a Palestinian who remained and became an Israeli citizen, who is deeply attached to his village of birth, located in the 'triangle', where his extended family still resides. But at the same time, he articulated a profound acknowledgment of shared history and

---

that was denied significant state funding, unlike Robben Island, where 'community' eventually stood for 'the nation'. See Annie E. Coombes, *Visual Culture and Public Memory in a Democratic South Africa* (Durham, NC: Duke University Press, 2003), pp. 118–21.

identity with Palestinian refugees. The Nakba was not an event that occurred to others a generation ago. In a real sense, it happened to him as well.

Gugulethu and District Six, then, highlighted the complexities of multiple attachment to place produced by displacement: on the one hand, refugees like Noma, who relates to place *in situ*, are 'working through' the trauma of dispersion by forging affective attachments with those who surround them; on the other hand, people, like Palestinians, who have experienced repeated displacements, have shown creativity by maintaining their attachment to lost places: through the organisation of space in refugee camps,[24] organising heritage trips for their descendants (see Chapter 4) or connecting with other exiles through the internet.

For the Palestinian members of the group, then, the museum served as what Navaro-Yashin called 'affective spaces' that exude a melancholia over a lost home and a yearning desire to reclaim it.[25] However, when we were taken to the vacant grounds that used to be District Six, the way we affectively experienced the open urban space radically changed. Under the blazing midday sun and punishing humidity, we were led through a plateau dotted with rubble, fragments of household items and personal belongings and exposed foundations. Some of the items were identifiable from our everyday life: a broken toilet here, a rusting old pot there; most remains though seemed like undistinguishable piles of garbage. Eitan Bronstein, founder of Zochrot, pointed to what seemed to him like the remains of streets. I followed these remains, which transformed the open field into a blueprint of a once lively neighbourhood, with a network of smaller alleyways off a wide thoroughfare, probably a busy local business district, teeming with shoppers, housewives and toddlers on their daily afternoon stroll, and noisy traffic. Our guide was Aslam, a former District Six resident who fought back tears as he was pointing to where his grandmother's house used to stand and where he spent countless afternoons playing with the neighbourhood's children. 'It felt like a tour of Zochrot,' mumbled Eitan, and those members of the Tel Aviv group within earshot silently nodded. Indeed, the resemblance to Zochrot's trademark Saturday Nakba tours was uncanny: carefully treading among rubble, listening to the

[24] Peteet, *Landscape*.
[25] Navaro-Yashin, *Make-Believe Space*, pp. 161–2.

stories of the witness-refugee and reflecting about the bleak reality of the state that ethnically cleansed vast populations and then refused to allow them to return. For us Israelis, District Six was an environment of destruction and loss that discharged melancholia and even despondency. Yet surprisingly, for our Palestinian counterparts, these landscapes scarred by forced removals and state violence invoked a sense of hope, even elation. In the outskirts of the area, revealed Aslam, new homes are being built for District Six returnees, some of whom have already reclaimed their keys from government officials in a formal ceremonial return, an annual ritual commemorating the anniversary of the neighbourhood's destruction. Silently, Salah kneeled down and inscribed on a large slab of concrete '*a'idun*' (Arabic, 'returning') and 'we will' in English (see Figure 6.2). He then took out the Palestinian flag from his backpack, proudly standing upon a nearby rock, joined by Naji and Nidal who chanted together 'from 'Ajur to District Six, we will return'. The rest of us watched them, tears in our eyes, cameras at hand (see Figure 6.3).

Following this symbolic act of solidarity, and still attempting to grapple with his emotions, Eitan posted the following text in his blog:

> I lived here, in District Six, until I was ten years old / My parents were born here, in 'Ajur village.
>
> Our house was near the northern edge of the neighborhood. The whites lived on the other side of the street / My father explained that our house was in the southern part of the village.
>
> Today, as you can see, there's a small parking lot there, and a wall / You can see that only a heap of stones is left.
>
> The area remained empty, so we can return, and we will. My father filled out the application forms and I hope he'll soon build us a new home in District Six / I want to return to Ajur even though I was never there. I'll return with my wife and daughters.
>
> My father was in jail because he was active politically against apartheid / I was jailed by Israel for activities opposing the occupation.
>
> The neighborhood will develop and again be inhabited by people of different backgrounds, like it was when I was a child / I want to live here along with my neighbors from the 'Aida refugee camp. Jews will live near the village, as in the past.

FEELING PALESTINE IN SOUTH AFRICA | 175

Figure 6.2   The inscription '*a'idun*' on the ruins of District Six. (Photo by Amaya Galili.)

Figure 6.3   Waving the Palestinian flag in District Six. (Photo by the author.)

> Aslam Levy talks to us as he stands next to a map of the District Six drawn on the floor of the museum at Cape Town that preserves its history. He cries when he remembers how his family tried to keep him from knowing his father was jailed / Salah Ajarma is filled with optimism when he sees a new neighborhood arising from the rubble of the one destroyed by the apartheid regime. Cape Town, 6/2/2012.[26]

Though this passage was based on what Salah and Aslam shared with the delegation, Eitan created an imagined dialogue using the first person 'I' between two refugees at the point of intersection between the places they were forced to leave behind and became inaccessible to them. District Six and 'Ajur partially merged and became a space of hope for both, a vantage point from which they could both imagine better futures for themselves and others, refugees and colonisers alike. Thus, the pile of rubble in the open field elicited fantasies of future for these three men, Aslam, Salah and Eitan, who imagined this conversation taking place at the site ('here'). Yet, this imagery also produces a reversal: the two refugees are reconstructed as mobile, en route back to their lost place of belonging, when, in our present reality, refugees and internally displaced persons are often confined to spaces of uprootedness, like refugee camps (which is indeed where Salah resides), their mobility severely confined by transnational aid regimes as well as states' security apparatuses. Eitan, the Israeli Jew whose mobility is unrestricted, reimagined himself here as staying in place, the 'white Jew' who will remain in the city and may live 'nearby' the returnees.

The differences I observed between the Palestinians' and the Israelis' affective reactions to District Six kept haunting me for the duration of my fieldwork. A year and a half later I finally explored the meanings of that site for some of the tour's participants. Naji was enthusiastic when I wrote to let him know I was coming for another visit to Deheishe. Accompanied by a colleague from my own department who was doing his fieldwork in Jerusalem at the time and had never visited the camp, we headed to Deheishe by public

---

[26] The English translation of this blog has since been taken off the internet, but this entry is still posted in Hebrew: Eitan Bronstein Aparicio, 'The Distance between 'Ajjur and District Six', *Zochrot*, 6 February 2012, http://zochrot.org/he/article/53404 (last accessed 7 January 2022).

transportation on a sweltering late summer day. I was keenly aware that as an Israeli citizen, I am not allowed to travel to Bethlehem, so we had to avoid the direct bus and opt for a different route: from Jerusalem to Beit Jala, and from there to Deheishe by taxi. Naji greeted us in his small office at the Lilac centre, located at the bottom edge of the hillside camp. He offered us coffee, and spoke at length about the centre, its activities and the international volunteers staying there. Occasionally, people kept coming in and interrupting us, and Naji, apologising each time, resumed his impassioned speech. When I asked him about District Six, he explained: 'A few years ago we visited Deir Aban (his ancestral village) and we carried the Palestinian flag with us. It [District Six] was the same,' immediately correcting himself, 'it felt the same.' Then he made an observation that escaped me during our visit to District Six:

> When you look, you can see white people living in the mountain and it's the same with the Jewish colony in Deir Abban ... I know it's different in South Africa, but those people [refugees from District Six] are thinking about this place, and ... thinking about coming back.

'In this case,' I asked him, 'how come you seemed to us so elated?' Naji grinned, as if he had heard the question before. 'People always ask us [Palestinians] how come we smile when we talk about Palestine ... We know our story, we are connected to the land, and we are living here.' For Palestinian refugees like Naji and Salah, then, the remains of District Six represented sites of memories of loss and spaces of hope – it is where their own ancestral villages, now demolished and inaccessible to them, and the neighbourhood that was depopulated intersected and converged. Landscapes of ruins turned into itineraries of expulsion but also of return. It was in Cape Town that Palestinians (and in different ways, Israeli Jews) were prompted to remap local, national, regional and global spaces. Where officially sanctioned maps drew borders, erased histories and life worlds, our own 'being in space' brought to our lines of vision places of old and those that have yet to be created, superimposed on one another. Our affective experiences in Western Cape gave new meanings to Alessandro's 'stereoscopic vision'; for a moment in District Six, traumatic memories and hopes for a future projected different places into one space: Naji's Deir Aban, Salah's 'Ajur, Manshiyyeh (for many of the Israeli Jews, including myself) and District Six itself.

The ways in which we experienced affect differently in District Six (and throughout our visit) were further elucidated by 'Umar. 'Umar, a Zochrot employee and a key figure in other return planning projects, was also the leader of the NGO's Jaffa group, and, together with Bassem from Badil, was also in charge of the South Africa itineraries and schedules imposed by our KAIROS hosts. I interviewed him in the offices of Zochrot, shortly before an event, as people occasionally shuffled into the adjoining meeting room and waved us hello. When I asked him about District Six, he explained that the elation I noted and was baffled by was because of the Palestinian flag:

> We experienced a flash as we heard a name of a place there that sounded like 'Ajur, which is when a refugee from 'Ajur [Salah] waved the Palestinian flag. [Unlike his village of origin], that [i.e District Six] was a space where that act was allowed, and [the sight made them] feel pride. The place reminded them of 'Ajur, and they can see it's in ruins, but there were also other possibilities nearby. There was hope not too far from the destruction ... and it made them feel hopeful.

The 'flash' 'Umar was referring to is the moment in which landscapes transform and merge with each other, as a new and unfamiliar place imbued with a new-old meaning. It becomes a place that is intimately familiar, even if one, like a Palestinian refugee, has never actually inhabited it. That 'flash' is the affective engagement of humans and sites, like a switch that goes off in one's imagination and sends electrical currents through one's body. 'Umar was not just referring to a cognitive act of meaning-making through comparison ('this site is similar to another'), but to an embodied response to a realisation, to being in place, that sends jolts of affect through the body, processed and generated emotion. For the Palestinians in the group, those emotions were hope and pride. For the Israeli-Jewish members, a mixture of despair, melancholia, and even doubt.

Sivan, for instance, reflects on her experiences in South Africa as saturated with melancholia. The museum, she said, attempted to promote a progressive narrative – from racial oppression, through apartheid to liberation and redress. However,

> you did not solve any of the problems! That area [where District Six used to be] remains vacant! It was a testament to everything that is not resolved ...

then when we walked around there I found it hilarious – that Nakba village in the midst of Cape Town.

The hilarity Sivan cited also denotes a sense of familiarity and commensurability. As a member of Zochrot, she had also visited countless destroyed Palestinian villages and towns during the Saturday tours. But for Sivan, that recognition, the same 'flash' that went through 'Umar and the other Palestinians produced a sense of despair and doubt, cynicism even. She could not, or would not, see 'other possibilities nearby' as genuine forms of redressing injustice. The melancholia shared by other Israelis in our group was a way to make sense of the commensurability (or 'cultural intimacy') of the landscapes of destruction and loss, their intersection with sites we frequent and silenced histories we are vocal about. Yet this familiarity was also coupled with realisation of the failures of the new regime in South Africa, our sense of dystopia and urban terror. Every night, members of the group ventured out to remove themselves from conversations about the day's events and the urge to process and work through their emotions. The double iron gates, surveillance cameras and security protocols at the guesthouse were our first introduction to what I come to consider 'dystopic urbanity'. Members of the delegation, both female and male, could not shake the feeling of imminent danger – of sexual violence, assault or robbery, and we were constantly warned by our hosts to avoid venturing out by ourselves. At different moments during the visit, we were wondering aloud whether this is how postcolonial Palestine might end up looking: crime-ridden, violent, with ever-increasing social disparities. This shared sense of melancholia can perhaps, then, be attributed to these darker sides of liberation as well as implicit and explicit fears, often voiced by Israeli Jews about being engulfed by the natives, taken over by demography or the return of the refugees. In one of Zochrot's events, someone sarcastically called this 'fear of the invasion of the barbarians'. This remark, although made in jest, perhaps to lighten a tense moment of heated discussion, conveys the coloniser's anxiety of the revenge of the coloniser, articulated by Frantz Fanon in *The Wretched of the Earth*. Decades of forced evictions, underdevelopment and incarceration would be avenged tenfold upon liberation, when the colonised, outnumbering his oppressor, finally rises up to rid himself of the occupier. In this dystopic scenario, the colonised is the one to determine the price for the horrors of occupation – claiming the coloniser's city, home, even the body of his wife as his own.[27] In this particular context, the Israeli Jews of Zochrot and their supporters, who embrace the right of return of the Palestinian refugees and undertake the task of imagining it, are articulating concerns about the future of the former-colonisers. While they reject the racist undertones of the demographic discourse perpetrated by the Israeli state, Zochrot members are keenly aware that dismantling the current regimes of power and colonial privileges would mean having to consider the possibility that some of the returnees might simply not want them around, and that reconciliation may be a challenging task.

Conclusion

Earlier in this chapter, I referred to the unexpected way by which a moment of recognition and the acknowledgment of the uncanny congeal to reveal 'horizons of possibility'. I was referring to a 'flashlike' recognition of what we did not realise was there prior, something that is new and yet painfully familiar. This sudden 'flash', as my analysis showed, is embodied and deeply affective, the moment participants in this tour identified the uncanny resemblance between places and along itineraries. Focusing on the ways in which place is affectively experienced made visible those moments of flashlike recognition of the uncanny and – significantly – the political valence of this embodied response. I argue that the lens of affect enables us to explore the ways in which Palestinians and Israeli Jews visiting Cape Town differentially identified and reacted to similarities and differences between Palestine and South Africa; recognising the uncanny resemblance made those two places commensurable, or, to quote one Palestinian member of the group, 'it felt the same'. For a few short weeks, Cape Town became a stage on which the future of Palestine played out, at least in our minds. But at the same time, Cape Town is a real place with its own complex history, which we knew very little of. In the preparatory meetings prior to our excursion, there was no systemic discussion of the colonial history of South Africa, the violent apartheid regime or its aftermath. In the final analysis, then, perhaps the 'uncanny resemblance' that we identified is rooted more in the primacy of the apartheid analogy in activist circles, and

---

[27] Frantz Fanon, *The Wretched of the Earth*, trans. Constance Farrington (New York: Grove Press, 1963), p. 39.

the ways in which the Palestinian members of the groups experience Israeli apartheid. This might also explain the responses I observed among the Israeli members of the group, myself included: as part of the colonising society, we are not on the receiving end of the apartheid regime; we are its beneficiaries. Moreover, like Ari said (quoted earlier in this chapter) in a moment of honesty (but in the absence of our Palestinian counterparts): 'if the return doesn't actually happen it would not be a great disaster'. All of us were, and remain, deeply committed to decolonisation and the implementation of the right of return. But Ari articulated the experiential fissures within the group and how this coloniser/colonised divide accounts for our radically different affective reactions that I described in this chapter.

The impulse of making the two sites commensurate is more than just identifying the familiar and uncanny in a history of racial segregation, forced removals and brutal political control; this recognition also provides Palestinians with a toolkit to challenge the settler colonial 'new normal' and forge a sense of hopefulness, a horizon of liberation that was made possible elsewhere, and can materialise in Palestine as well.[28] This is a payoff that is mostly closed off to Israelis, who are allies but not active participants in the resistance movement.

And finally, the south-south encounter of the kind I described here is productive beyond the bequeathal of resources of collective anticolonial resistance. Perhaps its most powerful, far-reaching political implications lie in the potential to create trans-regional conversations between formerly and currently colonised peoples over the heads of their colonisers. Earlier in this chapter I described how Eitan, an Israeli Jew, fantasised about a conversation between Aslam and Salah; the South African 'coloured' and the West Bank Palestinian refugee find common ground in the experience of displacement and draw on each other's histories in ways that are inaccessible to Israeli Jews, who are left outside the conversation. The force of this encounter and its potential can explain the outburst of optimism and elation expressed by the Palestinians in Cape Town, which evaded the Israelis who remained dwelling on the hurdles and impossibilities. While the remainder of this book focuses

---

[28] Another source of such potential encounter is with African-Americans: Rami Younis, 'Watch: Lauryn Hill, Angela Davis call for Black-Palestinian Solidarity', +*972 Magazine*, http://972mag.com/watch-lauryn-hill-angela-davis-call-for-black-palestinian-solidarity/ (last accessed 26 May 2016).

on the coloniser–colonised dynamics and the potential for their undoing, and the next chapter foregrounds the question of post-liberation 'living together', it is worthwhile to consider what the Cape Town journey implies not just for the anticolonial struggle in Palestine, but for potentially rethinking the circulation of ideas and the remaking of globalisation in the image of human solidarities, or what the Zapatistas, in the 1996 Fourth Declaration of the Lacandon Jungle called the 'international of hope':[29] unity that transcends and overcomes both national boundaries as well as the 'globalization of misery', the working of transnational bodies that regulate and control human activity, maintaining global resources and economic power in the global north.

---

[29] 'The Millennium Arrives: January 1, 1994', quoted in Rebecca Solnit, *Hope in the Dark: Untold Histories, Wild Possibilities* (Chicago: Haymarket Books, 2016), p. 45.

7

THE PALESTINE OF TOMORROW

> Why therefore should I not dream and Hope? For is not revolution the making real of dreams and hopes? So let us work together that my dream may be fulfilled, that I may return with my people out of exile, there in Palestine to live with this Jewish freedom-fighter and his partners, with this Arab priest and his brothers, in one democratic state where Christian, Jew and Moslem live in justice, equality, fraternity and progress.
>
> Yassir Arafat, UN address, 1974[1]

Shortly after our return from Cape Town, we heard that the Tel Aviv municipality had decided to name a small turnabout in Jaffa after Dr Fouad Dajani (1890–1940), scion of an elite family, a physician and Palestinian medical pioneer who had lived nearby. The roundabout is located right behind the Dajani family home and hospital founded by Dr Dajani. Both have been repurposed by the state and are used today as a geriatric centre. The ceremony was planned to be a public affair in the presence of the extended Dajani clan, including the physician's surviving son and his grandchildren, several of whom

---

[1] 'PLO Chairman Yasir Arafat: Address to the UN General Assembly (November 13, 1974)', in Walter Laqueur and Barry Rubin (eds), *The Israeli-Arab Reader: A Documentary History of the Middle East Conflict* (New York: Penguin Books, 2008), p. 181. Arafat makes references to Udi Adiv, an Israeli Jew convicted of treason and espionage for Syria, as well as to Bishop Hilarion Capucci, convicted by Israel of assisting the Palestinian resistance to smuggle arms.

were allowed back into the country for the first time.² A group of Zochrot activists, both Palestinian and Israeli Jews, planned to attend the ceremony and call for the implementation of the right of return rather than tokenising the Dajani family and the Palestinian-Arab history of the city in order to curry favour with Palestinian voters.³

Our group took position at the periphery of the large crowd, yet clearly visible, holding banners in English, Arabic and Hebrew calling for the right of return. One of the signs provocatively greeted the Dajani family members with 'welcome returnees'. Our presence was quickly acknowledged by members of the audience and the media. We were approached by architect and self-styled 'Tel Aviv expert' Samuel Giller, who, according to his account, facilitated the whole affair. Giller sternly demanded that we leave the scene, claiming that 'such provocations might discourage the municipal authorities from making similar gestures' and that moreover, the Dajani family was 'uncomfortable' with our presence.⁴ His claims were belied by the sheer enthusiasm of all members of the Dajani family, who came to shake our hands, expressing their gratitude, and insisting on having their photographs taken with the group and the banners (see Figure 7.1).

On the surface, this incident is reminiscent of the 'virtual returns' I discussed in Chapter 4; the Dajanis' visit consisted of the predictable elements: strolling the streets of 'Ajami, visiting the old family home and paying respects to their ancestors' graves. Yet at the same time, this 'return'

---

² The Jerusalem-based branch of the Dajani family rejected the invitation and published a public notice in the Palestinian media stating the refusal of the symbolic gesture by the Tel Aviv municipality 'under the Israeli flag'; see Yaffa48, 'Dajani family of the city of Jerusalem announces its refusal to participate in the naming ceremony of Dr. Fouad Dajani roundabout', 16 February 2012, *Yaffa48*, http://www.yaffa48.com/?mod=articles&ID=4934 (last accessed 9 January 2022).

³ Uncoincidentally, municipal elections were planned to take place the following year. Those instrumental in security naming the roundabout, in particular Ahmed Masharawi from Liberal Zionist party Meretz, where hoping to capitalise on this event. His local political rivals, in particular Tajamu' supporters, were conspicuously absent.

⁴ On the role of Samuel Giller behind the scenes of the naming ceremony, see Amir Eshel, *Futurity: Contemporary Literature and the Quest for the Past* (Chicago: University of Chicago Press, 2013), p. 160. Eshel mentions Giller in the context of contemporary Israeli prose on Jaffa and argues that incorporating the Palestinian story does not result in the diminishing of the Israeli self.

Figure 7.1 Members of the Dajani family with an activist from Zochrot. (Photo by Lia Tarachansky.)

was fraught enough to raise the ire of the Jerusalem-based branch of the clan. The Dajanis were *invited* by the Tel Aviv municipality as honoured guests into a well-orchestrated performance designed to cement its image as a 'cosmopolitan' city. Naming the roundabout after Dr Dajani was clearly meant to support the municipal's claim for inclusion of Palestinians in its official narratives, and contribute to marketing the 'new normal' as a success story. Standing for the local Palestinian community, the presence of the Dajanis was meant to symbolise the respect and tolerance of 'minorities' within the urban landscapes and Israeli society as a whole.

Any discomfort felt by the Dajanis themselves, by their own account, was not a result of the presence of a small group of activists who reminded the crowd about the ethnic cleansing in Jaffa and the plight of the refugees. Rather, the cause of their consternation was the fact that they were admitted into their ancestral homeland by virtue of an official invitation from what they see as an occupying authority.[5] The Dajanis' itinerary also included a visit to their old family home in Jaffa, not far from the roundabout and the hospital, where a Palestinian family now resides. The current occupant, a man by the name of Ramzi Jun, attempted to overcome the awkwardness by greeting the Dajanis: 'this is your home ... we will be honoured to welcome you here'.[6]

The Dajani incident, and in particular the hostile responses and discomfort of several Jewish members in the audience (as well as mayor Ron Huldai, who was quick to leave the scene) point to the profound anxiety prevalent in Israeli society surrounding the Nakba and the right of return. The Tel Aviv municipality celebrates diversity and cosmopolitanism, as long as its 'others' remain absent, or, at the very least, are briefly feted and then leave.[7] The longer those absentees linger, the more tangible their presence, as neither the settler colonial nor the Zionist nationalist logic can tolerate their claims to place. Furthermore, those Palestinians who are rooted in place and continue to live in Jaffa are considered either impediments to gentrification and urban renewal, or a source of political and social anxiety. Outside election season, Jaffa's Palestinian population and its needs are systematically neglected by the municipal authorities.[8] The group that picketed the ceremony consisted of those of us who had just returned from Cape Town.

---

[5] The visit and ceremony were documented by a family member and Dr Dajani's namesake: https://youtu.be/DSVPWF_yc-M.

[6] 'Immortalizing the Memory of the late Dr. Fouad Dajani by naming a roundabout in what remains of Jaffa after him' [in Arabic], 29 February 2012, *al-Quds*, p. 6.

[7] This dynamic is somewhat similar to the deliberate erasures of Turkey's 'others' from nationalist urban histories, but at the same time using 'traces of minority pasts' to celebrate an urban cosmopolitan culture. See Amy Mills, *Streets of Memory: Landscape, Tolerance and National Identity in Istanbul* (Athens, GA: University of Georgia Press, 2010).

[8] One such ongoing needs is a better local education system. Palestinians and Jews in Jaffa have been locked in a bitter struggle against the municipality over the city's bilingual education system; see for instance, Yarden Skoop, 'Tel Aviv backtracks, will not open bilingual school in Jaffa', *Haaretz*, 30 January 2015, http://www.haaretz.com/israel-news/.premium-1.639812 and Yarden Skoop, 'Parents and Tel Aviv Municipality in a row over the Bilingual education in the city' [in Hebrew], *Haaretz*, 28 January 2016, http://www.haaretz.co.il/news/educa tion/1.2833104 (last accessed 26 May 2016). In addition to Jaffa's education crisis, there has always been a shortage of accessible public transportation, and the majority of Palestinians who reside in Ajami and Jabaliyyeh are forced to walk considerable distance to Jerusalem Boulevard in order to catch a bus to Tel Aviv. Current municipal plans for the construction

We were in the midst of deliberating and writing our reports, and the obvious Israeli-Jewish anxious response to our intervention gave us pause. Additionally, the Dajanis' visit to their home currently occupied by another Palestinian contributed to heighten our sensitivities to the complexities of the process of decolonisation and return, including, for instance, questions of generational differences and what we came to frame as the 'secondary occupant' (see discussion below).

The purpose of this chapter is *not* to chart out a systematic vision or plan for the 'morning after' the return of the refugees, nor do I intend to grapple with the countless logistical issues that are part and parcel of a process of mass repatriation. Furthermore, none of the following directly addresses the question of how things will come about: what might be the political process that eventually leads to the final breakdown of settler colonialism in Palestine and precipitate the return of the refugees. Instead, in this chapter, I am attempting to probe the potential for 'living well together'. The aim is to tease out potential futures, and point to the way both Palestinians and Israeli Jews might engage in 'forward dawning' by imagining and bringing into consciousness that which is not yet here. In fact, by articulating these imaginaries, those who engage with the future already in a way bring it into being, giving it shape and form through language and making these possible futures, potentialities, legible. The vantage points from which individuals are able to imagine these futures, however, are situated in the present and saturated in personal grief and a profound sense of injury. For many Palestinians, the idea of reciprocal exchange with their oppressors, let alone the potential for reconciliation, remain unimaginable, and so is the notion of 'living together' that transcends the present formations of coexistence under colonialism. As I will demonstrate below, some eschew the mere idea of 'living together' and can only imagine a future existence without the presence of Israeli Jews.

First, I will return to the Cape Town 'detour', this time through the tangible products of our visit. Written as part of an ambitious project by Zochrot and Badil, two documents in particular reflect their engagement with the

---

of the light rail system will force Palestinians to traverse even longer distances and considerably limit their access to public transportation during years of construction along the boulevard.

future, one that is concerned with the language of rationality and civility, emphasising civil society and processual thinking.[9]

The next section of this chapter will shift to the world of fiction that, unlike the NGOised report-production genre, has always been the bedrock of human imagination and offers a creative outlet from the stagnant confines of the present into the realm of possibilities. Here, I will offer close readings of two short stories, by a Palestinian and an Israeli Jew, both imagine a post-return reality in Jaffa, but with sharp difference in tone: while the Israeli-Jewish author's engagement with the emergent future reality reflects hopefulness and sheer optimism, his Palestinian counterpart suggests that even when politically the path is open, 'real' return remains impossible. In a sense, literature is where fantasies come alive, because not only do the author's wildest and most profound desires become legible through the use of language and the narrative form, but they also demand the attention of the readers, entice them to entertain, even for a fleeting moment, the possibility of another life, and undermine binaries such as truth/lie, fantasy/reality and self/other. Readers are expected to partake in fantasy and imagine themselves assuming a role in another reality.

A group interview I held with a few of Balata's young men is the centrepiece of the third and final section of this chapter. It elucidates that the conditions of entrenched military occupation and collective trauma may inhibit, even foreclose, refugees' ability to imagine a reality that is the radical other of the life they were born into and are forced to endure. Furthermore, the youth's affective reactions to my questions also illustrate that the practice of 'imagining

---

[9] The genre 'trickled down' from the neoliberal business world, NGOised, and has become a prominent marker of a rationalised form of humanitarianism and other forms of activism. Donor foundations now expect annual reports presented in formats familiar to them and the governmental agencies that regulate them. These formats render information simple and easy to read since it requires short sentences, using a language that has been naturalised in the sphere of NGOs: 'facilitating', 'community-based grassroots initiatives', 'advocacy', 'coalition-building', 'knowledge-building', 'democratically organized', etc. Rationalising the language of humanitarianism, and therefore also activism, bestowing an air of universalism and transparency, obstructs from our line of vision the specific histories associated not only with these phrases, but also their linkages to the spheres of business and government bureaucracies. In fact, although its repeated redeployment creates an effect of coherence and transparency, the rationalised language remains opaque and hinders context-specific meanings. The Cape Town and Jaffa documents then, grapple with the limitations of the genre of 'the report'.

futures' and planning a post-return reality is the purview of the privileged few, who are able to take time away from everyday struggles to survive.

Living Well Together

A few years before his death, Jacques Derrida, who by the late 1990s had become a vocal critic of Israel, engaged with the idea of 'living together' in the context of Palestine. Specifically, Derrida was concerned with the question: how to live *well* together? If we take the present conditions of military occupation, forced displacements and ethnic segregation as our point of departure, then following Derrida, we must ask: how do we change these forms of living together, under settler colonialism and its constant application of violence, to something else, better? Moreover, what does this other, better way of living together entail, and what might it look like? Derrida explored an understanding of 'return' that meant revisiting a traumatic past in order to achieve a sense of closure through repentance and reconciliation. Derrida's idea of return is derived from the Jewish tradition of *teshuvah*, which literally shares the same Hebrew root and means 'a change for the better', or 'a return to oneself'.[10] If we follow his logic, then, the route for a new way of living together in Palestine necessitates reconciliation and forgiveness, which imply forms of reciprocity between colonisers and colonised that would open up possibilities for a better future for both. Indeed, Desmond Tutu, who I mentioned in the previous chapter, has argued that there is no future without forgiveness, a principle that directed his leadership of the post-apartheid Truth and Reconciliation Committee in South Africa.[11]

---

[10] Jacques Derrida, 'Avowing – The Impossible: "Returns", Repentance and Reconciliation', in Elisabeth Weber (ed.), *Living Together: Jacques Derrida's Communities of Violence and Peace* (NewYork: Fordham University Press, 2013), pp. 18–41. A repentant sinner is called *Hozer bi-Tshuvah* in Hebrew, a literal translation of which would necessitate repeating the word 'return', as the roots of both words mean 'return'.

[11] Desmond M. Tutu, *No Future without Forgiveness* (London: Rider, 1999). In this deeply Christian account, Tutu explicates the principles that guided the creation of the Truth and Reconciliation Committee in South Africa with the fall of the apartheid regime. In a similar manner to Derrida, he argues that perpetrators' confession and appeal for forgiveness from their victims is the only way to forge new relationships as individuals and collectives that are radically different than those who caused the injustices of the past. In this formulation, reconciliation is a national project aimed at producing a new society that embraces multiculturalism.

Derrida, however, remained on the abstract level when he spoke of the potentiality for 'living well together' in Palestine. He did not attend to the specific forms of oppression that the state of Israel has imposed on Palestinians, nor to the settler colonial occupation of Palestine, and remained particularly silent about the history of mass expulsions and spatial appropriations, which I discussed in the context of Jaffa in Chapter 2. Understanding histories of oppression is crucial for any discussion about the possibility of reconciliation and 'living well together'. For instance, refugees in West Bank camps have experienced military occupation, while their counterparts in Syria and Lebanon have been multiply displaced as a result of civil wars, revolutions and regime reprisals. Palestinians who remained and became citizens have endured political and economic marginality, and in recent years in Jaffa, as I mentioned in Chapter 5, are under an increasing threat of displacement as a result of rapid gentrification. This is not to argue that 'living well together' is not a useful concept and should be abandoned. Instead, I would like to argue that this approach is symptomatic of the prevailing discourse of 'negotiations' that produces false symmetries between occupied and occupier. This same approach ungirds commonplace notions of 'coexistence', reinforced by NGOs and the 'peace industry'. The symmetrical approach, then, should be overcome by thinking through 'living well together' through the lens of experience, accounting for particular forms of oppression as well as the contingencies of decolonisation.

My discussion of 'living well together' is therefore informed by these multiple histories and the way people relate to them. The possibilities of 'what might be' that I am concerned with here are deeply vexed and are rooted in present political contexts and multiple configurations of power relations, primarily colonial in nature. The long decades of exile have complicated refugees' sense of belonging. As Diana Allan argues, 'while the importance and legitimacy of the right of return is not in doubt, what it means for different generations of refugees, in particular those born and raised in exile, is less certain'.[12] As Quayson and others have argued, exile does not only mean absence from

---

[12] Diana Allan, *Refugees of the Revolution: Experiences of Palestinian Exile* (Stanford: Stanford University Press, 2014), p. 191.

one's 'place of origin'.[13] Dispersed refugees have travelled multiple routes, formed attachments to other places where children were born, immense loss and trauma occurred, and communities created (and dissolved). At the same time, newcomers resettled in places from where Palestinians were expelled, and made them their homes. In other words: since time has not stopped in 1948, we must account for the upheavals and transformations in the life of refugees and settlers alike, including all the places they now call 'home', and those spaces in between.

'If my House Still Stands'

All these considerations were discussed during the final two days in Cape Town that were devoted to the visit's concluding workshop. The joint delegation was divided into three sub-groups, each responsible for what we identified as a significant theme, broadly defined – working toward return, reparations and visions of a new state – then reconvened to share their main conclusions and proposals. While certain issues sparked lively, even heated, debates, others encountered consensus, in ways that were often surprising. The final product, which came to be known as 'The Cape Town document', is representative of the emotional journey undertaken by the delegation, but also reflective of the conundrum of collective imaginary this 'joint action' implies.

The introduction (which was written some time after the Cape Town trip and after the drafts of the other sections were finalised) positions this document on spatial and temporal scales: it charts specific itineraries, from various places in Palestine (and the diaspora) to Cape Town and back; itineraries within the Western Cape which generated particular narratives and insights while, at the same time, potentially hindering others. The introduction also acknowledges the challenge of making a spatio-temporal leap, between present geographical and human terrains, punctured by borders, checkpoints and

---

[13] Ato Quayson, 'Introduction: Area Studies, Diaspora Studies, and Critical Pedagogies', *Comparative Studies of South Asia, Africa and the Middle East*, vol. 27, no. 3 (2007), pp. 580–90; Ato Quayson and Girish Daswani, 'Introduction: Diaspora and Transnationalism, Scapes, Scales and Scopes', in A. Quayson and G. Daswani (eds), *A Companion to Diaspora and Transnationalism* (Hoboken: Wiley-Blackwell, 2013), pp. 1–26; Khachig Tölölyan, 'The Contemporary Discourse of Diaspora Studies', *Comparative Studies of South Asia, Africa and the Middle East*, vol. 27, no. 3 (2007), pp. 647–55.

walls: the territories under Israeli control (both inside 1948 and 1967), and the global Palestinian and Jewish diasporas. The difficulties of 'jointly imagining' and sustainable collaboration between Israeli-Jew anti-occupation activists and Palestinians who live under occupation have perhaps been partially mitigated by the shared experiences in Cape Town, and through the process of group discussions that are based on agreed-upon principles. Indeed, upon our return to Palestine, it was Naji who revealed to me that he considers Jewish members of our group closer to him than some of his Palestinian neighbours, a sentiment he probably would not have been able to share had it not been for this collaborative work in South Africa and beyond.

The document acknowledges the different ways in which participants engaged the challenge of imagining a post-liberation future: while for Israeli Jews, imagining a return may represent an outlet for a quest for justice, a possible avenue of political activism or merely an intellectual exercise, for Palestinians, particular those who live in refugee camps and/or under Israeli military occupation, the act of imagining means leaping over the daily struggle for liberation, overcoming injuries and working through trauma in order to envision a yet unformed future where not only the injuries cease, but one in which perpetrators and victims work towards reconciliation. These disparities are also clearly illustrative of the ways in which imagining futures is a privilege most colonised are deprived of. As I quoted Ari in the previous chapter, if the return does not occur, it's 'not a big deal' for 'us'. Israeli Jews can afford to preserve the status quo (and therefore their settler colonial privileges) and treat projects such as this one as an exercise of utopian thinking. For Palestinians, particularly refugees who live in the West Bank and contend with everyday forms of oppression, the threat of imminent violence, restrictions on movement and the struggle to maintain a semblance of normality leave very little space, time and resources for fantasy. Those very few Palestinians who participated in this project were able to do so because they were extracted from their everyday contexts into a different place where the act of imagining was made possible, and where they were able to engage in fantasy with members of the settler society.

At the same time, this project is not about decontextualised fancy or mere intellectual exercises; our extraction from the immediate context of life in Palestine along the coloniser/colonised divide was also a process of recontextualisation – in the sites in which we visited, but also affectively, with other places we imagine as eerily similar, just like Salah likened District Six to his ancestral village of 'Ajur, and the same site prompted the Saturday Nakba tours for the Israelis in the group. Thus, this document is very much a product of a particular moment, at the intersection of people and places, along specific itineraries. Nevertheless, the cultural intimacy that elicited our visions of the future also revealed the cleavages within the delegation, between colonised and members of the colonising society.

The basic premise of the Cape Town document is that there will be no forced removals, and that evictions of residents from their homes do not constitute a just solution. Moreover, the document advocates both actual and symbolic unsettling and 'overthrowing' geographical, ethnic and spatial boundaries, and props up the idea of 'mixing' as a strategy to overcoming colonial anxieties. Postcolonial de-Zionided society will thus eschew ethnic and racial enclaves, transforming Jewish-only locales (the way Tel Aviv is imagined today by the state, municipality and its residents) into shared communities.

Arguably, the most contentious point and a subject for a heated debate was the issue of 'the second occupant', shorthand for cases where the original pre-Nakba house is still standing and is currently occupied by someone who purchased it in good will. The guiding principle and the ideal resolution in these few cases is to prioritise a mediated and consensual solution, as long as the right to housing is guaranteed for both the Palestinian returnee and the current occupant. The declaration held the view that whereas legal title of the property reverts back to the original owner, it is the state's duty to find housing for the 'second occupant' and their heirs even when no agreement is reached.

The issue of 'the second occupant' proved to be the flashpoint for the question of collective imagining. As soon as the group introduced the topic of the 'second occupant', Salah's facial expression and demeanor suddenly changed; he interrupted the presentation and, visibly upset, exclaimed 'if my house still stands, I don't care who's in it. I just want my house back.' Salah's emotional reaction and his adamant refusal to debate the issue are indicative of the intimate attachment of refugees to memories of home, as a marker of justice, and a place of intimacy and security. Salah has never actually lived in the (hypothetical) house in question, yet he passionately claims his right of ownership and attachment to it. Nevertheless, as other discussants indicated, the so-called 'second occupant' also maintains their own attachment to the same house. These moments of unbridled affective outbursts disrupt the notion of 'joint action', and prove to be an unexpected result of a process aimed at producing a coherent vision for the future.

The Trouble with 'Mixing'

The question of a shared vision also inhabits another concern: what about those who are imagined as part of this future society, but who are overlooked, their desires and fantasies ignored or not taken into account? One of those groups is the population often referred to as 'second and third Israel', namely the Mizrahim, who are imagined in this document as a frontier contact zone in the post-Zionist polity. If the state of Israel settled them along its borders as a reluctant civilian policing force against Palestinian returnees,[14] the Zochrot-Badil document implicitly relegates them to a similar role, though for the opposite purpose. What I mean by that is that the document imposes on the Mizrahim the role of avant-guard postcolonial 'mixing'. Presently, most urban, semi-urban and rural communities within both the 1948 and the 1967 territories were designed and are maintained as either exclusively Arab or Jewish. Even within the so-called 'mixed cities' residents are spatially distributed by ethnicity and class.

Monterescu and Hazan argue that the nationalisation of space has also meant that even within a mixed city, physical proximity notwithstanding, neighbours are viewed as distant political and cultural 'others' to the point that any discussion of cohabitation in 'symbolic space', that is, bridging this imagined distance, is impossible.[15] This symbolic distance was particularly poignant when, during the summer of 2011, a coalition of Jaffa residents and social justice activists formed the tent encampment protesting government and municipal policy of house demolitions and mass evictions from public housing.[16] Notably absent from this celebration of protest were the impoverished Jewish

[14] See, for instance, Ella Shohat, 'Sephardim in Israel: Zionism from the Standpoint of its Jewish Victims', *Social Text*, no. 19/20 (1988), pp. 1–35.
[15] Haim Hazan and Daniel Monterescu, *A Town at Sundown: Aging Nationalism in Jaffa* [in Hebrew] (Jerusalem: Van Leer Institute and Hakibutz Hameukhad, 2011).
[16] Daniel Monterescu and Noa Shaindlinger, 'Situational Radicalism: The Israeli "Arab Spring" and the (Un)making of the Rebel City', *Constellations*, vol. 20, no. 2 (2013), pp. 1–25.

Mizrahi working-class neighbourhoods (Yafo Gimel, Yafo Dalet). Thus, symbolic distance overpowered class solidarities and inhibited a joint struggle that would have benefited Jewish and Palestinian residents both.[17]

The Cape Town document postulated that 'for the purposes of medium and long-term integration and reconciliation', the new state (or interim authority) is to encourage the creation of mixed communities by offering monetary incentives and housing subsidies.[18] Though not explicitly stated, the population targeted by these incentive packages is working-class Mizrahi Jews (as well as former camp dwellers). The document effectively allows the Ashkenazi middle class to maintain its segregated suburban communities while the Mizrahim would be once again subjected to limited housing choices, in newly constructed mixed public housing and other sites earmarked for this social engineering experiment of mixing. The Mizrahim, in particular those who originated in Arabic-speaking countries, have been forced by the Zionist state to abandon their rich non-Jewish cultural heritage. Adults were socialised through their school-age children to refrain from speaking Arabic (or Judeo-Arabic) or listening to Arabic music.[19] In fact, although certain elements of Arab culture have re-emerged in the past two decades, few Mizrahim would publicly identify as 'Arab-Jews' because of the social sanctions and political ramifications of such an act. Decades of forced alienation from everything Arab, compulsory military service, usually in low-ranking combat roles that entail close contact with the Palestinian population in the 1967 occupied territories, and continuous repression by hegemonic Ashkenazi elites (often identified as politically liberal or leftist) resulted in reluctance and often outright hostility toward Palestinians. A common (mis)representation of working-class Mizrahim (mostly among Ashkenazim) is of extreme right-wingers hurling racial slurs against Arabs. Though exaggerated and de-contextualised, the image of the Mizrahi as an 'Arab hater' is indicative of ethnic class tensions, emanating from state indoctrination and from the brutality of an everyday

---

[17] It is important to note that, briefly, some of the Mizrahim in Hatikva neighbourhood, a working-class area in southern Tel Aviv, joined the coalition with the Jaffa tent encampment on the condition of exclusion of all nationalist claims or symbols.

[18] Zochrot-Badil, *Study Visit to Cape Town* (Zochrot-Badil, 2012), p. 19.

[19] Shohat, 'Sephardim in Israel'; Sami Shalom Chetrit, *Intra-Jewish Conflict in Israel: White Jews, Black Jews* (London: Routledge, 2010).

survival struggle in the lowest social echelons.[20] This form of 'living together' in the sense of physical proximity within overlapping urban spaces is typical in 'mixed cities' such as Jaffa, and has been designed to produce intercommunal tensions. The purpose of this document is therefore to chart possible ways to overcome these forms of vexed coexistence and instead offer imaginaries of better ways to live together. Planning for the future of Palestine, then, must account for these enmities and devise policies to overcome these obstacles.

Although the social integration and reconciliation postulated in the document are desirable ideals, forced mixing might not encourage 'trust among individuals and communities' or 'bolster faith in the process of reconciliation',[21] especially if this mixing is artificially and reluctantly created. This reluctance to mix is often voiced by Palestinian refugees themselves. As we will see later in this chapter, a teen I interviewed in Balata was adamant that there is no possibility of reconciliation with Israeli Jews: 'Has your best friend died in your arms because the soldiers shot him? How could I ever live with these people?' And indeed, in an evening of discussion at Zochrot, a few months before our Cape Town excursion, when we discussed the prospect of return, one of the speakers had asked: 'all fine and well, but what if the Palestinians don't wish to see our ugly faces anymore?' This anxiety is prevalent among Israeli Jews as well as Palestinians. Countless times I have been told by random taxi drivers or store vendors they opted to move out of Jaffa because of the presence of 'Arabs'. When I moved into an apartment in the heart of 'Ajami, a group of Jewish repairmen who spent most of the day in our living room curiously inquired about our experience living in 'this kind of neighbourhood' with 'these people', and whether we were not afraid of a break-in or random acts of violence in the street. These types of utterances are indicative, on the one hand, of the profound sense of enmity that undergirds any kind of social exchange between Palestinians and Israeli Jews. For Palestinians suffering the brunt of military occupation, the experience of 'living together' has been so traumatic that sharing lived spaces with Israeli Jews seems unimaginable. On the other

---

[20] Smadar Lavie, *Wrapped in the Flag of Israel: Mizrahi Single Mothers and Bureaucratic Torture* (New York: Berghahn Books, 2014); Yossi Dahan and Gal Levi, 'Multicultural Education in the Zionist State – The Mizrahi Challenge', *Studies in Philosophy and Education*, vol. 19, no. 5–6 (November 2000), pp. 423–44.

[21] Zochrot-Badil, *Study Visit to Cape Town*, p. 23.

hand, Israeli Jews have internalised the Zionist state's core principle of ethnic and religious separation, and its spatial articulations of walls and fences. This internalisation also manifests in a desire to police those boundaries and maintain the status quo. These acts of policing are performed not just by the state's security apparatus, but by ordinary civilians.

Consider, for instance, one of the gated communities in Jaffa where my friend Ari resides. The complex is surrounded by a wall, and entry is possible only through designated gates with sophisticated electric panels that require a code. When he invited a few Palestinian children from the neighbourhood into the complex to play football, his neighbours were up in arms, denouncing his 'frivolous' act and voicing concerns about the possibility of 'break-ins'. Alternatively, Palestinian interviewees in a short Zochrot documentary filmed in Balata imagined their return into a network of such gated communities, where a wall would be built between them and the Jews. What seems to be absent from this document is a more thorough discussion about the deeply ingrained acceptance of the notion of segregation from racial 'others' and the ways in which a process of 'de-Zionisation' of space would also have to overcome such rooted convictions. At the same time, this perceived embrace of segregationist practices is underwritten by anxieties about self-preservation and cultural survival, especially for the colonised Palestinians.

Conversely, there are also many Palestinians like Naji, who repeatedly claimed: 'I feel closer to my friends from Tel Aviv than to my neighbours from the camp', and that as educated urbanites, he and his grown children would rather settle in Jaffa or Tel Aviv than in his ancestral village of Deir Aban. Consider, as well, 'Adel, who I mentioned in Chapter 4, originally from Abu Kabir neighbourhood in Jaffa and currently residing in 'Askar refugee camp near Nablus who would rather return to present-day Tel Aviv and live in a middle-class Jewish-majority neighbourhood than reclaim his house which is located in a 'slum'.

A Return to the Homeland

Geographer and right of return scholar Salman Abu Sitta has demonstrated that most of the destroyed Palestinian villages remain vacant; many have been simply annexed to kibbutzim or other Jewish settlements and are allocated as land reserves for future expansion, while others have been used by the Jewish

National Fund in their nationwide, vast forestation projects. The process of repatriation to these villages, argues Abu Sitta, should be the least complex, especially in the Galilee (north) and the Naqab/Negev (south), and that moreover, many of their former inhabitants would not even have to traverse vast distances: most of the refugees currently languishing in Lebanon hail from Galilee while those in the Gaza Strip and the southern parts of the West Bank originated in the Naqab region. Abu Sitta is therefore mainly concerned with the reconstruction of destroyed Palestinian villages and towns for the benefit of 'their' returnees.[22]

Zochrot and Badil's line of thinking offered an alternative: rather than recreate lost communities, it proposed taking into account realities on the ground, as well as the trajectories of refugees' lives. Thus, for instance, former peasants and their descendants have long abandoned the *falahi* lifestyle, and settled into their urban (proletarian) lives instead. In the 1950s, successive Israeli governments determined that Mizrahi Jews must all be 'natural peasants' and sought to resettle them in remote agricultural settlements, expecting them to tend to livestock and toil the land. These assumptions utterly ignored the large percentage of urban, middle- and lower-class Jews from the Maghreb (Morocco, Tunisia, Algeria and Libya) and the Fertile Crescent, especially Iraq. Bitter lessons learned from the Israeli experience require us to attend to contemporary experiences of refugees in whatever scenario of return.

Over the past few decades, refugees have built lives, created communities and called many other places 'home'. Imposing a 'return' to a place most have never known, and that looks nothing like the memories of elders, might not make sense to refugees. The pre-Nakba village cannot be resurrected, nor can Palestinians be forced to give up powerful attachments created in years of exile and to dissolve communities that crystalised in the camps and the diaspora. Attending to all this and to the will of the refugees themselves, Zochrot

---

[22] For Abu Sitta's ideas about the logistics of return and resettlement, see his *From Refugees to Citizens at Home: The End of the Palestinian-Israeli Conflict* (Palestine Land Society and Palestinian Return Centre, 2001) available online at https://www.plands.org/en/books-reports/books/from-refugees-to-citizens-at-home; 'The Implementation of the Right of Return', in Roane Carey et al. (eds), *The New Intifada: Resisting Israel's Apartheid* (New York: Verso, 2001), pp. 299–319; and his 'The Feasibility of the Right of Return', *ICJ and CIMEL*, June 1997, http://prrn.mcgill.ca/prrn/papers/abusitta.html.

and Badil proposed a return to the *homeland*, that is, the territory that used to be Mandatory Palestine, stressing routes over roots, lived experience over memories.

This approach offers several creative possibilities for refugees. For instance, provisions should be made for those who wish to exercise their right of return and those who do not; the latter could opt for a Palestinian citizenship, some in addition to the one they already hold from another state.[23] Those refugees who belong in the first category and wish to take residence in Palestine should be free to choose whether they wish to resettle in a new returnee community on the lands of their ancestral village, joining a Jewish settlement built on the lands of a former village thus making it a 'mixed community', or an existing Palestinian town. The shifting political realities in the entire region will also alter received spatial configuration; thus, for instance, a person can reside in Jerusalem but travel to Amman for work, since crossing borders will become routine practice. The flexibility of this approach will not only cater to returnees' needs but is also in line with the principle set by Zochrot and Badil (and inherent in the concept of transitional justice), firmly rejecting any further displacements, including those of Israeli Jews.

Returning to Jaffa

The follow-up document to the Cape Town document, which was publicly launched on Nakba Day 2013, focused on Jaffa and Tel Aviv. Zochrot's work in South Africa opened up possibilities of imagining the future of Jaffa-Tel Aviv while physically situated in the city and embedded within urban culture elicited concrete and place-specific imaginaries. The intimate familiarity of the group's members with these urban spaces elicited fantasies that completely transformed them in their minds to fit the new political realities: the 'green house' at Haj Kahil roundabout, a majestic villa at the heart of 'Ajami (see Figure 7.2), overlooking several falafel and shawarma places (all owned by the formidable Haj Kahil clan), where traffic often comes to a halt and

---

[23] See Lex Tekkenberg, 'The Search for Durable Solutions for Palestinian Refugees: A Role for UNRWA?', in Eyal Benvenisti, Haim Gans and Sari Hanafi (eds), *Israel and the Palestinian Refugees* (Berlin: Springer, 2007), pp. 373–86, as well as Yoav Peled and Nadim Rouhana, 'Transitional Justice and the Right of Return of the Palestinian Refugees' in the same volume, pp. 141–58.

Figure 7.2 The 'green house' at the heart of Ajami (built 1934), until recently used as a military court. (Photo by Haim Schwarczenberg, 2014.)

pedestrians scramble to safely navigate among the cacophony of honking impatient drivers, functions as a local courthouse to judge Israeli war criminals; the former site of the IDF museum, near the historic railway station in Manshiyyeh, as a memorial of the atrocities of occupation; the army radio station (Galatz) at Yehuda Hayamit Street, which leads from Jerusalem Boulevard (the epitome of modern Jaffa) towards the old port, as a local news station that would broadcast Arabic music.[24]

Although these locations were repeatedly discussed during the group's meeting, the Jaffa document focuses on one particular location: Beit Gidi, or the Etzel museum, located at Charles Clore Park in the area which was built on Irshid, a northern suburb of Jaffa. The structure is comprised of two main architectural elements: a modernist steel and glass cube superimposed on a

---

[24] For many years Galatz has been famous for its refusal to broadcast Mizrahi music, and was critiqued, among other things, as the bastion of the ruling Ashkenazi elite. Although in recent years it seems it has conceded and added selected Mizrahi music to its playlist, it never plays any Arabic music, despite the fact it is located at the Heart of Jaffa, surrounded by Palestinian residents.

stone Arab house, a scene of further symbolic violence wreaked on the battered city of Jaffa.[25] Because it is the only surviving pre-Nakba structure on the beach (with the exception of the Hassan Bek Mosque located nearby), participants reimagined Beit Gidi as the prototype of the new site of memory and a community centre. Its location and current use fuelled our planning: from a museum that commemorates occupation and its perpetrators, we willed it to become a site of remembrance of loss but also of return, an architectural embodiment of urban history and hopes for the future. Optimistically we envisioned the building in relation to its historical surroundings – the railway station across the street, which we planned as part of the complex. The two could be connected by underground passageways. These 'Manshiyyeh tunnels' were to be made of glass, so that visitors and passers-by will be able to view the remains of the neighbourhood homes, buried underneath the park. The group's members envisioned the historical museum section of the complex to be underground, the main floor would be dedicated to the present, and the top – to the future. The complex was going to be fitted with a glass roof, where visitors would be able to view the open sky but at the same time be shielded from the sun and the rain. And finally, the refurbished building should also include a spatial element linking it to the Mediterranean, symbolically reconnecting exiled *Yafawi* Palestinians back to the sea, from which many used to derive their livelihood prior to 1948, and by which many escaped and were expelled during the Nakba.

The most important factor in the building's redesign would be its embeddedness within the community. This multi-purpose complex would house community services attracting returnees, professionals, a tourist information centre and a point of departure for Nakba tours, and above all – a safe space for public performance addressing trauma and healing. In this context, healing means a process by which suffering as victimisation would be worked through and 'renounced' in order to forge a truly shared new urbanity.[26] 'Healing of

---

[25] Sharon Rotbard, *White City, Black City* [in Hebrew] (Tel Aviv: Bavel), pp. 235–40.
[26] This 'ethos of trauma' has been critiqued by indigenous scholars as an 'economy' that accompanies neoliberalism and that, in the final analysis, expects indigenous people to move on from injury without resolving its root cause, i.e. colonial violence. See, for instance, Dian Million, *Therapeutic Nations: Healing in an Age of Indigenous Human Rights* (Tucson: University of Arizona Press, 2013).

Figure 7.3 'Beit Gidi' – the Etzel (Irgun) Museum in Irshid. The base, the only surviving house in the entire quarter is used today as a site celebrating the city's fall and destruction and commemorating its conquerors. (Photo by the author.)

memories', then, are processes both separate, serving the needs of each community, and shared, where victim and victimiser mourn multiple losses: Palestinians would be encouraged to mourn the obliteration of their pre-1948 lifeworlds, but also of the new communities they had forged in the decades since – in exile, in refugee camps, along itineraries, even within 'landscapes of despair'.[27] Jews, on the other hand, should be allowed to reflect on the loss of the Zionist sociopolitical order, the only one they had known, which at the same time hinged on suffering as identity-endowing, and on the other hand, provided them with the power to dispossess and do violence unto others.

Even with the absence of Badil (who were not part of this section of the project), the problematics of 'joint action' or collective imagining resurfaced.

---

[27] The notion of 'healing of memories' is based on our experience at the Institute for Healing of Memories in Cape Town. See https://healing-memories.org/.

'Umar, for instance, argued that we had created a very 'Israeli' document which deploys

> psycho-social thinking, which I am not sure should be presented to the refugees. I am not sure they would accept the notion of 'healing' but instead maybe 'a new beginning', 'adjustment', and so on. The approach here creates a symmetry between the two sides, for instance, acknowledging each other's mourning. At present time, this symmetry is rather problematic. Even the creation of joint communities does not necessitate joint healing processes. These can be separate and respond to each sides' needs ... Besides, I am missing a more detailed description of the new society. How do you envision the transformations of Israeli society and culture?

'Umar voiced a concern about the idea of 'travelling theories', or the tacit assumption that ideas and notions, such as the 'healing of memories', can somehow travel and that they migrate between contexts. Walter Mignolo, for instance, argued that theoretical concepts are rooted in 'emotional foregrounding' or local sensibilities that link the body to specific places.[28] In this case, the complex concept of healing, with its particular dynamics that are rooted in specific histories of psychology, may resonate with a particular, middle-class segment of Israeli-Jewish society, but may seem alien and moreover – an imposition – not just to Palestinians, but also to many Mizrahi Jews who have been excluded from academic circles and from 'new age' trends. As I noted earlier, it will be Mizrahi Jews who might be positioned in the borderlands and contact zones of urban neighbourhoods that will inhabit returnees. Perhaps there should be further consideration about the ethics of 'mixing', spatial (re)designing and the politics of hope.

Finally, the issue of 'the second occupant' created a moment of disruption within the Zochrot group as well. 'Umar once again exhibited unease: 'but what about the refugees' lands? Why would the [Jewish] residents of Ramat Aviv remain in houses built atop these lands ... the right of the refugee over his land should be recognized.' Sivan attempted to explain that we should strive to avoid creating new forms of social injustice by avoiding emphasising

---

[28] Walter D. Mignolo, *Local Histories/Global Designs: Coloniality, Subaltern Knowledges and Border Thinking* (Princeton, NJ: Princeton University Press, 2000).

private property and that in fact we should focus on questions of reparations. Suddenly, the discussion takes a turn to the intimate and personal. Sivan explains that her parents 'worked very hard all their lives to afford their home in Ramat Aviv, and therefore it would be a gross injustice to force them to relinquish their right to their apartment, including the right to bequeath it'. 'Umar disagrees and insists ownership should revert to the refugee in all cases. Sivan is visibly frustrated: 'this in fact revokes the understandings and solutions agreed upon in Cape Town', she passionately argues, trying to reason with 'Umar. We take a vote. Most Jewish members of the group vote with Sivan, while the Palestinians side with 'Umar. The meeting is adjourned with obvious unresolved tensions in the air. The group never revisited the issue again.

Once more, the specific nature of 'return' and the question of a 'place of origin' proved to be the fault-lines between Israeli Jews and Palestinians. In Cape Town, it was Salah's emotional outburst refusing any compromise with the 'second occupant' that revealed a cleavage within the idea of 'joint action': for members of the colonising society, the notion of 'return' represents an opportunity for creativity, reconfiguring spaces of belonging, a position that enables ideas of symbolic returns. But for the displaced, like Salah, whose mobility is restricted by a security apparatus designed to keep him in place, it is a lost ancestral place that is an object of desire, an actual locus of hope and not merely a symbolic gesture.

The Jaffa document was eventually launched as part of Zochrot's activities for Nakba Day on 15 May 2013. The event was held at the Saraya theatre in the old city of Jaffa. Janet, who was the presenter, could not hide her excitement. After saying a few words in Hebrew, she switched to her native tongue of Arabic:

> Perhaps one day I will be able to speak in either language and everyone in the audience will be able to understand ... We are gathered here this evening to mark 65 years of the Nakba, not to mourn, but to speak about the vision for the return of the refugees. I wish to open with a story [about my grandfather] ... everything I know about this city comes from him. During the war, they [his family] sent him to Egypt on a ship, thinking he would return later. But he understood he would not be able to survive with only

one Lira, and therefore jumped ship, headed back to the port, and this is how we remained in Jaffa. It is difficult for me to speak of him, and I am anxious. This coincidence always perplexed me; I could not understand how come we remained here. This is not a story of heroism or courage, but of coincidence. Like many other residents I was preoccupied planning to leave because the reality here is unbearable. I escaped to the US to study, and there I understood what refugeeness feels like. I missed Jaffa, its scents and people ... Those of us who remained, are here, but the glory of Palestine had dimmed after the Nakba – the culture, books and scents – those kept vanishing. I hope tonight we will give back to Jaffa its pride and honour my grandfather used to speak of. Discussing the return will revive the possibility and the dream to return to Jaffa.

Janet's tearful speech invokes the rationale for our project: imagining the return of the refugees is a project designed to elicit discussions, as unresolved as they may be, and through them to also open 'cracks' in the walls of separation and silence, which in turn, become part of the 'cluster of promise'. Sites of enunciation, whether they are in Tel Aviv, Jaffa, Deheishe or Cape Town, or even the texts themselves as they circulate and generate a new kind of discourse – making the return thinkable within growing publics – bring into being that which is 'not yet here' and transform into spaces of hope. At the same time, these documents and the discussions around them reveal the tensions and potential pitfalls of the process of planning and the eventual return: decades of occupation, dispossession and refugee life have left their marks on both the settler and returnee society, and these fissures will have to be taken into account as well.

The New Manshiyyeh

The bilingual edited volume *Awda, Imagined Testimonies of Possible Futures*, which was launched at Zochrot's return conference I mentioned at the start of Chapter 5, advanced the NGO's work further by offering a broader readership through tangible and deeply personal narratives of post return 'experiences'. These experiences reflect the wide array of responses by Palestinian and Israeli-Jewish authors to the idea of radical post-liberation transformation, forcing them not only to make the temporal leap I mentioned earlier, but to position their imagined selves within a reality that has yet to emerge, and that moreover most people dismiss as an impossibility. In what follows, I will discuss two short stories from this volume, by an Israeli Jew and a Palestinian, that directly address the imagined futures of Jaffa. My discussion will pay special attention to the particularities of both visions, the emplacement of the respective protagonists and the ways these authors approach the possibility of return.

Tomer Gardi's 'A Story from Manshiyeh al-Jdeideh' deliberately confounds the reader with the dizzying interchange of temporalities, gender and truth claims: which parts in all this can be true? To confuse us even further, Gardi pauses to stress that every part of the story is pure fiction, yet at the same time, he mentions at least two very real people: Samir al-Youssef and his novel *The Illusion of Return*, and Zochrot's 'Umar al-Ghubari who co-edited the book *Awda* with Gardi. He even mentions 'Umar's embodied response to Gardi's joke, and his scowl, familiar to all who know him.[29] The reference to Samir al-Youssef's novella is especially instructive. Al-Youssef, originally a camp refugee, published *The Illusion of Return* in English, obviously intended for broad audiences. As the provocative title suggests, the right of return, held sacred by Palestinians, is dismissed by the story's protagonist as an 'unrealistic' idea that should be replaced with an unspecified form of a 'symbolic return'. Later in the story, the protagonist's collaborator friend Ali is articulating a similar idea that was instilled in him by his Jewish friend Bruno:

> It's a one-way journey! ... [A]s for those who claim to return to a place where they never were ... they are simply confusing the symbolic and metaphorical with the possible and actual ... The idea of a right of return in such a case is, he believed, no more than a claim on the past – the near or faraway past – and perhaps the only possibly legitimate claim for those who are faced by the inhospitality of the world. The idea of return is actually an attempt to escape the inhospitality of the present state of the world – the discrimination and persecution.[30]

---

[29] Tomer Gardi, 'A Story from Manshiyeh al-Jdeideh' [in Hebrew], in 'Umar al-Ghubari and Tomer Gardi (eds), *Awda: Imagined Testimonies of Possible Futures* (Tel Aviv: Pardes, 2013), p. 182. My transliteration of the place's name is faithful to the original text rather than the standard IJMES rules of Arabic-English transliteration.

[30] Samir al-Youssef, *The Illusion of Return* (New York: Melville House, 2007), pp. 144–45.

Articulating a 'failed nationalist' voice, like the majority of the characters, al-Youssef grapples with the right of return as an impossibility for Palestinians; significantly, he considers the locus of enunciation of Palestinian return advocates, namely, those refugees who have been confined to the camps, unable to migrate or assimilate. Al-Youssef, the author, was even more explicit:

> The idea that every single person whose parents came from Palestine should have an automatic right of return is ridiculous. People who make that claim don't give a toss about the refugees, whether Palestinians live or die, they just to continue the war with Israel ... I don't believe in the right of return, he says, and don't want to return, but I do want an acknowledgment from Israelis that I don't come from nowhere.[31]

Later in the story, as I discuss below, it is the fictionalised al-Youssef that becomes the plot's catalyst, as Gardi reveals that in his imagined future, al-Youssef was proven wrong by the (relative) success of the return project, and eventually settled in Haifa himself. That Gardi consciously chose to challenge an outspoken Palestinian critic of the right of return is by itself significant. As an Israeli Jew, Gardi claims that an acknowledgement of injustice is not sufficient redress, and that moreover, as a member of the settler society, he is taking upon himself the burden of finding a way out of the present impasse and imagines a future that is not only simply 'not yet' here, but that many, including Palestinians like al-Youssef, are not even capable of conceiving.

Gardi opens his story with an anecdote that could be real and that he actively tries to convince us has occurred: finding al-Youssef's book in a second-hand Tel Aviv bookstore in what seems like the present day.[32] The store's owner priced the book higher than it should be because of a handwritten dedication by the author to an unknown Lisa. In jest, Gardi proposes to change his own name to Lisa to make the steep price, 100 NIS (New Israeli Shekels, the official currency), worth his while.

---

[31] Mathew J. Reisz, 'Samir el-Youssef: At Home with the Heretic', *The Independent*, 18 January 2007, http://www.independent.co.uk/arts-entertainment/books/features/samir-el-youssef-at-home-with-the-heretic-432650.html (last accessed 10 January 2022).

[32] Gardi mentions the book he was editing, *Awda*, which ostensibly locates the bookstore anecdote firmly in present times, i.e. before the return.

And so, the next time the story returns to al-Youssef, Gardi has morphed into Lisa. When the story picks up again after the interlude of meeting 'Umar, the male protagonist is now female, and the story takes place in the future, in the 'new Manshiyeh' of post-return Jaffa. Manshiyeh al-Jdeideh is, apparently, the creation of 'ridiculous architects', an artificial island overlooking the old Manshiyeh, which, we are made to assume, is now repopulated with returnees. The island's 'mixed diasporic' neighbourhood is a new, yet crowded, residential area that houses returnees and old-timer Palestinians and Jews, 'full of complaints and happy'.[33] Gardi implies that everyone on the island remains a refugee: they can see Jaffa from the sea, from the point Palestinians gazed upon the city the day of their expulsion – and Jews, as they migrated into Palestine. At the same time, their unique vantage point also endows them with a particular identity: being there, and/of Jaffa, and not in it. Only a bridge connects the new Manshiyeh to the mainland, a tangible marker of the 'ridiculousness' of the existence of the island, but at the same time reflects a necessity: the Jaffa-Tel Aviv metropolis continued to attract migration after the return and planners were forced to resort to creative housing solutions.

At the same time, Gardi implies that living on the artificial island would not be anyone's preference, and that in addition to the crowdedness, the neighbourhood also housed several 'cheap bars' but 'no money'. Manshiyeh al-Jdeideh then is a working-class neighbourhood where those down on their luck found cheaper accommodation in a neoliberal housing market. The joy of return was marred by the decisive victory of neoliberalism over its political opponent, anarcho-communism, which resulted in the production of a highly stratified society: affluent elite returnees managed to restore their previous economic status, while the huddled masses of former peasants and tenants were squeezed once again into the economic and political margins.[34]

---

[33] Gardi, 'Manshiyeh al-Jdeideh', pp. 184–5. Gardi uses the biblical word *Sha'atnez*, referring to the divine prohibition to wear garments containing wool and linen together. Its usage here denotes mixing of two things that should not be united, perhaps hinting at the inherent difficulties of imagining a post-return reality and the challenge of overcoming the colonial logic of segregation.

[34] The monetary currency in this post-return reality is the *khubeizeh*, the popular Arabic name for a species of mallow, an edible plant indigenous to Palestine used in various dishes. *Khubeizeh* is the poor man's bread, *khubz* in Arabic.

Despite these structural inequalities, when Gardi scales down to the personal, it is clear that in the realm of the social, the return utterly transformed the life of both Palestinians and Jews, returnees and old-timers. First, the ethnic and sectarian organisation of space that currently undergirds the colonial Zionist order was replaced with what seems like a normative approach to mixing. But, as I cautioned earlier in this chapter, the poor and the economically disadvantaged face few choices and usually end up living within working-class enclaves. Still, when Lisa is faced with the challenge of treasure hunting, the first person she turns to for help is Manar, her Palestinian neighbour. Manar's immediate agreement to drop everything on a moment's notice and accompany her neighbour further attests to a sense of closeness between the two women. This is also the final tone of the story: Gardi stresses that once they ran back across the bridge onto the island, they both stopped and gazed into each other's eyes, a gesture demonstrating their affinity and sense of intimacy.[35]

Samir al-Youssef, the author whose novel launched this story, became a protagonist in Gardi's fantasy, just like Lisa from the book's dedication. Al-Youssef's dismissive approach towards the possibility of return in 'our' present reality is belied by his return to Haifa in Gardi's story. Moreover, in this alternate future, al-Youssef is an editor of a volume not unlike *Awda*, except that in his case, the prose is to document and testify to the actual return rather than 'possible futures', whereas Lisa (a female version of Gardi) is a freelance writer, literally starved for employment. The paths of the two intersect again when al-Youssef calls Lisa and offers her to contribute a story for his edited volume. When Lisa demands compensation, al-Youssef, after an initial enraged refusal ('you Jews have only money on your mind!'),[36] proposes to guide her to a treasure his grandfather hid in a wall in their Jaffa home before they left in 1948. Lisa, suspending her disbelief, accepts the barter, enlists her friend Manar and together they head to the house in question, now owned by a rich French Jew by the name of Jean-Louis, who they convince to join the treasure hunt.

---

[35] In fact, Gardi repeats the last few words twice, *Isha Be'eyney Hashniyah* – [one] woman [gazing] into the eyes of the other.
[36] Gardi, 'Manshiyeh al-Jdeideh', p. 183.

Lisa, Manar and Jean-Louis' efforts come to naught, however, when their persistent attempts to tear the house's walls in search of the treasure bring about the collapse of the entire house. The collapse of the house marks the end of the story and gestures towards a contradiction already present in the story: on the one hand, it was the former home of the al-Youssef family, representing Palestinian Arab rootedness in Jaffa that survived the Nakba, the Israeli occupation and the eventual return. Its destruction then is a powerful symbol for the final abandonment of the myth of 'paradise lost' prevalent among diaspora Palestinians today; it is a departure from a traumatic past in the form of a house that has haunted the Israeli-Jewish psyche with the notable absence of its original owners. On the other hand, the fact that in the story, the house is owned by a French Jew, an agent of neoliberal gentrification and dispossession, represents a flicker of hope for Gardi. The destruction of the house through the collective effort of two women, a Palestinian and a Jew, with the aid of a greedy French occupant, hints at a possibility for another, more egalitarian future, where social relations can flourish in the absence of state-imposed segregation and class solidarity can score occasional victories even against hegemonic and powerful neoliberal power structures.

The Closing of the Path

Contrary to Tomer Gardi, who has spent most of his life in Israel (but now resides in Berlin), Husam 'Uthman, author of 'Our Father's House', was born in al-Yarmuk refugee camp in Syria, and resided in several different countries before being allowed back into Palestine and settled in Ramallah as a result of the Oslo Accords.[37] This poignant 'return' at the sufferance of the occupier, which left him few choices, also severely limited 'Uthman's mobility: the return foreclosed travel across the Middle East and North Africa and confined him to the West Bank, where he is encircled by the separation barrier, a network of checkpoints and a strict permit regime.

'Uthman also dwells on real and symbolic itineraries traversed by his protagonists, brothers Saleh and Shweikat, as they travel between the Jalazun refugee camp near Ramallah to Jaffa and back in order to stake their claim to their

---

[37] Juliane Hammer, *Palestinians Born in Exile: Diaspora and the Search of a Homeland* (Austin: University of Texas Press, 2005).

family's home in the old city. The first thing they notice is how empty the road seems without Israel's military presence. The observation and the initial arrival into Jaffa's iconic clock tower square fill the brothers with joy and longing for their deceased father, who experienced the horrors of expulsion. But soon thereafter, as their vision is adjusted to see what is there rather than how it used to be 'before', doubt creeps in. And the seed of doubt grows over the course of the story until it completely takes over Saleh's horizon and expectations and effectively results in a 'blocked path'.

Already on their way to Jaffa's post office, presumably the historical building in today's Jerusalem Boulevard, Saleh notices the presence of 'light-haired' Jews and wonders where they fit in the new order: 'could they be our neighbours?' Unlike Gardi's Lisa and Manar, sharing urban spaces or a homeland with the former colonisers is not an option Saleh welcomes. He is further taken aback by the presence of 'light-haireds' at the office for returnees claims and opts to speak only with a 'woman of eastern, Arab, facial features, whose dark hair marks her as a true daughter of Jaffa',[38] and whose presence alleviates their consternation. When he gets back to Jalazun, his wife Amina exacerbates his anxiety, warning him that the Jews at the claims office might steal the *kushans* (land deed documents) he left with them, steal their property and turn them into eternal refugees. The possibility of losing their claim would then confine them to the refugee camp indefinitely without a glimmer of hope of getting out. This anxiety is rooted in the desire to strip their refugee status and stake a claim to the place where they believe they belong:

> From now on, we will not be called refugees and the only blue colour remaining for us is the colour of the sea. No more UNRWA clinics and hospitals, not more refugee camp committees. This, here, will be our homeland. This is where the dream ends and reality begins.[39]

Returning to Jaffa and locating his family's property does not allay his anxieties. On the contrary; perhaps echoing Kanafani's *Returning to Haifa* that I discussed in chapter three, the longer he spends on the road to his ancestral

---

[38] Husam 'Uthman, 'Our Father's House' [in Arabic], in 'Umar al-Ghubari and Tomer Gardi (eds), *Awda: Imagined Testimonies of Possible Futures* (Tel Aviv: Pardes, 2013), p. 82.
[39] Husam 'Uthman, 'Our Father's House', p. 83.

home, the farther his destination seems. Thus, for instance, he wonders what would become of the Jewish settlements that puncture the Palestinian landscapes and whether their occupiers would just leave the country, now that its 'true' sons and daughters are back to reclaim it. Moreover, he discovers that his family's house, like that of his acquaintance's Abu Rashid, is currently occupied by a Jewish family, and that it may take elaborate litigation to take possession of it. A large portion of land belonging to his family is lost to a paved asphalt road. Even meeting Haim, an Israeli Jew who had supported the return and believes in a democratic state for all, does not cheer him up: if there are so many bureaucratic hurdles to claiming my home, 'what do I get out of it?' he wonders.[40]

It is at the moment of realising the refugee's dream, that Saleh realises that the 'paths are closing in his face',[41] and the future he had hoped for disappears. The dream of return was never to become a reality. Even when political circumstances made the return a possibility, for the refugees themselves, the dream turned into a nightmare:

> I don't know whether to return there or remain here [in the camp]. This is where I was born, grew up and came of age. Here everyone is family and friends. Over there, everyone will be family and friends, but I will be the stranger, son of a foreign land.[42]

This sense of strangeness of Palestinian returnees echoed Gardi's story as well: Samir al-Youssef was a 'migrant returnee', relocating to where he had never left, just like 'Uthman himself. These two short stories could not be more different in tone; Gardi, the Israeli Jew, wholeheartedly embraces the fall of settler colonialism and the return of the refugees, even if the outcome is far from ideal. Jaffa of tomorrow is a place of contradictions, tensions of class, and a lingering sense of exile, but at the same time, it is, as Lisa 'testifies', a 'happy' place that enables forms of social interactions unavailable under Israeli colonial rule. 'Uthman, on the other hand, articulates a desire prevalent among Palestinians in the diaspora, who have not had sustained and meaningful social

---

[40] Ibid., p. 88.
[41] Ibid., p. 88.
[42] Ibid., p. 88.

interactions with Israeli Jews (that were not uniformed soldiers): that the liberation of Palestine would entail the departure of the Israelis who have settled in the country from 1948.[43] This departure is perceived as a zero-sum game, where Palestinian absence depends on Jewish presence and vice versa. It is the inability to move beyond this fantasy and acknowledge that while Palestinian society was refashioned by exile, Palestine itself has irrevocably changed by decades of settler colonial rule and mass Jewish migration. This realisation drives both Saleh and 'Uthman to conclude bitterly that exile has become homeland, and that the dream of return is merely a pie in the sky, so unrealistic, in fact, that by the end of the story, Saleh is grateful his father, of *jil Filastin*, is deceased and was not forced to accept the bitter reality.

From Balata to Jaffa?

The fate of the settlers also loomed large in conversations I had with people in Balata refugee camp. On one particular occasion, I conducted a group interview with Muhammad, Ihab and 'Anan, three young men between the ages of nineteen and twenty-three. I had met them at the Yafa Cultural Centre, and during a rare lull in my usually hectic schedule of visits and interviews with elderly refugees, Ahmad, the camp's 'fixer', suggested I speak with some of the young men and hear their perspectives about the return.

Muhammad's grandfather hailed from Jamasin al-Gharbi, a small village that bordered with Tel Aviv on one side, and Ramat Gan on the other. By March 1948, the villagers were forced out because of their defencelessness in the face of increasing violence from the Zionist militias.[44] Muhammad, twenty-three at the time of the interview, dominated the conversation; he related some of the stories he had heard from his grandfather, about the idyllic life in Jamasin before it was lost, and dwelled on its proximity to the Mediterranean ('only a few minutes bike ride to the sea'). Palestinians, they all

---

[43] A Zochrot-produced short film documented diasporic Palestinian points of view about the possibility of return, including the possibility of living together with the (former) colonisers. The film was first screened during the Israeli Independence Day activities at Zochrot, 2012: https://youtu.be/zxeRcIe01ps?list=PLF32C600FA6433540.

[44] Benny Morris, *The Birth of the Palestinian Refugee Problem, 1947–1947* [in Hebrew] (Tel Aviv: Am Oved, 1991), pp. 62, 81–2.

explained to me, are barred from reaching the sea: 'We just want to see it, not even swim, just to see.'

Muhammad is painfully aware of the current condition of his grandfather's village. Months after the depopulation of Jamasin, the vacant houses became home to impoverished Jewish migrants from various Middle Eastern countries as well as those known as the 'refugees': Jews who previously lived in proximity to Jaffa or surrounding villages and had been displaced during the hostilities. Over the decades, Jamasin became known as Givat Amal, a working-class neighbourhood of Tel Aviv that incrementally fell prey to real-estate moguls. The remnants of Givat Amal are sandwiched between the affluent Bavli quarter and the newer Akirov high rises, residential skyscrapers that are home to some of the Israel's millionaires.[45]

When I tell Muhammad about the current landscapes of Jamasin, he sighs and notes: 'I cannot connect the memories of my grandfather with the reality of those big towers. [This is why] I cannot imagine how it is going to be [after the return]. We do not know our land anymore.' The others concurred. Irrevocably changed, their places of origin have become opaque for them, and so has the ability to imagine a future where they live anywhere but the camp, the only place they now call home. Just like 'Uthman/Saleh, these young men acknowledge that even though they have a right to repatriate, 'people are not going to go back, they are settled here'. A third generation of the Nakba, Muhammad and his friends embody the tension between homeland and home: as national subjects and as refugees who grew up commemorating Palestine's 'lost paradise', they articulate profound links to a homeland they do not know, and places they had not visited and yet trace part of their identities to them. But having come of age at the refugee camp and its particular histories of violence and trauma (which they related to me over the course of our discussion), these young men and their peers have formed affective communities that are based on their experiences of military incursions, incarceration and devastating loss.

---

[45] By the end of 2021, the last remaining residents in Givat Amal Bet were forcibly evicted by police. See Oren Ziv, 'Farewell to Givat Amal: Police Evict last Residents of Mizrahi Neighbourhood', *+972 Magazine*, 15 November 2021, https://www.972mag.com/givat-amal-eviction-mizrahim/.

These traumatic histories are also constitutive of Muhammad's approach towards the possibility living with his current occupiers:

> How can you live with the person who killed your brother or imprisoned your brother and father? Even if it's a peaceful person who has nothing to do with the army, you can't even look at them, because when you do, you remember everything that happened to you. Imagine you are 16 years old waking every morning to the sound of the mosque announcing a new martyr. You can't face them and live like neighbours. Are we going to have to see them every day?

For Muhammad, who lived through the Second Intifada (2000–5) and a three-week Israeli siege of the camp, Israelis are constant reminders of his loss, like the death of his best friend in his arms, from bullets fired by the invading Israeli army. He believes that Palestinians should 'stick together as one group' and 'kick the Israelis out, like they did to us in 1948'. Muhammad refuses to imagine the particularities of return, but he insists on one thing: the absence of the Israeli settlers as a precondition for liberation and collective healing. Ideas about the eventual departure of Israeli Jews have been commonplace among refugees, modelled after the Algerian experience. The single democratic state, the vision for Palestine formally accepted by the Fatah-controlled PLO in the late 1960s that I mentioned in my introduction was created as a response to these ideas of mass departure. Nevertheless, a segment of Palestinian refugees still holds on to this idea. Ihab and 'Anan may not share Muhammad's idea of liberation, but they are equally sceptical about Zochrot's vision of shared urban spaces:

> I don't think they will leave. We should respect them as humans, but I don't know exactly how that's going to be. If they allow us to return, are they going to accept us? Because now they are calling us 'terrorists'. I don't see an ultimate solution that will solve all the problems; maybe one that would bring some peace but it's not like everyone will be happy.

Contrary to the optimistic tone of the Zochrot and Badil return documents, Ihab voices doubt: can former coloniser and colonised actually form social relations that are not based on asymmetrical military power? Moreover, politically, what does it mean to ask Palestinians currently living under Israel's military occupation to extract themselves from ongoing struggles for liberation and engage in imagining a reality where their oppressors are *former* colonisers? Ihab's response inhabits this tension: on the one hand, he cannot quite extract himself from the current colonial relations of power ('they are calling us terrorists'). He later added that he did not wish to feel compassion towards Israelis, because Palestinians are locked in an intense struggle with them, and he needed to remain resolved to be part of this struggle. But on the other hand, Ihab is clearly willing to entertain the possibility of postcolonial coexistence that, just like in Gardi's story, will not make everyone happy, and will no doubt, maintain certain social tensions, but at the same time will provide at least a partial solution that is preferable to a violent present.

Conclusion

In a short documentary prepared by Zochrot for the launch of the 'Planning the Return' project, residents of Balata of all ages were asked to imagine the possibility of their return to Jaffa. An elderly woman joyfully responds: 'Back there I left my cows, my sheep and my crops. We want to live as we did before.'[46] This romantic vision of restoration of the past invertedly elides decades of occupation and Judaicisation of Jaffa, and its mere enunciation can be read as a form of resistance to and rejection of the 'new normal'.

However, Palestinian refugees are well aware of the profound transformations their places of origin have gone through over decades of Israeli occupation and resettlement of Jewish migrants. The Zochrot-Badil documents, as well as the works of fiction I discussed above and my conversations with Balata youth clearly reflect this. The radical differences in outlook and tone that I noted here are rooted in the ways people imagine 'mixing': while the Cape Town and Jaffa documents clearly advocate ethnic and confessional mixing as the path towards reconciliation, Gardi also cautions us about its inherent tensions. Conversely, the author Husam 'Uthman and Balata's young men are highly sceptical of the possibility of living together with the same people who are currently perpetrating violence and that have settled on their ancestral lands, effectively 'closing the path' of return. The high rises of Jamasin and

---

[46] 'Yafa Refugees Talk about Return', *YouTube*, https://youtube/HzdRFA6edUM (last accessed 10 January 2022).

French-owned mansions in Jaffa literally obstruct the horizons of possibility from the refugees' line of sight.

This closure also challenges Derrida's notion of 'living well together' that the Cape Town document articulated, and points to the potential failure of their prescribed forced 'mixing', and the work of reconciliation that should be done before former colonisers and colonised develop other forms of social relations, that are based trust and reciprocity. The literary and ethnographic examples I discussed in this chapter elucidate the tension between return-as-repatriation and 'return' the way Derrida advocated – revisiting a tainted past in order to fashion a new way of living. Viewed in this light, Lisa and Manar's friendship in Gardi's short story reflects this process, as the working-class 'mixing' on the island of 'New Manshiyyeh' represents a possibility for 'living well together' that transcends the understandable suspicion and distrust of former colonisers by Palestinians, on the one hand, and the normalised acceptance of ethnic segregation prevalent among Israeli Jews.

The reluctance, even outright hostility, that some Palestinian express towards 'living together' reveal a profound suspicion of the concept of reconciliation, especially if, in the liberal logic, it means reconstructing a version of the past that accommodates both victims and perpetrators.[47] For Palestinians, most of whom are displaced, the past represents not merely a place of belonging, but of grave injury and a demand for justice. The question of justice in this context opens up the absence of settler colonialism as a theoretical framework and point of departure in Derrida's intervention, and raises the issue of the unforgivable act that both Hannah Arendt and Derrida (in another piece) attempted to address.[48] Can willed colonial violence be 'overcome' and forgiven? This question is notably absent from Derrida's engagement with 'living together' as well as the Zochrot and Badil documents and Gardi's short story, where somehow, former colonised and coloniser transcend the present history of continued dispossession. The outright suspicion expressed by 'Uthman and my Balata interviewees reveal that thorny issues of injustice and forgiveness

---

[47] On this, see David Scott, *Omens of Adversity: Tragedy, Time, Memory, Justice* (Durham, NC: Duke University Press, 2014), p. 13.
[48] Hannah Arendt, *The Human Condition* (Chicago: University of Chicago Press, 1998), pp. 236–43; Jacque Derrida, 'On Forgiveness', in J. Derrida, *On Cosmopolitanism and Forgiveness*, trans. Mark Dooley and Michael Hughes (London: Routledge, 2001), pp. 25–60.

cannot be glossed over. This suspicion cannot be overcome by forced 'mixing' or suppressing histories of violence for the sake of reconciliation, but through replacing guilt with responsibility, not just for past injustice, but for a future that is the radical other of the present. 'Living together', then, should be recast not as a romantic fantasy of reconciliation and the erasure of suspicion, but as a process of becoming and of overcoming.

Perhaps the artificial island of 'New Manshiyyeh' can serve us as an apt metaphor here: its inhabitants' vantage point maintains Jaffa as an unobtainable object of desire, within a short distance, yet out of reach, while new, if imperfect, forms of communities and social relations are fostered. Maybe this is all one can hope for in the neoliberal present.

CONCLUSION: THE WAY HOME

At moments like this, when destinations, glimpsed, just there, at the bottom of the road, slip away, all you have is the journey, the not-much-deliberated, unfulfilled attempt to go there.[1]

Home is more lovely than the way home [al-bayt ajmal min al-tariq ila al-bayt].[2]

In May 2014, Zochrot led a day-long Nakba tour promoted under the title 'From Yafa to Beirut'. Signalling a departure from their trademark Saturday tours to a specific site of a former Palestinian village, this event highlighted the refugees' path to their forced exile. The meet-up spot 'Umar, the tour organiser, chose, was symbolically ironic: 48 Hakovshim (Hebrew, 'conquerors') Street. Located in the heart of what used to be Manshiyyeh, it is named after the Irgun Zionist militants who the Israeli state credits with the occupation of Jaffa that began with the shelling and depopulation of Manshiyyeh in the spring of 1948 (see Chapter 1). From there, the group of middle-class Israeli tour participants walked to two local key sites: the Hasan Bek Mosque, the only

---

[1] Ishtiyaq Shukri, 'Palestine Journey', in Jon Soske and Sean Jacobs (eds), *Apartheid Israel: The Politics of an Analogy* (Chicago: Haymarket Books, 2015), p. 16.
[2] Nouri al-Jarrah, 'Mahmoud Darwish: Home is more Lovely than the Way Home', *al-Jadid*, vol. 3, no. 19 (June 1997), http://www.aljadid.com/content/mahmoud-darwish-home-more-lovely-way-home#sthash.XwHM (last accessed 11 January 2022).

complete surviving pre-Nakba structure that still functions as a house of worship for Jaffa's Muslim community, and Beit Gidi, currently occupied by the historical museum of the Irgun (see Chapter 7). After a relatively brief historical introduction by 'Umar, the group was led to a bus parked by the mosque, and began the journey north, making brief stops at Qaysariyah (Caesarea), Bir'im and al-Bassa (inside the Jewish settlement of Shlomi in the Acre district), all Palestinian communities that were ethnically cleansed in 1948. Our destination was Rosh Hanikra, or as it is known in Arabic, Ras al-Naqurah, the northwestern (closed) border crossing to Lebanon.

The narrow passageway leading to the locked gate was the end point of our tour; we did not reach Beirut after all. Ras al-Naqurah became our 'unfulfilled destination', where a large sign directs visitors to Beirut and Jerusalem in three languages,[3] but the path north leads nowhere. By virtue of settler colonial conquest and war, Ras al-Naqurah became a site of closure: even the locked gate is covered so visitors cannot get a glimpse of what lies beyond. Moreover, tunnels blasted in the rocks during the late British Mandate, designed to connect Istanbul and Cairo via rail, were sealed by Israel in 1949, ending its railway in the Jewish town of Nahariyah, just south of Ras al-Naqurah. It is, perhaps, metonymic to the state of the country and its citizens, cut off from the rest of the region, self-condemned to isolation behind locked gates, walls and barbed wires, as former Prime Minister Benjamin Netanyahu argued, to 'keep the predators out'.[4]

An outsider would have been greatly disappointed by the failure of the tour organisers to deliver on the promise implicit in its title 'From Yafa to Beirut'. However, the intention of 'Umar and Zochrot was never to somehow illicitly traverse the 1949 armistice line, Israel's de facto border with Lebanon, and reach Beirut. Rather than focus on the commemoration of one depopulated

---

[3] Notably, Jerusalem is translated into Arabic as Urshalim, which is not in common use. Palestinians and Arabs in general use al-Quds, whereas Urshalim is only used today by the Israeli state. See Umar al-Ghubari, 'How Israel Erases Arabic from the Public Landscape', *+972 Magazine*, 22 November 2015, https://www.972mag.com/how-israel-is-erasing-arabic-from-its-public-landscape/ (last accessed 10 January 2022).

[4] Herb Keinon, 'Netanyahu: Israel Needs Fences on all Borders to Keep out "Predators" in the Region', *The Jerusalem Post*, 9 February 2016, http://www.jpost.com/Arab-Israeli-Conflict/Netanyahu-Israel-needs-fences-on-all-borders-to-keep-out-beasts-in-region-444358 (last accessed 10 January 2022).

CONCLUSION | 221

Figure 8.1 'Umar introducing the history of demise of Manshiyyeh in front of Beit Gidi. (Photo by the author.)

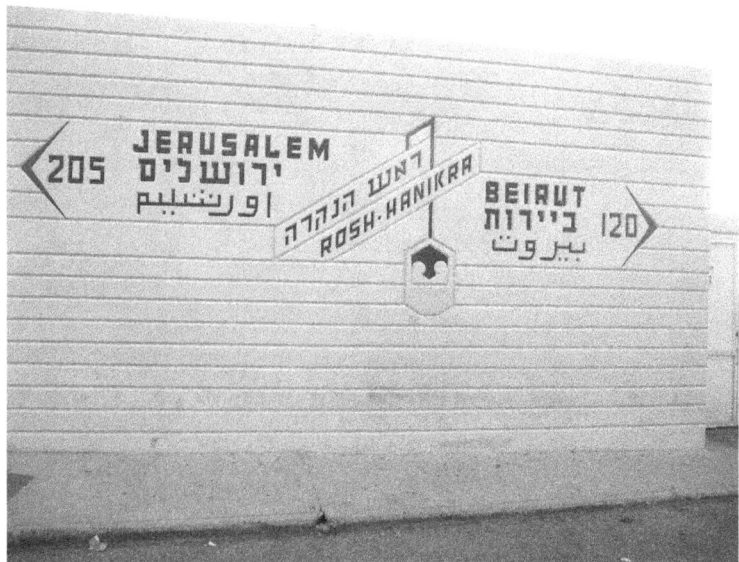

Figure 8.2 The sign at the Israeli–Lebanese northwestern border in Ras al-Naqurah, pointing north to Beirut and southeast to Jerusalem. (Photo by the author.)

village or town, 'Umar chose to highlight the journey of Palestinian refugees such as Ghassan Kanafani, forced to flee from Jaffa northward and find solace in Lebanon, hoping for a reprieve and fast resolution. Instead, the gate was locked behind them and their path back home was closed indefinitely. Those locked gates only allow movement in a single direction and for Israel's military only. In fact, two Israeli middle-aged men in the group quietly joked that they have, in fact, been to Beirut, and that the distance from Ras al-Naqurah seemed shorter aboard military jeeps and tanks.

Imagining Futures

This book joins a growing body of scholarly interventions that eschew the narrow focus on political histories of negotiations and military conflict, centring on 'archival imagination of and for the future, to quote literary scholar Gil Hochberg'.[5] This new focus displaces the traditional archives as the source of authoritative knowledge – and therefore of historians as its gatekeeprs. This intervention is especially needed in the case of Palestine, as the state has taken on a clear role of organising the archives, imbuing them with meaning that serves its purposes, and actively concealing any traces that undermine its own legitimacy. Therefore, instead of mining what crumbs state archives toss our way for traces of a past that is an 'open secret', scholars have shifted to archival assembleges that are highly contingent and in flux, and that offer us the opportunity to search for traces of the future. A future-oriented approach frees us from disciplinary confines and hierarchies of knowledge; more importantly, it offers colonised peoples an avenue of expression that is beyond the reach of the coloniser and the international web of institutional knowledge-production that prioritises officialdom and its written records. Unlike Hochberg, who dismisses the archives as obsolete since they reveal no new knowledge, I am interested in the architecture of archival silences, the play between revelation and concealment, and in the ways to challenge their power. In other words: Israel's archives are a vital part of the state's decades-long investment in strategic erasures, both the symbolic and the physical ones. This is why this book's point of departure is what is knowable about the past by reading 'along the grain' of declassified archival records.

---

[5] Gil Hochberg, *Becoming Palestine: Toward an Archival Imagination of the Future* (Durham, NC: Duke University Press, 2021).

Moreover, as I have demonstrated, Palestinians cherish the pre-1948 past just as they retell painful memories of displacement and refugeehood. History plays a vital role in the construction of multi-generational Palestinian identity as it informs refugees relationship with the present and an engagement with potential futures, as we have seen in Chapter 7. Depopulated villages as records of ruination also serve an NGO like Zochrot to educate Israelis about the violence that enabled the creation and maintenance of the Jewish state. These material traces are revered and preserved by successive generations of displaced persons, as we have seen in Chapter 6. All this to say that perhaps one should not dismiss records of the past as obsolete or useless; rather, what I attempted here is to de-centre both the authority of the archives and the primacy of the past. Instead, I opted to explore the ways in which Palestinians challenge these multiple regimes of erasure that the state has imposed upon them and wrest away not just history but also the potential for liberation and the undoing of the colonial.

This monograph has also examined Palestinians' profound attachment to home while simultaneously also challenging nationalist discourses about belonging. The ways in which Palestinians continue to identify as *Yafawiin*, whether or not they actually reside in Jaffa, are spatially fluid, as identity and locality are contingently formed through the intersection of places of origin, sites of refuge, and the paths traversed in between. Put differently: against the nationalist doxa that is centred on the idea of origin, Palestinians articulate belonging in much more creative and unpredictable ways that highlight multiple origins, intimate commitments and affective attachments. Thus, for instance, the refugee camp figures both as a site of collective and personal trauma and as a vibrant if disenfranchised community with locally embedded support networks.

These multiple and interconnected enunciations of belonging are also vital for the way Palestinians engage with ideas about return. If refugees eschew received nationalist wisdom about restoration to the place of origin, or turning the clock back to 1947, then imaginaries of the return are anything but predictable: a 'stereoscopic' approach, like the one employed by DAAR (see Chapter 6), has attempted to project places of refuge into sites of origin while for members of Zochrot and Badil, the road to envisioning the return went through the post-apartheid landscapes of Cape Town.

To return to Diana Allan's caveat about the 'airy purity of solidarity rhetoric',[6] overemphasising return to a place of origin overrides the lived experiences of Palestinians since the Nakba, their embeddedness in multiple places, the complexities of social commitments and the multidirectionality and contingent sense of belonging that I have attempted to chart here.[7] Being attentive to how Palestinians themselves think of the possibility of return also allows for scepticism, fear and even the outright rejection of the idea. Thinking of return as an impossibility or as a potential dystopia challenges both nationalist doxa and prevailing discourses among committed scholars and solidarity activists that position Palestinians as bearers of memory, places of origin such as Jaffa as 'Nakba museums' and the future as a unidirectional reversal of exile, from the camp back 'home'. And finally, shifting our scholarly spotlight to itineraries of displacement and the multiple experiences of exile expands our horizon of possibility to think of return to a homeland and refashioning lives in ways that are meaningful to Palestinians. In other words: visions of the return are crafted out of Palestinians' experiences since 1948 in all the places they have been exiled to, and the lives they have made for themselves.

Although I have referred to Palestinians who reside outside of historic Palestine as 'diasporic' (often interchangeably with 'exile'), the category is problematic in its own right; upholding what is perceived as the Jewish diasporic history as paradigmatic, scholars have been debating the level of 'diasporicity' of various ethnic groups, or how others, including Palestinians, measure up in comparison with the Jews as the 'ideal type'.[8] Universalising Jewish experience

---

[6] Diana Allan, *Refugees of the Revolution: Experiences of Palestinian Exile* (Stanford: Stanford University Press, 2014), p. 213.

[7] Allan also interviewed camp Palestinians who would rather pack up and move to Europe or elsewhere in the West, essentially giving up the hope of return. While my interlocutors repeatedly professed their commitment to return, I have met countless other Palestinians who have despaired of the entrenched occupation of Palestine and instead expressed their wish to migrate elsewhere.

[8] See William Safran, 'Diasporas in Modern Societies: Myths of Homeland and Return', *Diaspora: A Journal of Transnational Studies*, vol. 1, no. 1 (Spring 1991), pp. 83–99, his 'Comparing Diasporas: A Review Essay', *Diaspora: A Journal of Transnational Studies*, vol. 8, no. 3 (Winter 1999), pp. 255–91, as well as 'The Jewish Diaspora in a Comparative and Theoretical Perspective', *Israel Studies*, vol. 10, no. 1 (Spring 2005), pp. 36–60; Robin Cohen, *Global Diasporas: An Introduction* (London: Routledge, 2008); Stéphane Dufoix, *Diasporas*, trans. William Rodarmor (Berkeley: University of California Press, 2008); Clifford pointed

in such a way has led Safran, for instance, to imply that Palestinians do not quite constitute a diasporic group since they share 'language, culture and religion' with their 'Arab hosts',[9] replicating the Israeli claims that justify its policy against the return of the refugees. Conversely, insisting on the diasporicity of Palestinians can potentially 'dislodge the politics of return', according to Julie Peteet, especially if it replaces refugeehood and stresses the level of integration of Palestinians in host societies.[10]

The way in which Jewish diasporic experiences has been universalised, and in particular the unproblematic naturalisation of its attendant concepts of 'return' and 'homeland' have obstructed our understanding of the violence they have unleashed: the mass displacement of Palestinians and the settlement of Jewish migrants in their stead, on the one hand, and the elision of rich Jewish diasporic cultural traditions, sidelined by the monolithic Zionist ideal of the 'new Jew'. Situated within the history of settler colonialism in Palestine, displacing the universality of 'return' would reveal the violent practices it entails and the complicity of scholars in maintaining a colonial state formation that passes itself off as a 'restoration' of national independence. In the future, scholars need to better attend to what ways the deployment of hegemonic diaspora paradigm boosts nation states and their exclusionary and oppressive practices in other contexts, especially towards 'minorities', or groups that self-identify in ways that dissent from the hegemonic categories in terms of ethnicity, race, religion or sexuality.

Rather than just being there, waiting to be reclaimed, homelands are made. These place-making practices are often absent from narratives about diasporic returns; in the Zionist case, these practices involved ethnic cleansing, expulsions and spatial appropriations, of which Jaffa is merely one notable example (see Chapter 2). However, for many Palestinians, who live in the colonial present, 'homeland' is future-oriented, not a simple restoration of a place lost to others, but an invocation of their right to belong and to remake the world in

---

to several problems arising from this paradigmatic approach, see James Clifford, 'Diasporas', *Cultural Anthropology*, vol. 9, no. 3, Further Inflections: Towards Ethnographies of the Future (August 1994), pp. 302–38.

[9] Safran, 'Comparing Diasporas', p. 259.

[10] Julie Peteet, 'Problematizing a Palestinian Diaspora', *International Journal of Middle East Studies*, vol. 39, no. 4 (November 2007), p. 636.

their own image.[11] To return to the epigraphs at the top of this conclusion, this 'homeland' is both the journey forward, towards what might be merely a glimpse of the unknown, *and* an eventual destination, to a place of belonging and that truly feels like home.

Heeding a recent call to reframe scholarship of Palestine in the context of settler colonialism in addition to space and time,[12] I argue that in addition to revealing the 'continuity between 1948, 1967 and the present', and 'the consistency of the Zionist project' from its inception to contemporary practices of containment and separation,[13] this analytical framework is instructive for futuristic projects such as 'imagining the return of the refugees' that aim to undo the 'new normal'. Settler colonialism as a political force has profoundly shaped the lives of Palestinians (and Israeli Jews) at least since the Nakba, radically reorganising spatiotemporal resources in Palestine for the benefit of the Jewish colonisers. Undoing a 'nationalist-inflected' conceptual framework reveals that the Palestinian demands for justice and Zionist colonisation are not competing claims over territory. Using settler colonialism as analytical framework not only de-exceptionalises the history of Zionist occupation of Palestine, locating it within a broader context of settler colonial formations elsewhere, as I explained in Chapter 6, but moreover, it encourages us to imagine the decolonial: overcoming the suspicion of the colonised in liberal processes of 'reconciliation' and undoing violent histories of expulsion and expropriations and claim responsibility for shaping a different future. Put differently: 'living well together' in the future is made possible only through a sustained understanding of the settler colonial present.

Being attentive to lived realities and historical transformations forces us to consider the fate of the colonisers. Imagining the return is also a project of repositioning Israeli Jews not as colonisers, and this is, arguably, the more challenging task. As I demonstrated in this book, for Palestinians, thinking beyond the call for one democratic state for all meant to imaginatively transcend their sense of injury by making place for Israeli Jews, for instance, through 'mixing'

---

[11] See also Julie Peteet, *Landscape of Hope and Despair: Palestinian Refugee Camps* (Philadelphia: University of Pennsylvania Press, 2005), p. 216.

[12] Julie Peteet, 'Language Matters: Thinking about Palestine', *Journal of Palestine Studies*, vol. 45, no. 2 (Winter 2016), pp. 24–40.

[13] Peteet, 'Language Matters', p. 31.

or by negotiating the status of the 'second occupant' (see Chapter 7). The fact that authors like Husam 'Uthman or my Balata youth interlocutors were not able to overcome the coloniser/colonised divide and insisted that they cannot even imagine living with the Jews proves my point: that entrenched settler colonialism in Palestine with its practices of violent displacement and forced segregation, has, at least partially, cemented the 'new normal' and almost completely foreclosed potential different trajectories.

This last point is crucial; the ability to imagine that which is not yet present, and to expand our horizon of possibilities is vital in order to overcome settler colonialism, undo its legacy of violence and rebuild lives destroyed by decades of refugeehood, military occupation and siege. The particular settler colonial formation in Palestine means that Israeli Jews, though conscripted by the state, willingly, in most cases, as a means to cement the removal of the native and take his place, are not about to leave with the onset of decolonisation. No matter how the return of the refugees shapes up, former colonised and coloniser – irrespective of the latter's level of complicity in colonial oppression – will have to adjust to living together in a way that will necessarily be different than what it is today.

Since it is clear that neither Palestinians nor Israeli Jews are likely to leave Palestine and will be faced with the need to recreate a 'shared homeland', the role of the imagination as a means to forge new potential futures is crucial. Moreover, Edward Said has once charged that 'if we are all to live ... we must capture the imagination not just of our people, but of our oppressors'.[14] Said, then, also recognised the importance of the imagination in the struggle against settler colonialism in Palestine, and that the liberation struggle cannot afford, in the long run, to exclude Israeli Jews. Perhaps against nationalist logic, Said entices Palestinians to reach out to the colonisers, despite and maybe because of a profound sense of injustice, and 'capture their imagination'. What he meant by this, I think, is to understand the imaginaries that fuel Zionism and makes it appealing for Israeli Jews – literally understand what makes them tick – in order to address their fears, desires and hopes as humans. In other words, if Netanyahu, for example (as did Jabotinsky before him), deploys images of walls and fences to mobilise the Jewish masses to rally for the state,

---

[14] Edward Said, 'The Only Alternative', *al-Ahram Weekly Online*, no. 523, 1–7 March 2001.

what Said is effectively saying is that Palestinians should fully understand this logic and the power it sways over the colonisers in order to undo it. Put differently: the way to undoing physical cement barriers, walls and barbed wires goes through dismantling affective barriers. Admittedly, so far, the Palestinian liberation struggle, and in particular the idea of return, has failed to capture the imagination of Israeli Jews, with the exception of a tiny minority, such as the Zochrot activists and artists like Gil Mualem-Doron and Tomer Gardi, whose activities I discussed in previous chapters.

My point is that the path to decolonisation goes through the imagination, ideally of both colonised and coloniser. Imagination and hopefulness are mutually constitutive: our capacity to imagine a future that is radically different than the present propels revolutionary action in order to realise that future. But at the same time, action is what opens up horizons of possibility. When I was still a graduate student, I attended a lecture by a renowned veteran black scholar and activist who argued that any counterhegemonic action, as small and insignificant as it may seem, works not only to undermine the entrenched present political order, but produces unpredictable avenues for revolutionary action, literally refashioning futures. I have forgotten the speaker's name and much of everything about that time, but that message still invigorates me to this day.

BIBLIOGRAPHY

Abramson, Larry. 'What does Landscape Want? A Walk with W. J. T. Mitchell's Holy Landscape', *Culture, Theory & Critique*, vol. 50, no. 2–3 (2009), pp. 275–8.

Abu el-Haj, Nadia. *Facts on the Ground: Archaeological Practice and Territorial Self-Fashioning in Israeli Society* (Chicago: University of Chicago Press, 2001).

Abu Iyad with Eric Roulaeu, *My Home, My Land: A Narrative of the Palestinian Struggle*, trans. Linda Butler Koseoglu (New York: Times Books, 1978).

Abu Lughod, Ibrahim. 'Altered Realities: The Palestinians since 1967', *International Journal*, vol. 28, no. 4 (Autumn 1973), pp. 648–69.

Abu Lughod, Lila. 'Return to Half-Ruins: Memory, Postmemory, and Living History in Palestine', in Ahmad H. Sa'di and Lila Abu-Lughod (eds), *Nakba: Palestine, 1948, and the Claims of Memory* (New York: Columbia University Press, 2007), pp. 77–104.

Abu Saad, Ismael. 'Separate and Unequal: The Role of the State Educational System in Maintaining the Subordination of Israel's Palestinian Arab Citizens', *Social Identities: Journal for the Study of Race, Nation and Culture*, vol. 10, no. 1 (2004), pp. 101–27.

Abu Sitta, Salman. 'Al Nakba Anatomy', *From Refugees to Citizens at Home*, http://www.plands.org/en/books-reports/books/right-of-return-sacred-legal-and-possible (last accessed 26 May 2016).

—— 'The Feasibility of the Right of Return', *ICJ and CIMEL*, June 1997, http://www.arts.mcgill.ca/MEPP/PRRN/papers/abusitta.html (last accessed 15 March 2016).

—— 'The Implementation of the Right of Return', in Roane Carey *et al.* (eds), *The New Intifada: Resisting Israel's Apartheid* (New York: Verso, 2001), pp. 299–319.

—— *The Logistics of Return: From Refugees to Citizens at Home*, http://www.plands.org/books/book%2001-12.html (last accessed 30 October 2015).

Abu Sitta, Salman, and Terry Rempel. 'The ICRC and the Detention of Palestinian Civilians in Israel's 1948 POW/Labor Camps', *Journal of Palestine Studies*, vol. 43, no. 4 (Summer 2014), pp. 11–38.

AbuKhalil, As'ad. 'George Habash and the Movement of Arab Nationalists: Neither Unity nor Liberation', *Journal of Palestine Studies*, vol. 28, no. 4 (Summer 1999), pp. 91–103.

Abulhawa, Susan. 'Because we are not Children of a Lesser God', *Aljazeera*, 20 June 2015, http://www.aljazeera.com/indepth/features/2015/06/magazine-children-lesser-god-palestinian-refugees-150615110526283.html (last accessed 26 May 2016).

Abusalim, Jehad. 'The Great March of Return: An Organizer's Perspective', *Journal of Palestine Studies*, vol. 47, no. 4 (Summer 2018), pp. 90–100.

Aderet, Ofer. 'War Crimes and "Unpleasantness": Israel's Censorship List', *Haaretz*, 20 October 2021, p. 7.

AFP, 'Dozens of Bodies Found at Mass Grave in Jaffa', *The Jerusalem Post*, 1 June 2013, http://www.jpost.com/National-News/Dozens-of-bodies-found-at-mass-grave-in-Jaffa-315073 (last accessed 26 May 2016).

—— 'Israel Plans Law against Using Facebook for "Terror"', *Yahoo News*, 22 June 2016 (last accessed 26 June 2016).

Ahmed-Farajeh, Hisham, *Ibrahim Abu Lughod: Resistance, Exile and Return* (Birzeit: Ibrahim Abu Lughod Institute of International Studies, 2003).

Akinwumi, Akin. 'The Will to Transform: Nation-Building and the Strategic State in South Africa', *Space and Polity*, vol. 17, no. 2 (2013), pp. 145–63.

Alami, Musa. 'The Lesson of Palestine', *Middle East Journal*, vol. 3, no. 4 (October 1949), pp. 373–405.

al-Bireh, Norah. 'Angular Identities of the Palestinian Diaspora', *Sixteen Minutes to Palestine*, 18 June 2015, http://smpalestine.com/2015/06/18/the-angular-identities-of-the-palestinian-diaspora/ (last accessed 26 May 2016).

al-Dabbagh, Mustafa Murad. *Biladuna Filastin [Our Country Palestine, Volume 4, Part 2: The Jaffa Area]* (Beirut: Dar al-Tali'ah, 1972). [Arabic]

Aleksandrowicz, Or. 'Gvulot shel Niyar: Ha-Historia ha-Mehukah shel Neveh Shalom' ['Paper Boundaries: The Erased History of Neveh Shalom'], *Theory and Criticism*, vol. 41 (Summer 2003), pp. 181–2. [Hebrew]

Al-Ghubari, 'Umar. 'How Israel Erases Arabic from the Public Landscape', *+972 Magazine*, 22 November 2015, https://www.972mag.com/how-israel-is-erasing-arabic-from-its-public-landscape/.

Al-Ghubari, 'Umar, and Tomer Gardi (eds). *Awda: 'Eduyot Medumyanot me-'Atidim Efshariim [Awda: Imagined Testimonies of Possible Futures]* (Tel Aviv: Pardes, 2013). [Hebrew and Arabic]

al-Hardan, Anaheed. 'Al-Nakbah in Arab Thought: The Transformation of a Concept', *Comparative Studies of South Asia, Africa and the Middle East*, vol. 35, no. 3 (2015), pp. 622–38.

al-Hout, Shafiq. *My Life in the PLO: The Inside Story of the Palestinian Struggle*, trans. Hader al-Hout and Laila Othman (New York: Pluto Press, 2011).

Al-Ja'fari, Kamal, Hadas Lahav and Asaf Adiv. *Jaffa Facing the New Judaization Plan* (Jerusalem: Dar al-Sharara, 1992). [Arabic]

al-Jarrah, Nouri. 'Mahmoud Darwish: Home is more Lovely than the Way Home', *al-Jadid*, vol. 3, no. 19 (June 1997), http://www.aljadid.com/content/mahmoud-darwish-home-more-lovely-way-home#sthash.XwHM (last accessed 26 May 2016).

Allan, Diana. *Refugees of the Revolution: Experiences of Palestinian Exile* (Stanford: Stanford University Press, 2014).

Allegra, Marco, Ariel Handel and Erez Maggor (eds). *Normalizing Occupation: The Politics of Everyday Life in the West Bank Settlements* (Bloomington: Indiana University Press, 2017).

Allen, Diana. *Refugees of the Revolution: Experiences of Palestinian Exile* (Stanford: Stanford University Press, 2014).

Allen, Lori. *The Rise and Fall of Human Rights: Cynicism and Politics in Occupied Palestine* (Stanford: Stanford University Press, 2013).

al-Youssef, Samir. *The Illusion of Return* (New York: Melville House, 2007).

Anziska, Seth. 'The Erasure of the Nakba in Israel's Archives', *Journal of Palestine Studies*, vol. 49, no. 1 (Fall 2019), pp. 64–76.

Arab Office, The. *The Future of Palestine* (London: The Arab Office, 1947).

Arendt, Hannah. *The Human Condition* (Chicago: University of Chicago Press, 1998).

Ashton, Nigel J. 'Pulling the Strings: King Hussein's Role during the Crisis of 1970 in Jordan', *The International History Review*, vol. 28, no. 1 (2006), 94–118.

Atshan, Sa'ed. 'The Anthropological Rise of Palestine', *Journal of Palestine Studies*, vol. 50, no. 4 (2021), pp. 3–31.

Auron, Yair. 'Breaking the Silence: The Poem that Exposed Israeli War Crimes in 1948', *Haaretz*, 18 March 2016, http://www.haaretz.com/israel-news/.premium-1.709439 (last accessed 18 March 2016).

Badil, 'Badil-Zochrot Joint Action: Practical Approaches to Refugee Return', *The Struggle for Palestinian Rights: New Strategies in a Changing Middle East*, no. 46 (Summer 2011), http://www.badil.org/en/component/k2/item/1687-art7 (last accessed 26 May 2016).

Badran, Amneh Daoud. *Zionist Israel and Apartheid South Africa: Civil Society and Peace Building in Ethnic-National States* (London: Routledge, 2010).

Beauchamp, Zack. 'A New Study Reveals the Real Reason Obama Voters Switched to Trump', *Vox*, 16 October 2018, https://www.vox.com/policy-and-politics/2018/10/16/17980820/trump-obama-2016-race-racism-class-economy-2018-midterm (last accessed 29 December 2021).

Begin, Menachem. *Ha-Mered [The Revolt]* (Jerusalem: Achiasaf, 1950). [Hebrew]

Ben Gal, Yaacov. 'Mignana ve-Mitkafa' ['Defense and Offense'], in Yosef Arikha (ed.), *Yafo: Mikraah Historit-Sifrutit [Jaffa: A Historical-Literary Reader]* (Tel Aviv: Tel Aviv Municipality, 1957), pp. 239–40. [Hebrew]

Benjamin, Walter. 'Paris, the Capital of the Nineteenth Century (1935)', in W. Benjamin, *The Arcades Project*, trans. Howard Eiland and Kevin McLaughlin (Cambridge, MA: The Belknap Press of Harvard University, 1999), pp. 3–13.

—— 'Theses on the Philosophy of History', in W. Benjamin, *Illuminations*, trans. Harry Zohn (New York: Schocken Books, 1968), pp. 253–64.

Beska, Emanuel. 'Political Opposition to Zionism in Palestine and Greater Syria: 1910–1911 as a Turning Point', *Jerusalem Quarterly*, vol. 59, no. 55 (2014), pp. 54–67.

Billingsley, Amy. 'Hope in a Vice: Carole Pateman, Judith Butler, and Suspicious Hope', *Hypatia*, vol. 30, no. 3 (Summer 2015), pp. 597–612.

Bishara, Marwan. *Palestine/Israel: Peace or Apartheid – Occupation, Terrorism and the Future* (London: Zed Books, 2002).

Bloch, Ernst. *The Principle of Hope*, trans. Neville Plaice, Stephen Plaice and Paul Knight (Cambridge, MA: MIT Press, 1986).

Brand, Laurie A. 'Palestinians and Jordanians: A Crisis of Identity', *Journal of Palestine Studies*, vol. 24, no. 4 (Summer 1995), pp. 46–61.

Brejzek, Thea. 'From Social Network to Urban Intervention: On the Scenographies of Flash Mobs and Urban Swarms', *International Journal of Performance Arts and Digital Media*, vol. 6, no. 1 (2010), pp. 109–22.

Bronstein Aparicio, Eitan. 'The Distance between 'Ajjur and District Six', *Zochrot*, 6 February 2012, http://zochrot.org/he/article/53404 (last accessed 26 May 2016).

Bussow, Johann. *Hamidian Palestine, Politics and Society in the District of Jerusalem, 1872–1908* (Leiden: Brill, 2011).

Campos, Michelle U. 'Between "Beloved Ottomania" and "The Land of Israel": The Struggle over Ottomanism and Zionism among Palestine's Sephardi Jews, 1908–1913', *International Journal of Middle East Studies*, vol. 37 (2005), pp. 461–83.

—— *Ottoman Brothers: Muslims, Christians, and Jews in Early Twentieth-Century Palestine* (Stanford: Stanford University Press, 2011).

Carter, Jimmy. *Palestine: Peace, Not Apartheid* (New York: Simon & Schuster, 2006).

Chamberlin, Paul Thomas. *The Global Offensive: The United States, the Palestine Liberation Organization, and the Making of the Post-Cold War Order* (Oxford: Oxford University Press, 2012).

—— 'The Struggle against Oppression Everywhere: The Global Politics of Palestinian Liberation', *Middle Eastern Studies*, vol. 47, no. 1 (2011), pp. 24–41.

Chelouch, Aharon. *Mi-Galabiya le-Kova Tembel [From Jalabia to Kova Tembel]* (Tel Aviv: Kol Seder, 1991). [Hebrew]

Chelouch, Yosef Eliyahu. *Parashat Hayay [The Story of my Life]* (Tel Aviv: Bavel, 2005) [Hebrew].

Chetrit, Sami Shalom. *Intra-Jewish Conflict in Israel: White Jews, Black Jews* (London: Routledge, 2010).

Clifford, James. 'Diasporas', *Cultural Anthropology*, vol. 9, no. 3, Further Inflections: Towards Ethnographies of the Future (August 1994), pp. 302–38.

Cohen, Dan. 'Thousands of Palestinians Mark Nakba Day at March of Return', *Mondoweiss*, 8 May 2014, http://mondoweiss.net/2014/05/thousands-palestinian-citizens.html (last accessed 26 May 2016).

Cohen, Robin. *Global Diasporas: An Introduction* (London: Routledge, 2008).

Collins, John. *Occupied by Memory: The Intifada Generation and the Palestinian State of Emergency* (New York: New York University Press, 2004).

Coombes, Annie E. *Visual Culture and Public Memory in a Democratic South Africa* (Durham, NC: Duke University Press, 2003).

Cosmas, Desmond. *The Discarded People: An Account of African Resettlement in South Africa* (Harmondsworth: Penguin, 1971).

Coursen-Neff, Zama. *Second Class: Discrimination against Palestinian Arab Children in Israel's School* (New York: Human Rights Watch, 2001).

Crapanzano, Vincent. 'Reflections on Hope as a Category of Social and Psychological Analysis', *Cultural Anthropology*, vol. 18, no. 1 (2003), pp. 3–32.

Dahan, Yossi, and Gal Levi. 'Multicultural Education in the Zionist State – The Mizrahi Challenge', *Studies in Philosophy and Education*, vol. 19, no. 5–6 (November 2000), pp. 423–44.

Davidson, Lawrence. 'Remembering Hisham Sharabi (1927–2005)', *Journal of Palestine Studies*, vol. 34, no. 3 (Spring 2005), pp. 57–64.

Davis, Rochelle A. *Palestinian Village Histories: Geographies of the Displaced* (Stanford: Stanford University Press, 2011).

Davis, Uri. *Apartheid Israel: Possibilities for the Struggle Within* (London: Zed Books, 2003).

—— *Israel, an Apartheid State* (Atlantic Highlands: Zed Books, 1987).

de Cesari, Chiara. *Heritage and the Cultural Struggle for Palestine* (Stanford: Stanford University Press, 2019).

Derrida, Jacque. 'Avowing – The Impossible: "Returns", Repentance and Reconciliation', in Elisabeth Weber (ed.), *Living Together: Jacques Derrida's Communities of Violence and Peace* (New York: Fordham University Press, 2013), pp. 18–41.

—— 'On Forgiveness', in J. Derrida, *On Cosmopolitanism and Forgiveness*, trans. Mark Dooley and Michael Hughes (London: Routledge, 2001), pp. 25–60.

Doumani, Beshara. *Rediscovering Palestine: Merchants and Peasants in Jabal Nablus, 1700–1900* (Berkeley: University of California Press, 1995).

Dufoix, Stéphane. *Diasporas*, trans. William Rodarmor (Berkeley: University of California Press, 2008).

Eldar, Akiva. 'Be-14 be-Yuni 1967 Hem kvar Nishu Heskem' ['In 14 June 1967 They Already Drafted an Agreement'], *Haaretz*, 4 June 2007, http://www.haaretz.co.il/misc/1.1415076 (last accessed 26 May 2016). [Hebrew]

Elkayam, Mordekhai. *Yafo, Neve Tsedek: Reshita shel Tel Aviv [Jaffa, Neve Tsedek: The Beginnings of Tel Aviv]* (Tel Aviv: Misrad Habitahon, 1990). [Hebrew]

el-Khazen, Farid. *The Breakdown of the State of Lebanon, 1967–1976* (London: I. B. Tauris and the Centre for Lebanese Studies, 2000).

Emergui, Sal. 'Returning to Jaffa: The Triumphant Odyssey of Palestinian Refugee Hassan Hijazi', *MR Zine*, 17 May 2011, http://mrzine.monthlyreview.org/2011/emergui170511.html (last accessed 26 May 2016).

Erakat, Noura. 'It's not Wrong, it's Illegal: Situating the Gaza Blockade between International Law and the UN Response', *UCLA Journal of Islamic and Near Eastern Law*, vol. 11, no. 37 (2011–2012), pp. 1–34.

Erakat, Noura, and Mark Lamont Hill. 'Black-Palestinian Transnational Solidarity: Renewals, Returns, and Practice', *Journal of Palestine Studies*, vol. 48, no. 4 (2019), pp. 7–16.

Eshel, Amir. *Futurity: Contemporary Literature and the Quest for the Past* (Chicago: University of Chicago Press, 2013).

Esmeir, Samera. 'A Guide for the Perplexed: On the Return of the Refugees', *Middle East Research and Information Project*, 28 April 2014, http://www.merip.org/mero/interventions/guide-perplexed (last accessed 26 May 2016).

Falah, Ghazi. 'The 1948 Israeli-Palestinian War and its Aftermath: The Transformation and De-Signification of Palestine's Cultural Landscape', *Annals of the Association of American Geographers*, vol. 86, no. 2 (June 1996), pp. 256–85.

Fanon, Frantz. *The Wretched of the Earth*, trans. Constance Farrington (New York: Grove Press, 1963).

Feldman, Keith. *A Shadow over Palestine: The Imperial Life of Race in America* (Minneapolis: University of Minnesota Press, 2015).

Fishman, Louis. *Jews and Palestinians in the Late Ottoman Era, 1908–1914: Reclaiming the Homeland* (Edinburgh: Edinburgh University Press, 2020).

Fisk, Robert. *Pity the Nation: Lebanon at War* (Oxford: Oxford University Press, 2001).

Foucault, Michel. *Fearless Speech*, ed. Joseph Pearson (Los Angeles: Semiotext(e), 2001).

Frantzman, Seth J. 'The Dark Narrative of Israel's Rhodesia Fantasy', *+972 Magazine*, 24 September 2015, http://972mag.com/the-dark-narrative-of-israels-rhodesia-fantasy/111926/ (last Accessed 26 May 2016).

Freud, Sigmund. 'The Uncanny, 1919', in David Sandner (ed.), *Fantastic Literature: A Critical Reader* (Westport: Praeger, 2004), pp. 74–101.

Gardi, Tomer. 'A Story from Manshiyeh al-Jdeideh' [in Hebrew], in 'Umar al-Ghubari and Tomer Gardi (eds), *Awda: Imagined Testimonies of Possible Futures* (Tel Aviv: Pardes, 2013).

Gerner, Deborah J. 'Missed Opportunities and Roads not Taken: The Eisenhower Administration and the Palestinians', *Arab Studies Quarterly*, vol. 12, no. 1/2 (Winter/Spring 1990), pp. 67–100.

Golan, Arnon. 'The Battle for Jaffa, 1948', *Middle Eastern Studies*, vol. 48, no. 6 (November 2012), pp. 997–1101.

—— 'European Imperialism and the Development of Modern Palestine: Was Zionism a form of Colonialism?' *Space & Polity*, vol. 5, no. 2 (2001), pp. 127–43.

—— 'From Palestinian-Arab to Israeli Towns, 1948–1967', *Middle Eastern Studies*, vol. 39, no. 4 (October 2003), pp. 121–39.

Goodman, Tanya. 'Performing a "New" Nation: The Role of the TRC in South Africa', in Jeffrey C. Alexander, Bernhard Giesen and Jason L. Mast (eds), *Social Performance: Symbolic Action, Cultural Pragmatics, and Ritual* (Cambridge: Cambridge University Press, 2006), pp. 169–92.

Goren, Tamir. 'The Struggle to Save the National Symbol: Jaffa Port from the Arab Revolt until the Twilight of the British Mandate', *Middle East Studies*, vol. 51, no. 6 (November 2015), pp. 863–82.

Green, Penny, and Amelia Smith. 'Evicting Palestine', *State Crime Journal*, vol. 5, no. 1: Palestine, Palestinians and Israel's State Criminality (Spring 2016), pp. 81–108.

Gren, Nina. *Occupied Lives: Maintaining Integrity in a Palestinian Refugee Camp in the West Bank* (Cairo: The American University in Cairo Press, 2015).

Gresh, Alain. *The PLO, the Struggle Within: Towards an Independent Palestinian State* (London: Zed Books, 1988).

Griffiths, Ron. 'Cultural Strategies and New Modes of Urban Intervention', *Cities*, vol. 12, no. 4 (August 1995), pp. 253–65.

Grinberg, Lev. *The Histadrut Above All* (Jerusalem: Nevo, 1993). [Hebrew]

Gustafson, Erni, and Nabil Nabil Alawi. 'Aliens, but Friends: Practice Placement at Balata Refugee Camp, Palestine', *European Journal of Social Work*, vol. 18, no. 3 (2015), pp. 397–411.

Gutman, Yifat. 'Past before Future: Memory Activism in Israel-Palestine', PhD dissertation, New School for Social Research, 2011.

Hadawi, Sami. *Bitter Harvest: A Modern History of Palestine* (New York: Olive Branch Press, 1991).

—— *Village Statistics, 1945: A Classification of Land and Area Ownership in Palestine* (Beirut: Palestine Liberation Organization Research Center, 1970).

Hage, Ghassan. *Against Paranoid Nationalism: Searching for Hope in a Shrinking Society* (Annandale: Pluto Press Australia: 2003).

Hammer, Juliane. *Palestinians Born in Exile: Diaspora and the Search of a Homeland* (Austin: University of Texas Press, 2005).

Hart, Deborah M. 'Political Manipulation of Urban Space: The Razing of District Six, Cape Town', *Urban Geography*, vol. 9, no. 6 (1988), pp. 603–28.

Hart, Rachel. 'Yafo ve-Tel Aviv ba-Marah ha-Kefula shel ha-'Itonut ha-'Aravit, 1881–1930' ['Jaffa and Tel Aviv through the Double Prism of the Arab Press, 1881–1930'], *Kesher*, no. 39 (2009), pp. 92–101. [Hebrew]

Hasson, Nir. 'Experts Battle over whether Jaffa's Mass Graves Stem from World War I or 1948', *Haaretz*, 10 June 2013, http://www.haaretz.com/news/national/.premium-1.528786 (last accessed 26 May 2016).

Hatuka, Tali, and Rachel Kallus. 'Loose Ends: The Role of Architecture in Constructing Urban Borders in Tel Aviv-Jaffa since the 1920s', *Planning Perspectives*, no. 21 (January 2006), pp. 23–44.

Hazan, Haim, and Daniel Monterescu. *A Town at Sundown: Aging Nationalism in Jaffa* (Jerusalem: Van Leer Institute and Hakibutz Hameukhad, 2011). [Hebrew]

Heikal, Yusuf, and Imad el-Haj. 'Jaffa ... as it was', *Journal of Palestine Studies*, vol. 13, no. 4 (Summer 1984), pp. 3–21.

Hirst, David. *The Gun and the Olive Branch: The Roots of Violence in the Middle East* (New York: Harcourt Brace Janovich, 1977).

—— 'Shameless in Gaza', *The Guardian Weekly*, 21 April 1997.

Hochberg, Gil. *Becoming Palestine: Toward an Archival Imagination of the Future* (Durham, NC: Duke University Press, 2021).

—— *Visual Occupations: Violence and Visibility in a Conflict Zone* (Durham, NC: Duke University Press, 2015).

Honig-Parnass, Tikva. *False Prophets of Peace: Liberal Zionism and the Struggle for Palestine* (Chicago: Haymarket Books, 2011).

Howard, Ebenezer. *Garden Cities of To-Morrow* (London: Swan Sonnenschein, 1902).

Howe, Marvine. 'Palestinians in Lebanon', *Middle East Policy*, vol. 12, no. 4 (December 2005), pp. 145–55.

Hudson, Michael C. 'The Palestinian Factor in the Lebanese Civil War', *Middle East Journal*, vol. 32, no. 3 (Summer 1978), pp. 261–78.

Jabbar, Fuad. 'The Arab Regimes and the Palestinian Revolution', *Journal of Palestine Studies*, vol. 2, no. 2 (Winter 1973), pp. 79–101.

Jacobson, Abigail. 'From Empire to Empire: Jerusalem in the Transition between Ottoman and British Rule, 1912–1920', PhD dissertation, University of Chicago, 2006.

Jacobson, Abigail, and Moshe Naor. *Oriental Neighbors: Middle Eastern Jews and Arabs in Mandatory Palestine* (Waltham: Brandeis University Press, 2016).

Jamal, Amal. *The Palestinian National Movement: Politics of Contention, 1967–2005* (Bloomington: Indiana University Press, 2005).

Jameson, Frederic. *Marxism and Form: Twentieth-Century Dialectical Theories of Literature* (Princeton, NJ: Princeton University Press, 1971).

Kadish, Alon, and Avraham Sela. 'Myths and Historiography of the 1948 Palestine War Revisited: The Case of Lydda', *The Middle East Journal*, vol. 59, no. 4 (October 2005), pp. 616–34.

Kadman, Noga. *Erased from Space and Consciousness: Israel and the Depopulated Villages of 1948* (Bloomington: Indiana University Press, 2015).

Kana'an, Ruba. 'Two Ottoman Sabils in Jaffa (c.1810–1815): an Architectural and Epigraphic Analysis', *Levant*, vol. 33, no. 1 (January 2001), pp. 189–204.

Kanafani, Ghassan. 'The Land of Sad Oranges', in G. Kanafani, *Men in the Sun and other Palestinian Stories*, trans. Hilary Kilpatrick (Boulder: Lynne Rienner Publishers, 1999), pp. 75–80.

—— 'Returning to Haifa', in G. Kanafani, *Palestine's Children: Returning to Haifa and Other Stories*, trans. Barbara Harlow and Karen E. Riley (Boulder: Lynne Rienner Publishers, 2000), pp. 95–165.

Kanazi, Remi. *Before the Next Bomb Drops: Rising up from Brooklyn to Palestine* (Chicago: Haymarket Books, 2015).

Kark, Ruth. *Jaffa: A City in Evolution, 1799–1917*, trans. Gila Brand (Jerusalem: Yad Izhak Ben Zvi, 1990).

Karpel, Dalia. 'Ha-Bayt be-Manta Ray Pinat Banana Beach' ['The House in Manta Ray, Corner of Banana Beach'], *Haaretz*, 2 February 2012, http://www.haaretz.co.il/magazine/1.1631243 (last accessed 26 May 2016). [Hebrew]

Kattan, Victor. *From Coexistence to Conquest: International Law and the Origins of the Arab-Israeli Conflict, 1891–1949* (New York: Pluto Press, 2009).

Kazziha, Walid W. *Revolutionary Transformation in the Arab World: Habash and his Comrades from Nationalism to Marxism* (London: C. Knight, 1975).

Kedar, Hadas. 'Tseva ha-Kesef (Yored be-Mayim)' ['The Colour of Money (Washes in Water)'], *Hagadah Hasmalit*, 29 June 2014, http://hagada.org.il/2014/06/29/ה-לש-הדמשה-סזינכמב-סיורג-סירוב-תובקעב/ (last accessed 26 May 2016). [Hebrew].

Keinon, Herb. 'Netanyahu: Israel Needs Fences on all Borders to Keep Out "Predators" in the Region', *The Jerusalem Post*, 9 February 2016, http://www.jpost.com/Arab-Israeli-Conflict/Netanyahu-Israel-needs-fences-on-all-borders-to-keep-out-beasts-in-region-444358 (last accessed 26 May 2016).

Kenosi, Lekoko. 'Records, National Identity, and Post-Apartheid South Africa: The Role of Truth Commission Records in Nation-Building', *Archives and Manuscripts*, vol. 36, no. 2 (2008), pp. 76–87.

Khalidi, Raja, and Sobhi Samour. 'Neoliberalism as Liberation: The Statehood Program and the Remaking of the Palestinian National Movement', *Journal of Palestine Studies*, vol. 40, no. 2 (Winter 2011), pp. 6–25.

Khalidi, Rashid. *The Iron Cage: The Story of the Palestinian Struggle for Statehood* (Boston, MA: Beacon Press, 2006).
—— *Palestinian Identity: The Construction of Modern National Consciousness* (New York: Columbia University Press, 2010).
—— *Under Siege: PLO Decisionmaking during the 1982 War* (New York: Columbia University Press, 1986).
Khalidi, Walid. *All that Remains: The Palestinian Villages Occupied and Depopulated by Israel in 1948* (Washington, DC: Institute for Palestine Studies, 1992).
—— 'Introduction to Spiro Munayyer's *The Fall of Lydda*', *Journal of Palestine Studies*, vol. 27, no. 4 (1988), pp. 80–98.
—— 'Plan Dalet: The Zionist Master Plan for the Conquest of Palestine', *Middle East Forum*, vol. 37, no. 9 (1961), pp. 22–8.
—— 'Why did the Palestinians Leave? Revisited', *Journal of Palestine Studies*, vol. 34, no. 2 (Winter 2005), pp. 42–54.
Kimber, Imogen. 'Gentrifying Jaffa', *Middle East Eye*, 17 September 2015, http://www.middleeasteye.net/in-depth/features/gentrifying-jaffa-1476207527 (last accessed 26 May 2016).
Klein, Menachem. 'Arab Jews: Neither Oxymoron nor Aspersion', in M. Klein, *Lives in Common: Arabs and Jews in Jerusalem, Jaffa and Hebron*, trans. Haim Wartzman (London: C. Hurst & Co., 2014), Digital Edition.
—— 'Between Right and Realization: The PLO Dialectics of "The Right of Return"', *Journal of Refugee Studies*, vol. 11, no. 1 (1998), pp. 1–19.
—— *Lives in Common: Arabs and Jews in Jerusalem, Jaffa and Hebron*, trans. Haim Wartzman (London: C. Hurst & Co., 2014).
Kosellek, Reinhart. *Futures Past: On the Semantics of Historical Time*, trans. Keith Tribe (New York: Columbia University Press, 2004).
Lannegren, Olivia, and Hiroshi Ito. 'The End of the ANC Era: An Analysis of Corruption and Inequality in South Africa', *Journal of Politics and Law*, vol. 10, no. 4 (2017), pp. 55–9.
Laqueur, Walter, and Barry Rubin (eds). *The Israel-Arab Reader: A Documentary History of the Middle East Conflict* (New York: Penguin, 2008).
Lavie, Smadar. *Wrapped in the Flag of Israel: Mizrahi Single Mothers and Bureaucratic Torture* (New York: Berghahn Books, 2014).
Lazar, Haim. *The Occupation of Jaffa* (Tel Aviv: Misrad Habitahon, 1951). [Hebrew]
Lear, Jonathan. *Radical Hope: Ethics in the Face of Cultural Devastation* (Cambridge, MA: Harvard University Press, 2006).
LeBor, Adam. *City of Oranges: Arabs and Jews in Jaffa* (London: Bloomsbury, 2006).

Leibovitz, Arik Ariel. *Kedushat ha-Status Quo: Israel ve-Sugiyat ha-Plitim ha-Falestinim, 1948–1967 [The Sanctity of the Status Quo: The Palestinian Refugees Issue in Israel Foreign Policy, 1948–1967]* (Tel Aviv: Resling, 2015). [Hebrew]

Levi, Avi. 'Hakol 'al ha-Arihim ha-Me'utarim ha-Yefefiim shel Tel Aviv' ['Everything on Tel Aviv's beautifully adorned tiles'], *Xnet*, 21 April 2013, http://xnet.ynet.co.il/design/articles/0,14563,L-3100596,00.html (last accessed 26 May 2016). [Hebrew]

Levi, Gal, and Muhammad Massalha. 'Yaffa: A School of their Choice?' *British Journal of Sociology of Education*, vol. 31, no. 2 (2010), pp. 171–83.

LeVine, Mark. 'Nationalism, Religion and Urban Politics in Israel: Struggles over Modernity and Identity in "Global" Jaffa', in Daniel Monterescu and Dan Rabinowitz (eds), *Mixed Towns, Trapped Communities: Historical Narratives, Spatial Dynamics, Gender Relations and Cultural Encounters in Palestinian-Israeli Towns* (Aldershot: Ashgate, 2007), pp. 281–302.

—— *Overthrowing Geography: Jaffa, Tel Aviv and the Struggle for Palestine, 1880–1948* (Berkeley: University of California Press, 2005).

Lewis, Bernard. *The Middle East and the West* (New York: Harper & Row, 1964).

—— *The Muslim Discovery of Europe* (New York: W.W. Norton, 1982).

—— 'The West and the Middle East', *Foreign Affairs*, vol. 76, no. 1 (January–February 1997), pp. 114–31.

Lloyd, David. 'Settler Colonialism and the State of Exception: The Example of Palestine/Israel', *Settler Colonial Studies*, vol. 2, no. 1 (2012), pp. 59–80.

Lockman, Zachary. 'Land, Labour and the Logic of Zionism: A Critical Engagement with Gershon Shafir', *Settler Colonial Studies*, vol. 2, no. 1 (2012), pp. 9–38.

Löwy, Michael. *Fire Alarm: Reading Walter Benjamin's 'On the Concept of History'*, trans. Chris Turner (London: Verso, 2005).

Mabin, Alan. 'Comprehensive Segregation: The Origins of the Group Areas Act and its Planning Apparatuses', *Journal of Southern African Studies*, vol. 18, no. 2 (1992), pp. 405–29.

Majadala, Haneen. 'Your Honour, This is a History Lesson', *Haaretz*, 4 August 2021, https://www.haaretz.co.il/opinions/.premium-1.10084247 (last accessed 5 August 2021).

Mallison, Thomas, and Sally V. Mallison. *An International Law Analysis of the Major United Nations Resolutions Concerning the Palestine Question*, UN ST/SG/SER.F/4 (New York: UN, 1979).

—— 'The Right of Return', *Journal of Palestine Studies*, vol. 9, no. 3 (Spring 1980), pp. 125–36.

Mamdani, Mahmood. *When Victims Become Killers: Colonialism, Nativism, and the Genocide in Rwanda* (Princeton, NJ: Princeton University Press, 2002).

Manaa, Adel. 'The Palestinian Nakba and its Continuous Repercussions', *Israel Studies*, vol. 18, no. 2 (Summer 2003), pp. 86–99.

Mandel, Neville. J. *The Arabs and Zionism Before World War I* (Berkeley: University of California Press, 1976).

Marshall, Mark. 'Rethinking the Apartheid Paradigm', *Journal of Palestine Studies*, vol. 25, no. 1 (Autumn 1995), pp. 15–22.

Martin, Alison, *et al*. 'Israel Tightens the Blockade, Civilians Bear the Brunt', *Oxfam*, 27 July 2018, http://hdl.handle.net/10546/620527.

Masri, Hasan. 'For Palestinian Artists, the Freedom of Speech is Anything but Guaranteed', *+972 Magazine*, 20 June 2015, http://972mag.com/for-palestinian-artists-freedom-of-speech-is-anything-but-guaranteed/107997/ (last accessed 26 May 2016).

Matar, Haggai. 'Netanyahu Threatens New TV Station for Palestinian Citizens of Israel', *+972 Magazine*, 19 June 2015, http://972mag.com/netanyahu-threatens-new-tv-station-for-palestinian-citizens-of-israel/107971/ (last accessed 26 May 2016).

Mazawi, André, and Makram Khouri-Makhoul. 'Politica Merhavit be-Yafo: 1948–1990' ['Spatial policy in Jaffa: 1948–1990'], in Haim Lusky (ed.), *'Ir ve-Utopia [City and Utopia]* (Tel Aviv: Israel Publishing Company, 1991), pp. 62–74. [Hebrew]

Mbembe, Achile. 'The Power of the Archive and its Limit', in Carolyn Hamilton *et al*. (eds), *Refiguring the Archive* (Dordrecht: Springer, 2002), pp. 19–27.

McAlister, Melani. *Epic Encounters: Culture, Media, and U.S. Interests in the Middle East since 1945* (Berkeley: University of California Press, 2001), pp. 155–97.

McEachern, Charmaine. 'Mapping the Memories: Politics, Place and Identity in the District Six Museum, Cape Town', *Social Identities: Journal for the Study of Race, Nation and Culture*, vol. 1, no. 3 (1998), pp. 499–521.

Mignolo, Walter D. *Local Histories/Global Designs: Coloniality, Subaltern Knowledges, and Border Thinking* (Princeton, NJ: Princeton University Press, 2000).

Million, Dian. *Therapeutic Nations: Healing in an Age of Indigenous Human Rights* (Tucson: University of Arizona Press, 2013).

Mills, Amy. *Streets of Memory: Landscape, Tolerance and National Identity in Istanbul* (Athens, GA: University of Georgia Press, 2010).

Mills, David, *et al*. 'Structural Violence in the Era of a New Pandemic', *Lancet*, 26 March 2020.

Miyazaki, Hirokazu. *The Method of Hope: Anthropology, Philosophy and Fijian Knowledge* (Stanford: Stanford University Press, 2004).

Monterescu, Daniel. 'The Ghettoization of Israel's "Mixed Cities"', *+972 Magazine*, 5 December 2015, http://972mag.com/the-ghettoization-of-israels-mixed-cities/114536/ (last accessed 10 December 2015).

—— 'The "Housing Intifada" and its Aftermath: Ethno-Gentrification and the Politics of Communal Existence in Jaffa', *Anthropology News*, 21 December 2008.

—— *Jaffa, Shared and Shattered: Contrived Coexistence in Israel/Palestine* (Bloomington: Indiana University Press, 2015).

—— 'Zehut lelo Kehila, Kehila Mehapeset Zehut: Politica Merhavit be-Yafo' ['Identity without Community, Community in Search of Identity: Spatial Politics in Jaffa'], *Megamot*, vol. 47, no. 3–4 (2011), pp. 484–517. [Hebrew]

Monterescu, Daniel, and Noa Shaindlinger. 'Situational Radicalism: The Israeli "Arab Spring" and the (Un)Making of the Rebel City', *Constellations*, vol. 20, no. 2 (2013), pp. 1–25.

Morris, Benny. *Israel's Border Wars, 1949–1956: Arab Infiltration, Israeli Retaliation, and the Countdown to the Suez War* (New York: Oxford University Press, 1993).

—— *Leydata shel Be'ayat ha-Plitim ha-Falestinim, 1947–1949 [The Birth of the Palestinian Refugee Problem, 1947–1949]* (Tel Aviv: Am Oved, 1991). [Hebrew]

—— 'Operation Dani and the Palestinian Exodus from Lydda and Ramle in 1948', *Middle East Journal*, vol. 40, no. 1 (Winter 1986), pp. 82–109.

Mualem-Doron, Gil. *Mind the Gap: Transgressive Art and Social Practices* (artist's independent publication).

—— 'Sogrim et ha-Sha'ar' ['Closing the Gate'], *Jaffa Portal*, 20 October 2011, http://www.yaffo.co.il/article_g.asp?id=2818 (last accessed 26 May 2016). [Hebrew]

—— 'Urban Interventions and the Possibility of Radical Democratic Space', in City Mine(d), *Generalized Empowerment: Uneven Development and Urban Interventions*, http://www.citymined.org/index.php and http://www.generalizedempowerment.org/ (last accessed 26 May 2016).

Munoz, Jose Esteban. *Cruising Utopia: The Then and There of Queer Futurity* (New York: New York University Press, 2009).

Naber, Nadine. 'The US and Israel make the Connections for Us: Anti-Imperialism and Black-Palestinian Solidarity', *Critical Ethnic Studies*, vol. 3, no. 2 (Fall 2017), pp. 15–30.

Nabulsi, Karma. 'Nakba Day: We Waited 63 Years for This', *The Guardian*, 19 May 2011, http://www.theguardian.com/commentisfree/2011/may/19/nakba-day-palestinian-summer (last accessed 26 May 2016).

Nachmias, Ben-Zion. *Tel Aviv ke-Hazit u-Mefakda Michael Ben-Gal [Tel Aviv as a Frontier and its Commander Michael Ben-Gal]* (Tel Aviv: Irgun Havrey Hahagana, 1998). [Hebrew]

Nahmani, Yonat. 'Tsayer li Ritspa' ['Draw me a Floor'], *Calcalist*, 5 November 2014, http://www.calcalist.co.il/real_estate/articles/0,7340,L-3644034,00.html (last accessed 26 May 2016). [Hebrew]

Nakdimon, Shlomo, *Altalena* (Tel Aviv: Idanim, 1978). [Hebrew]

Naor, Moshe. 'Israel's 1948 War of Independence as a Total War', *Journal of Contemporary History*, vol. 43, no. 2 (2008), pp. 241–57.

Nassar, Jamal R. 'The Culture of Resistance: The 1967 War in the Context of the Palestinian Struggle', *Arab Studies Quarterly*, vol. 19, no. 3 (Summer 1997), pp. 77–98.

—— *The Palestine Liberation Organization: From Armed Struggle to the Declaration of Independence* (Westport, CT: Praeger, 1991).

Navaro-Yashin, Yael. *The Make-Believe Space: Affective Geography in a Postwar Polity* (Durham, NC: Duke University Press, 2012).

Neocosmos, Michael. 'The Politics of Fear and the Fear of Politics: Reflections on Xenophobic Violence in South Africa', *Journal of Asian and African Studies*, vol. 43, no. 6 (December 2008), pp. 586–94.

New Arab, The. 'Israel asks US to push Palestinians to accept Sheikh Jarrah "Compromise"', *The New Arab*, 5 August 2021, https://english.alaraby.co.uk/news/israel-asked-us-apply-pressure-sheikh-jarrah-case-0 (last accessed 5 August 2021).

Norris, Jacob. *Land of Progress: Palestine in the Age of Colonial Development, 1905–1948* (Oxford: Oxford University Press, 2013).

Noy, Orly. 'Gaza's Great Return March: 234 Killed, 17 Investigations, One Indictment', *+972 Magazine*, 25 November 2020, https://www.972mag.com/gaza-return-march-idf/ (last accessed 3 August 2021).

Owen, Roger. *The Middle East in the World Economy, 1800–1914* (London: Methuen, 1981).

Palumbo, Michael. *The Palestinian Catastrophe: The 1948 Expulsion of a People from their Homeland* (London: Quartet Books, 1987).

Pappé, Ilan. *The Ethnic Cleansing of Palestine* (London: One World Publications, 2006).

—— *The Forgotten Palestinians: A History of the Palestinians in Israel* (New Haven: Yale University Press, 2011).

—— 'An Indicative Archive: Salvaging Nakba Documents', *Journal of Palestine Studies*, vol. 49, no. 3 (Spring 2020), pp. 22–40.

—— (ed.). *Israel and South Africa: The Many Faces of Apartheid* (London: Zed Books, 2015).

Pasi, Rozalyah. *Ha-Bulgarim shel Yafo [The Bulgarians of Jaffa]* (Tel Aviv: Misrad Habitahon, 1993). [Hebrew]

Pearl, Joel. *The Question of Time: Freud in the Light of Heidegger's Temporality* (Amsterdam: Rodopi, 2013).

Peled, Yoav, and Nadim Rouhana. 'Transitional Justice and the Right of Return of the Palestinian Refugees', in Eyal Benvenisti, Haim Gans and Sari Hanafi (eds), *Israel and the Palestinian Refugees* (Berlin: Springer, 2007), pp. 141–58.

Perugini, Nicola, and Neve Gordon, *The Human Right to Dominate* (New York: Oxford University Press, 2015).

Pessar, Patricia. 'Women's Political Consciousness and Empowerment in Local, National and Transnational Contexts: Guatemalan Refugees and Returnees', *Identities: Global Studies in Culture and Power*, vol. 7, no. 4 (2001), pp. 461–500.

Peteet, Julie. *Landscape of Hope and Despair: Palestinian Refugee Camps* (Philadelphia: University of Pennsylvania Press, 2005).

—— 'Language Matters: Thinking about Palestine', *Journal of Palestine Studies*, vol. 45, no. 2 (Winter 2016), pp. 24–40.

—— 'Problematizing a Palestinian Diaspora', *International Journal of Middle East Studies*, vol. 39, no. 4 (November 2007), pp. 627–46.

—— 'The Work of Comparison: Israel/Palestine and Apartheid', *Anthropological Quarterly*, vol. 89, no. 1 (Winter 2016), pp. 247–81.

Pinder, D. 'Subverting Cartography: The Situationists and Maps of the City', *Environment and Planning A*, vol. 98 (1996), pp. 405–27.

Platzky, Laurine, and Cherryl Walker. *The Surplus People: Forced Removals in South Africa* (Johannesburg: Ravan Press, 1985).

Plocher, Lyle. 'Foreigner's Guide to Property Market: Living in Jaffa', *The Jerusalem Post*, 12 May 2011, http://www.jpost.com/Business/Real-Estate/Foreigners-guide-to-property-market-Living-in-Jaffa (last accessed 26 May 2016).

Prashad, Vijay. *The Poorer Nations: A Possible History of the Global South* (London: Verso, 2012).

Puchner, Martin. 'Society of the Counter-Spectacle: Debord and the Theatre of the Situationists', *Theatre Research International*, vol. 29, no. 1 (March 2004), pp. 4–15.

Quandt, William B. *Peace Process: American Diplomacy and the Arab-Israeli Conflict after 1967* (Washington, DC: Brookings Intitution Press, 2005 [1993]).

Quandt, William B., Fuad Jaber and Ann Mosely Lesch, *The Politics of Palestinian Nationalism* (Berkeley: University of California Press, 1973).

Quayson, Ato. 'Introduction: Area Studies, Diaspora Studies, and Critical Pedagogies', *Comparative Studies of South Asia, Africa and the Middle East*, vol. 27, no. 3 (2007), pp. 580–90.

Quayson, Ato, and Girish Daswani. 'Introduction: Diaspora and Transnationalism, Scapes, Scales and Scopes', in A. Quayson and G. Daswani (eds), *A Companion to Diaspora and Transnationalism* (Hoboken: Wiley-Blackwell, 2013), pp. 1–26.

Quigley, John. 'Apartheid Outside Africa: The Case of Israel', *Indiana International & Comparative Law Review*, vol. 2, no. 1 (1991), pp. 221–51.

—— 'Displaced Palestinians and the Right of Return', *Harvard International Law Journal*, vol. 39, no. 1 (Winter 1998), pp. 171–229.

Rabinow, Paul. *French Modern: Norms and Forms of the Social Environment* (Chicago: University of Chicago Press, 1989).

Rabinowitz, Dan, and Daniel Monterescu. 'Introduction: The Transformation of Urban Mix in Palestine/Israel in the Modern Era', in Daniel Monterescu and Dan Rabinowitz (eds), *Mixed Towns, Trapped Communities: Historical Narratives, Spatial Dynamic, Gender Relations and Cultural Encounters in Palestinian-Israeli Towns* (Aldershot: Ashgate, 2007), pp. 1–32.

—— 'Reconfiguring the "Mixed Town": Urban Transformations of Ethno-National Relations in Palestine/Israel', *International Journal of Middle East Studies*, vol. 40, no. 2 (2008), pp. 195–226.

Rabinowitz, Dan, and Khawla Abu Baker. *Coffins on our Shoulders: The Experience of the Palestinian Citizens of Israel* (Berkeley: University of California Press, 2005).

Radai, Itamar. *Between Two Cities: Palestinian Arabs in Jerusalem and Jaffa* (Tel Aviv: Tel Aviv University Press, 2015). [Hebrew]

—— 'Jaffa, 1948: The Fall of a City', *The Journal of Israeli History*, vol. 3, no. 1 (March 2011), pp. 23–43.

Ram, Hanna. *Ha-Yishuv ha-Yehudi be-Yafo ba-'Et ha-Hadasha: mi-Kehila Sefaradit le-Merkaz Tsiony [The Jewish Community in Jaffa from Sephardic Community to Zionist Center]* (Jerusalem: Carmel, 1996). [Hebrew]

Rapoport, Meron. 'History Erased: the IDF and the post-1948 Destruction of Palestinian Monuments', *Journal of Palestine Studies*, vol. 37, no. 2 (Winter 2008), pp. 82–8.

Rassool, Ciraj. 'Memory and the Politics of History: in the District Six Museum', in N. Murray, N. Shepherd and M. Hall (eds), *Desire Lines: Space, Memory & Identity in the Post-Apartheid City* (London: Routledge, 2007), pp. 113–28.

Raz, Adam. 'Arab Citizens behind Barbed Wire', *Haaretz Weekend*, 28 May 2020, p. 11.

—— 'History in Shreds', *Haaretz Weekend*, 25 June 2021, pp. 5, 11.

—— *Looting of Arab Property during Israel's War of Independence* [*Bizat ha-RereKhush ha-'Aravi be-Milhemet ha-'Atzmaut*] (Jerusalem: Carmel, 2020).

Real News Network, The. 'Up to Six Mass Graves Discovered in Jaffa, with Hundreds of Victims from 1948', 11 June 2013, http://therealnews.com/t2/index.php?option=com_content&task=view&id=31&Itemid=74&jumival=10298 (last accessed 26 May 2016).

Reisz, Mathew J. 'Samir el-Youssef: At Home with the Heretic', *The Independent*, 18 January 2007, http://www.independent.co.uk/arts-entertainment/books/features/samir-el-youssef-at-home-with-the-heretic-432650.html (last accessed 26 May 2016).

Reuters, '"It was always my Dream to Reach Jaffa," Syrian Infiltrator Says', *Haaretz*, 16 May 2011, http://www.haaretz.com/news/diplomacy-defense/it-was-always-my-dream-to-reach-jaffa-syrian-infiltrator-says-1.362166 (last accessed 26 May 2016).

Richter-Devroe, Sophie. '"Like Something Sacred": Palestinian Refugees' Narratives on the Right of Return', *Refugee Survey Quarterly*, vol. 32, no. 2 (2013), pp. 92–115.

Robinson, Shira. *Citizen Strangers: Palestinians and the Birth of Israel's Liberal Settler State* (Stanford: Stanford University Press, 2013).

Rodinson, Maxime. *Israel: A Colonial-Settler State?*, trans. David Thorstad (New York: Monad Press, 1973).

Romano, Claude. *Event and World*, trans. Shane Mackinlay (New York: Fordham University Press, 2009).

Rosenne, Shabtai. 'On Multi-Lingual Interpretation – UN Security Council Resolution 242', *The Israel Law Review*, vol. 6, no. 3 (1971), pp. 360–6.

Rothard, Sharon. *Ir Levana, Ir Shehora [White City, Black City]* (Tel Aviv: Bavel, 2005). [Hebrew]

Roth, Natasha. 'Wiping Palestinian History off the Map in Jaffa', *+972 Magazine*, 4 June 2016, http://972mag.com/wiping-palestinian-history-off-the-map-in-jaffa/119688/ (last accessed 26 June 2016).

Rothberg, Michael. *Multidirectional Memory: Remembering the Holocaust in the Age of Decolonization* (Stanford: Stanford University Press, 2009).

Rothchild, Alice. 'In Balata, the Occupation is not just of Body, but of Mind', *Mondoweiss*, 21 June 2013, http://mondoweiss.net/2013/06/balata-occupation-body (last accessed 26 May 2016).

Sa'di-Ibraheem, Yara. 'Settler-Colonial Temporalities, Ruinations and Neoliberal Urban Renewal: The Case of Suknet al-Huresh in Jaffa', *GeoJournal*, vol. 87 (2020), pp. 661–75, https://doi.org/10.1007/s10708-020-10279-0.

Sadler, Simon. *The Situationist City* (Cambridge, MA: MIT Press, 1998).

Safran, William. 'Comparing Diasporas: A Review Essay', *Diaspora: A Journal of Transnational Studies*, vol. 8, no. 3 (Winter 1999), pp. 255–91.

—— 'Diasporas in Modern Societies: Myths of Homeland and Return', *Diaspora: A Journal of Transnational Studies*, vol. 1, no. 1 (Spring 1991), pp. 83–99.

—— 'The Jewish Diaspora in a Comparative and Theoretical Perspective', *Israel Studies*, vol. 10, no. 1 (Spring 2005), pp. 36–60.

Said, Edward. 'My Guru', *London Review of Books*, vol. 23, no. 24 (13 December 2001), pp. 19–20.

—— 'The Only Alternative', *al-Ahram Weekly Online*, no. 523, 1–7 March 2001.

—— 'Permission to Narrate', *Journal of Palestine Studies*, vol. 13, no. 3 (Spring 1984), pp. 27–48.

Salhab, Akram. 'A Report from Badil-Zochrot Joint Actions: Practical Approaches to Refugee Return', *Zochrot*, May 2011, http://zochrot.org/en/content/report-badil-zochrot-joint-actions-practical-approaches-refugee-return (last accessed 26 May 2016).

Sassen, Saskia. 'Making Public Interventions in Today's Massive Cities', *Generalized Empowerment*, http://www.generalizedempowerment.org/ (last accessed 26 May 2016).

Sayigh, Rosemary. *The Palestinians: from Peasants to Revolutionaries* (London: Zed Books, 1979).

—— *Too Many Enemies* (London: Zed Books, 1994).

Sayigh, Yezid. *Armed Struggle and the Search for a State: The Palestinian National Movement, 1949–1993* (Oxford: Clarendon Press, 1997), pp. 71–80.

—— 'Reconstructing the Paradox: The Arab Nationalist Movement, Armed Struggle, and Palestine, 1951–1966', *Middle East Journal*, vol. 45, no. 4 (Autumn 1991), pp. 608–29.

Schielke, Samuli. *Egypt in the Future Tense: Hope, Frustration, and Ambivalence Before and After 2011* (Bloomington: Indiana University Press, 2015).

Scholch, Alexander. *Palestine in Transformation, 1856–1882: Studies in Social, Economic, and Political Development*, trans. William C. Young and Michael C. Gerrity (Washington, DC: Institute for Palestine Studies, 1993).

Schlor, Joachim. *Tel Aviv*, trans. Helen Atkins (London: Reaktion, 1999).

Scott, David. *Omens of Adversity: Tragedy, Time, Memory, Justice* (Durham, NC: Duke University Press, 2014).

Seale, Patrick. *Abu Nidal: A Gun for Hire* (London: Hutchinson, 1992).

Segev, Tom. 'Ze Hithil be-Karameh' ['It started in Karameh'], *Haaretz*, 23 January 2008, http://www.haaretz.co.il/misc/1.1558623 (last accessed 26 May 2016). [Hebrew]

Seikaly, Sherene. *Men of Capital: Scarcity and Economy in Mandate Palestine* (Stanford: Stanford University Press, 2015).

Sela, Rona. 'Rokmin et ha-Shinuy: Aktivism ve-Shinuy mi-Shnat 2000 ba-'Arim ha-Du-Leumiyot be-Israel' ['Weaving the Change: Activism and Transformation from 2000 in Israel's Bi-national Cities'], in *Tsisa: Diyur, Safa, Historia – Dor Hadash be-'Arim ha-Yehudiot-'Arviot [Effervescence: Housing, Language, History, A New Generation in Jewish-Arab Cities]* [exhibition catalogue] (Tel Aviv: Nahum Gutman Museum of Art, 2013), pp. 214–33. [Arabic and Hebrew]

Shafir, Gershon. *Land, Labor and the Origins of the Israeli-Palestinian Conflict, 1882–1914* (New York: Cambridge University Press, 1989).

Shaqra, Sama. 'Ani Hayiti Itam' ['I Was With Them'], in Yossi Granovsky, Yonatan Kunda and Roman Vater (eds), *Sfat Yafo [Jaffa's Language]* (Jerusalem: Carmel, 2009), p. 158. [Hebrew]

Sharabi, Hisham. *Embers and Ashes: Memoirs of an Arab Intellectual*, trans. Issa J. Boullata (Northampton, MA: Olive Branch Press, 2008).

—— 'Liberation or Settlement: The Dialectics of Palestinian Struggle', *Journal of Palestine Studies*, vol. 2, no. 2 (Winter 1973), pp. 33–48.

—— *Palestine Guerillas: Their Credibility and Effectiveness* (Washington, DC: The Center for Strategic and International Studies, 1970).

Shehadeh, Raja. 'My Father's Peace Proposal', *The Daily Beast*, 11 September 2012, http://www.thedailybeast.com/articles/2012/11/09/my-father-s-peace-proposal.html (last accessed 26 May 2016).

—— *Strangers in the House: Coming of Age in Occupied Palestine* (South Royalton: Steerforth Press, 2002).

Shenhav, Yehouda. *Beyond the Two State Solution: A Jewish Political Essay* (Cambridge, MA: Polity Press, 2012).

Shohat, Ella. 'Sephardim in Israel: Zionism from the Standpoint of its Jewish Victims', *Social Text*, no. 19/20 (1988), pp. 1–35.

Shvarts, Shifra. 'B'nai B'rith-Sha'ar Zion Hospital in Jaffa (1891–1921): The First Jewish Community Hospital in Palestine', *Judaism*, vol. 47, no. 3 (Summer 1998), pp. 358–70.

Siddiq, Muhammad. *Man is a Cause: Political Consciousness and the Fiction of Ghassan Kanafani* (Seattle: University of Washington, 1984).

Siklawi, Rami. 'The Dynamics of Palestinian Political Endurance in Lebanon', *The Middle East Journal*, vol. 64, no. 4 (Autumn 2010), pp. 597–611.

Sikseck, Ayman. 11 June 2015, [video], http://www.i24news.tv/en/tv/replay/i24newsen/4289682474001 (last accessed 26 May 2016).

Sirriyeh, Hussein. 'Jordan and the Legacies of the Civil War, 1970–71', *Civil Wars*, vol. 3, no. 3 (2000), pp. 74–86.

Skoop, Yarden. 'Ha-horim ve-Iryat Tel Aviv be-Maavak 'al ha-Hinikh ha-Du Leshoni be-Yafo' ['Parents and Tel Aviv Municipality in a Row Over the Bilingual Education in the City'], *Haaretz*, 28 January 2016, http://www.haaretz.co.il/news/education/1.2833104 (last accessed 26 May 2016). [Hebrew]

—— 'Tel Aviv Backtracks, Will Not Open Bilingual School in Jaffa', *Haaretz*, 30 January 2015, http://www.haaretz.com/israel-news/.premium-1.639812 (last accessed 26 May 2016).

Slyomovics, Susan. *The Object of Memory: Arab and Jew Narrate the Palestinian Village* (Philadelphia: University of Pennsylvania Press, 1998).

Smooha, Sami. 'Minority Status in an Ethnic Democracy: The Status of the Arab Minority in Israel', *Ethnic and Racial Studies*, vol. 13, no. 3 (July 1990), pp. 389–413.

Solnit, Rebecca. *Hope in the Dark: Untold Histories, Wild Possibilities* (Chicago: Haymarket Books, 2016).

Soske, Jon, and Sean Jacobs (eds). *Apartheid Israel: The Politics of an Analogy* (Chicago: Haymarket Books, 2015).

Sparr, Thomas. *German Jerusalem: The Remarkable Life of a German-Jewish Neighborhood in the Holy City*, trans. Stephen Brown (London: Haus Publishing, 2021).

Stein, Rebecca L. 'Souvenirs of Conquest: Israeli Occupations as Tourist Events', *International Journal of Middle East Studies*, vol. 40, no. 4 (2008), pp. 647–69.

Strickland, Patrick O. 'Palestinian Refugees Mark One Year of Return to Destroyed Village', *Electronic Intifada*, 15 August 2014, http://electronicintifada.net/content/palestinian-refugees-mark-one-year-return-destroyed-village/13757 (last accessed 26 May 2016).

Sukarieh, Mayssoun. 'The Hope Crusades: Culturalism and Reform in the Arab World', *PoLAR: Political and Legal Anthropology*, vol. 35, no. 1 (May 2012), pp. 115–34.

Supplement to Survey of Palestine: Notes Compiled for the Information of the United Nations Special Committee on Palestine, June 1947 (Washington, DC: The Institute for Palestine Studies, 1991).

Surkes, 'Facebook, Twitter, Removing 70% of Harmful Posts', *The Times of Israel*, 7 June 2016, http://www.timesofisrael.com/70-of-harmful-facebook-twitter-posts-said-removed/ (last accessed 26 June 2016).

Swedenburg, Ted. '12 The Kufiya', in Asef Bayat (ed.), *Global Middle East: Into the Twenty-First Century* (Berkeley: University of California Press, 2021), pp. 162–74.

Tait, Robert. 'Israel Prime Minister Benjamin Netanyahu Rejects Calls to Admit Syrian Refugees', *The Daily Telegraph*, 6 September 2015, http://www.telegraph.co.uk/news/worldnews/middleeast/israel/11847304/Israel-prime-minister-Benjamin-Netanyahu-rejects-calls-to-admit-Syrian-refugees.html (last accessed 26 May 2016).

Tamari, Salim. ''Issa al-Issa's Unorthodox Orthodoxy: Banned in Jerusalem, Permitted in Jaffa', *Jerusalem Quarterly*, vol. 59, no. 17 (2014), pp. 29–31.

—— *Year of the Locust: A Soldier's Diary and the Erasure of Palestine's Ottoman Past* (Berkeley: University of California Press, 2011).

Tamari, Salim, and Rema Hamami. 'Virtual Returns to Jaffa', *Journal of Palestine Studies*, vol. 27, no. 4 (Summer 1998), pp. 65–79.

Tekkenberg, Lex. 'The Search for Durable Solutions for Palestinian Refugees: A Role for UNRWA?', in Eyal Benvenisti, Haim Gans and Sari Hanafi (eds), *Israel and the Palestinian Refugees* (Berlin: Springer, 2007), pp. 373–86.

Teppo, Annika, and Myriam Houssay-Holzschuch. 'Gugulethu™: Revolution for Neoliberalism in a South African Township', *Canadian Journal of African Studies*, vol. 47, no. 1 (2013), pp. 51–74.

Terril, W. Andrew. 'The Political Mythology of the Battle of Karameh', *Middle East Journal*, vol. 55, no. 1 (Winter 2001), pp. 91–111.

Thompson, Elizabeth E. *Justice Interrupted: The Struggle for Constitutional Government in the Middle East* (Cambridge, MA: Harvard University Press, 2013).

Tilley, Virgina (ed.). *Beyond Occupation: Apartheid, Colonialism and International Law in the Occupied Palestinian Territories* (London: Pluto, 2012).

Tolkowsky, S. *The Gateway of Palestine: A History of Jaffa* (London: G. Routledge and Sons, 1924).

Tölölyan, Khachig. 'The Contemporary Discourse of Diaspora Studies', *Comparative Studies of South Asia, Africa and the Middle East*, vol. 27, no. 3 (2007), pp. 647–55.

Trouillot, Michel-Rolph. *Silencing the Past: Power and the Production of History* (Boston, MA: Beacon Press, 1995).

Tutu, Desmond M. *No Future without Forgiveness* (London: Rider, 1999).

Waked, Ali, and Yuval Peys. 'Hitpar'uyot Kashot seviv Misgad Hasan Bek ve-Abul'afiya' ['Severe Rampage around the Hasan Bek Mosque and 'Abulafiya'], *Ynet*, 3 June 2001, http://www.ynet.co.il/articles/0,7340,L-783369,00.html (last accessed 26 May 2016). [Hebrew]

Weizman, Eyal. *Hollow Land: Israel's Architecture of Occupation* (New York: Verso, 2012).

Western, John. *Outcast Cape Town* (Cape Town: Human & Rousseau, 1981).

Yacobi, Haim. *The Jewish-Arab City: Spatio-Politics in a Mixed Community* (London: Routledge, 2009).

Yaffa48, ''Ailat al-Dajani fi Madinat al-Quds Ta'alan Rafaduha al-Musharikah fi Hifl Tadshin Duwar Yahmal Ism Doktor Fuad al-Dajani' ['Dajani family of the city of Jerusalem announces its refusal to participate in the naming ceremony of Dr. Fouad Dajani roundabout'], *Yaffa48*, 16 February 2012, http://www.yaffa48.com/?mod=articles&ID=4934 (last accessed 26 May 2016). [Arabic]

Ynet. 'Syrian Infiltrator Recounts Journey to TA', *Ynet*, 16 May 2011, http://www.ynetnews.com/articles/0,7340,L-4069686,00.html (last accessed 26 May 2016).

Younis, Rami. 'Watch: Lauryn Hill, Angela Davis call for Black-Palestinian Solidarity', *+972 Magazine*, http://972mag.com/watch-lauryn-hill-angela-davis-call-for-black-palestinian-solidarity/ (last accessed 26 May 2016).

Ze'evi, Dror. 'Back to Napoleon? Thoughts on the Beginning of the Modern Era in the Middle East', *Mediterranean Historical Review*, vol. 19, no. 1 (2004), pp. 73–94.

Zeitoun, Yoav, and Elior Levi, 'The IDF Killed Terrorists that Fired on Soldiers; 16 Killed Yesterday in Gaza', *Ynet*, 31 March 2018, https://www.ynet.co.il/articles/0,7340,L-5211505,00.html (last accessed 3 August 2021).

Zochrot-Badil. *Study Visit to Cape Town* (Zochrot-Badil, 2012).

Zochrot et al-Lydd [Remembering al-Lydd] (Tel Aviv: Zochrot, 2012).

Zochrot et Manshiyyeh (Yafo) [Remembering al-Manshiyyeh (Jaffa)] (Tel Aviv: Zochrot, 2010). [Hebrew and Arabic]

Zochrot et Shekhunat 'Ajami be-Yafo [Remembering Jaffa's al-Ajami Neighbourhood] (Tel Aviv: Zochrot, 2007).

Zureiq, Constantine. *The Meaning of Disaster*, trans. R. Bayly Winder (Beirut: Khayat's College Book Cooperative, 1956).

INDEX

Abu Iyad (*nom de guerre* of Salah Khalaf), 44–5, 82–9, 92, 93, 95
Abu Kabir, 107, 109–10
Abu Lughod, Ibrahim, 93–4, 95, 144
Abu Lughod, Lila, 144
Abu Shehadeh, Isma'il, 43
Abu Sitta, Salman, 197–8
African American, working class, 16
African National Congress (ANC), 155, 169
agriculture, 28
Ahuzat Bayit, 33; *see also* Tel Aviv
Ajami ghetto, 48, 131, 139, 196
  'Arab Jaffa', 57–60, 62–8, 135
  'green house', 199–200
al-'Ayn camp *see* Balata refugee camp
al-Feneiq cultural centre, 162–3
al-Haq (Palestinian human rights organisation), 103
Allan, Diana, 20, 190
al-Naksa see Six Day War (1967)

al-Rabita (League for Jaffa's Arabs), 121, 133
al-Saraya (theatre), 163
al-Shabiba al Yafiyya (Jaffa youth), 121
Ana Loulou, 163
anthropological scholarship, 19
apartheid analogy, 156–7
Arab Democratic School for Science and Technology, 128, 129, 135, 139
'Arab Houses for Sale', Platform art fair, 140–8
Arab Nationalist Movement (ANM), 74–5, 76
Arabic (language and culture), 130, 132, 195
Arafat, Yasser, 5, 81, 95
  Declaration of Independence (1988), 6
  at UN General Assembly, 88
archives
  elisions in, 60

Israeli state archives (ISA), 8, 20
Palestinian alternative, 9, 20
Arendt, Hannah, 217
Ashkenazi Jews, 145–6, 195
'Askar refugee camp, 104, 105
Association of Arab-American
    University Graduates (AAUG),
    87, 94
Avner, Major General Elimelekh, 63
Awda, Imagined Testimonies of Possible Futures, 205–13
Ayam collective, 122–3, 150

Badil (refugee rights NGO), 153, 155;
    see also Zochrot-Badil project,
    'Envisioning'
Balata refugee camp, 104–5, 106, 110, 158, 213
Ba'thists, 80
Begin, Menachem, 44
Beirut, 18, 57, 93, 94
Beit Gidi (Etzel museum), Irshid, 200–2
Benjamin, Walter, 12–14, 72, 73
Bethlehem, 177
Bibi, Haj Ali, 128
Bibi, Walid, and family, 130, 131, 136–7
'Bibi's House' (urban intervention), 128–39
binationalism, 21
Black Lives Matter movement, 16
'Black September', 87
Bloch, Ernst, 9, 10–11, 15–16
Boycott, Divestment and Sanctions (BDS) movement, 18, 156
British Mandate, 34–5
    end of, 39
    and Jaffa, 37–8

    and Tel Aviv, 36
    and Zionism, 27, 35
Bronstein, Eitan, 173, 174–6
Bulgarian Jews, 60–1

Cairo Accord (1969), 81
Cape Town document, 153, 191–9, 217
Cape Town, South Africa, 164–80
Carleton, Richard, 70–2
censorship, 64
Charles Clore Park, 135–6, 200–2
checkpoints (military), 52, 55–6, 103, 108, 161
Chelouche, Aharon, 67
Chelouche, Yosef Eliyahu, 30, 67
Chetrit,, Minister of Minority Affairs, 57
Chizik, Itzhak (governor of Jaffa), 52
Chizik, Itzhak (military governor of Jaffa), 53–4
Christian Maronites, 29
coffee shops, 64, 67
Committee of the Internally Displaced Persons, 159
Crapanzano, Vincent, 19
Custodian of Absentee Properties, 66

DAAR (Decolonizing Architecture Art Residency), 162
Dajani, Fouad, 183
Dajani family, 183–7
Darna (The Popular Committee for Land and Housing Rights, 121
Darwish, Mahmoud, 6
Declaration of Independence (1988), 6
decolonisation, 65

Deheishe refugee camp, 160, 162, 168, 176–7
demolitions of villages and towns, 7, 13–14, 39, 111
Derekh Hasafa ('through language'), 122
Derrida, Jacques, 189–90, 217
detention and house arrest, 65
District Six, Cape Town, 169–72, 173–80
District Six Museum, 170–2, 173, 178
Dulles, John Foster, 94

East Jerusalem, Israel's conquest of, 75
economy, Zionism and, 32
Egypt, 28, 88
Emergency Committee, Jaffa, 51–2, 54, 57, 58–9, 65–6
employment, menial labour, 108–9
'Envisioning' project, 152–5, 159–80
erasure, discourses of, 114
Erem, Moshe (née Kazanovzky), 57–8
Erez-Barak, Daphne (Justice), 4
ethnic cleansing, 4, 39
Etzel museum *see* Beit Gidi (Etzel museum)
exile, 190–1, 198, 213, 214

Faisal, King, 121
Fanon, Frantz, 179
fascism, modernity and, 12–13
Fatah, 5, 81, 89, 102, 215
  founding of, 82, 85–6
  rise of (after 1967), 75
  see also Arafat, Yasser
Fayyad, Salam, 17
feminism, 17

'For Sand thou are and unto Dust shalt thou Return', 148–9
futurity, 15, 20

Galilee, 198
Garden Cities, 34
Gardi, Tomer, 'A Story from Manshiyeh al-Jdeideh', 206–10, 217
gated communities, 197
Gaza Strip, 145
  Great Return March, 3–4, 159
  Israeli occupation, 7, 75, 146
  NGOs and, 103–4
  operations Cast Lead and Protective Edge, 68, 148–9
  Oslo Process and, 6
General Security Services (GSS), 68
gentrification, 190; *see also under* Jaffa
Ghubari, 'Umar al-, 206
Givat Amal, 214
Golan Heights, 1, 146
Great Return March, 3–4, 159
Group Areas Act, 170
Gugulethu, Cape Town, 165–7, 173
Gurion, Ben, 54–5, 56–7, 145

Habash, George, 74, 76
Hagana, 41, 42, 52, 107, 110–11
Hage, Ghassan, 19
Haifa, 57–8
Hamami, Rema, 'Virtual Returns to Jaffa', 97–9
'haunting', 23–4
Hawatma, Nayef, 74
Hazan, Haim, 194
healing, concept of, 203
Hijazi, Hassan, 1–2

Histadrut, 35
historians of Palestine and Palestinians, 20
Hochberg, Gil, 126
hope, 10–11, 15–17, 19
Hourani, Albert, 65
Howard, Ebenezer, 34
human agency, 16–17
Hussein, King of Jordan, 72, 87

IDF (Israeli Defense Forces), 52, 53, 57, 62, 80, 107, 132
Ilani, Yehudit, 133
Im Tirtzu (Zionist nationalist NGO), 152
'Independence Day', Israel, 159
International Court of Justice, on the separation barrier, 18
international support for Palestinian cause, 87
Intervals art festival, 148–9
Intifada, Second, 18, 109, 121, 215
Iraq/Iraqis, 59, 121, 198
Irgun, 41, 42, 43–4, 44, 62, 78, 129
Irshid, Beit Gidi (Etzel museum), 200–2
Israeli Defence Forces *see* IDF (Israeli Defense Forces)
Israeli liberal-Zionist left, 7
Israeli state archives (ISA), 8, 20

Jaffa
  13 May agreement, 51–2
  Abu Lughod's return to, 94
  annexed to Tel Aviv, 63
  battle for, and Nakba, 41–5
  British Mandate, and 1936 revolt, 38
  collapse of (1948), 37
  Dajani roundabout, 183–7
  demographic boom and spatial expansion, 28–9, 36–7
  demolitions and spatial appropriations, 7–8
  end of military rule, 67–8
  gated communities, 197
  gentrification, 120–2, 126, 133–4
  hostilities with Tel Aviv, 36
  Irgun assaults on, 43–4
  'Jaffa tiles', 119–20
  as a mixed city, 21
  modernity and, 27–31, 34
  'new normal', 50–1, 55, 126, 158
  Palestinian returnees, 1–2
  PLL in, 35–6
  reimagined, 157
  Sharabi and, 90, 93
  Shehadeh's returns to, 100–2
  'spaces of hope', 163
  tourism, 8
  transformed into 'Jewish Jaffa', 57, 62, 63
  urban social relations, 29–30
  'virtual returns' to, 97–9
  as Zionist centre, 31
  see also Ajami; Manshiyyeh; Mualem-Doron, Gil
Jaffa document, 199–202, 204–5
Jaffa Project and *Jaffa 2030*, 122–5
Jamasin al-Gharbi, 213–14
Jazzar, Ahmed al-, 28
Jerusalem, Palestinian Arabs, 37
Jewish migration, 30, 31
Jewish militias *see* Irgun; Stern Gang
Jordan, 80–1, 87, 88

June 1967 war, 103; *see also* Six Day War (1967)

KAIROS, 155
Kanafani, Ghassan, 70–2, 82
   Returning to Haifa, 75–80, 96, 211
Karameh, battle of, 80–1
keffiyeh, 119
Khalaf, Salah (Abu Iyad), 44–5, 82–9, 92, 93, 95
Kiryati brigade, 61–2
Kissinger, Henry, 88
Koselleck, Reinhart, 15

labour markets, 32, 35–6
Laniado, Meir, 52, 54, 60, 66
   Operation Nine, 56–7
   special licences, 64
Lapid, Yair, 3
Lebanon
   Civil War, 82, 113, 190
   end of French mandate, 65
   Israeli assault on, 68
   multiple displacement, and refugees, 6, 190
   Palestinian refugee camps, 81
   PLO in, 87
LeVine, Mark, 29
liberation struggle, purpose of, 92
Likud party, 146
lobbying, 32
Lydd, 107

Madrid Summit, 18
Maghrebi Jews, 30, 198
Makhnes, Gad, 53
Mandela Park, refugee camp, 167–9

Manor, Ehud, 145–6
Manshiyyeh, 112, 129, 135, 135–6, 142, 144, 146, 200
Mapai (Land of Israel Worker's Party), 95, 145, 146
MAPAM party, 57
mass expropriation of houses, 54, 66
Mbembe, Achile, 8
media/news outlets, Arab-language, 31, 35, 67
media/news outlets, Israeli, 2, 4
Meir, Golda, 95
Mignolo, Walter, 16, 203
Ministry of Interior Affairs, 62
Ministry of Internal Affairs, Arab Affairs, department of, 67
Ministry of Minority Affairs, 53
mixed communities, 194–5
Miyazaki, Hirokazu, 19
Mizrahi Jews, 59, 67, 110, 146, 194–6, 198
modernity, 26, 27–31
Monterescu, Daniel, 21, 194
Mualem-Doron, Gil, 120–1, 125–31
   'Arab Houses for Sale', 140–8
   collages at Intervals, 148–9
   'My Jaffa' installation, 133–5

Nablus, refugee camps, 104–5
Nakba, 1, 8, 38–9, 39
   denial of, 127
   immediate aftermath of (1948–9), 48–68
   Sharabi on, 91
Nakba and Return film festival, 118–19
Nakba Day, 2013, launch of Jaffa document, 199–202, 204–5

INDEX | 257

Napoleon, 28
Naqab region, 198
Nasser, Gamal Abdel, 80, 82
National Expropriation Committee, 61n
Navaro-Yashin, 173
Nazism, 12
neoliberalism, 16, 17
Netanyahu, Benjamin, Prime Minister, 220
Neveh Shalom, 29
Neveh Tsedek, 29
NGOs, 103–4, 121; *see also* Zochrot (Israeli NGO); *specific names of individual NGOs*
Nuzha (Jaffa), 29

Obama, Barack, 16
October War (1973), 88
Open House Tel Aviv festival, 130
'Operation Dani', 107
Operation Nine, 56–7
operation Protective Edge, 148–9
Oslo Process and Accords, 6, 18, 92
Ottoman Empire/Ottomanism, 28, 29, 30, 65, 119
'Owdeh, Naji, 160, 162, 168, 177, 192

Palestine Labour League (PLL), 35–6
Palestine Liberation Organization (PLO), 5, 6, 215
　Abu Lughod and, 94
　elevation of, in the international community, 95
　Fatah-led, 102
　at Karameh, 80–1
　and King Hussein of Jordan, 87
　see also Fatah

Palestinian Arabs, 27, 31
Palestinian Authority (PA), 17, 20, 169
Palestinian militias, 107
Palestinian National Charter (1968), 5–6, 86
Palestinian National Council (PNC), resolution (1974), 6, 86
Palestinian villages, pre-Nakba, reconstruction and repatriation, 197–8
paramilitary organisations, 41, 107; *see also* Irgun; Stern Gang
Parrhesia (artistic collective), 122, 150
PASSOP (People Against Suffering, Oppression and Poverty), 168
'Pedagogic Acts', 135–6
permits system, 64, 68, 108–9
Persitz, Akiva, 61
Peteet, Julie, 81, 156
Plan Dalet, 39
Platform art fair, 'Arab Houses for Sale', 140–8
Popular Front for the Liberation of Palestine (PFLP), 76
'progress' narrative, 12, 13

Radai, Itamar, 37
Ramallah, 99, 103
Red Cross, 54
refugee camps (Palestinian), 7, 20, 73–4, 162
　Lebanon, 81–2
refugee camps (South Africa), 167–9
Rodinson, Maxime, 156
Rosetta (film), 118–19
Rouleau, Eric, 82

Saba, Nicola, 66–7
Sabra and Shatila massacres, 113n
Sadat, Anwar al-, 88
Sa'deh, Antun, 90, 93
Said, Edward, 6, 72, 95
Salameh, 41
'second occupant', 193–4, 203–4
separation barrier, 103
Sephardi Jews, 30, 67
settler colonialism, 11–12, 14, 21–2; see also Zionism
SHABAK, 68
Shafir, Gershon, 31–2
Sharabi, Hisham, 87, 90–4, 95
Shaykh Muwannis, 152
Shehadeh, Aziz, 100–3
Shehadeh, Raja, 99–100, 103–4
Shimoni, Yaacov, 55
Six Day War (1967), 75, 80, 91, 94, 104, 146
South Africa, and settler colonialism, 154–5
spatial appropriations, Jaffa, 7–8
spatial resistance, 114, 121–7
stereoscopic vision, 162, 163
Stern Gang, 41, 42, 43, 62
Supreme Court, Israel, 4
Syrian Social Nationalist Party (SSNP), 90
Syria/Syrians, 3, 65, 190, 210

Tamari, Salim, 'Virtual Returns to Jaffa', 97–8
Tanzimat, 28
Tel Aviv, 31, 100
 Abu Kabir, 109–10
 British Mandate, 36, 37
 Dajani roundabout, 183–6
 Eretz-Israel museum, 152
 establishment, 33–4
 Givat Amal, 214
 hostilities with Jaffa, 36, 41–5
 and Manshiyyeh see Manshiyyeh
 new port, 38
teshuvah, 189
tiles, 'Jaffa style', 119–20
tourism
 Jaffa, 8, 56, 135
 Occupied Territories, 75
trade and commerce, Palestine, 27
'trickle down' economics see neoliberalism
Trump, Donald, 16
Truth and Reconciliation Commission (TRC), 155, 189
Turk, Iftikhar, 44
Tutu, Desmond, 164–5, 189
'two states solution', 6–7, 89

uncanny, 23–4, 127, 157
United Nations Relief and Works Agency (UNRWA), refugee camps, 7, 104
United Nations (UN)
 partition, 38
 Resolution 181, 39–40
 Resolution 242, 83
United Nations (UN), General Assembly
 Arafat at, 88
 resolution 194, 4
United States of America, 91, 94
'Uthman, Husam, 'Our Father's House', 210–13

'Walls Talk' (sound installation), 130–1
'We Returned to the Land to Build and be Rebuilt' (installation), 136–9
website, Palestinian artists/activists, 122–3
West Bank
   Israeli occupation, 7, 75, 146, 190
   NGOs and, 103–4
   Oslo Process and, 6
   Palestinian refugees, 192
   post-1967 war and occupation, 103
witness testimonial, 153
World War I, 31

Yafa Cultural Centre, 105, 106, 213
Yafawiin, 29, 37, 55, 114; *see also* Abu Iyad; Kanafani, Ghassan; Sharabi, Hisham
Yehuda Hayamit Street, Jaffa, 120–1, 139
Yemen, 16
Youssef, Samir al-, 206–7, 209, 212

Zionism, 14
   (state) on ethnic/religious separation, 197
   Abu Iyad on, 84–5
   under British Mandate, 35
   and European colonial narratives, 26–7, 35
   Jaffa and, 30, 31–2
   and settler colonialism, 32
Zochrot (Israeli NGO), 118
   conference on right of return, 152
   Dajani roundabout, 184–7
   guided tours and memory activism, 152–3, 179, 219–20
Zochrot-Badil
   Cape Town document, 153, 191–9, 217
   Jaffa document, 199–202, 204–5, 215
   project, 'Envisioning', 152–4, 155, 159–80
Zureiq, Constantine, 38

EU representative:
Easy Access System Europe
Mustamäe tee 50, 10621 Tallinn, Estonia
Gpsr.requests@easproject.com

www.ingramcontent.com/pod-product-compliance
Lightning Source LLC
Chambersburg PA
CBHW051119160426
43195CB00014B/2264